# The
# CHARLESTON, SAVANNAH & COASTAL ISLANDS
# Book

*A Complete Guide*

Wade Spees

# THE CHARLESTON, SAVANNAH & COASTAL ISLANDS BOOK

## A Complete Guide

THIRD EDITION

## CECILY McMILLAN

Berkshire House Publishers
Lee, Massachusetts

The Charleston, Savannah & Coastal Islands Book: A Complete Guide
© 1993, 1997, 1998 by Berkshire House Publishers
Cover and interior photographs ©1993, 1997, 1998 by Wade Spees and other credited sources

**Library of Congress Cataloging-in-Publication Data**

McMillan, Cecily.

    The Charleston, Savannah & coastal islands book : a complete guide / Cecily McMillan. — 3rd. ed.
             p.        cm. — (The great destinations series, ISSN 1056-7968)
    Includes bibliographical references and indexes.
    ISBN 1-58157-001-5
    1. Charleston (S.C.)—Guidebooks. 2. Savannah (Ga.)—Guidebooks. 3. Sea Islands—Guidebooks. 4. Charleston Region (S.C.)—Guidebooks. 5. Savannah Region (Ga.)—Guidebooks. I. Title. II. Series: Great Destinations.
    F279.C43M38               1998
    917.57'9150443—dc21                        98-35817
                                                CIP

ISBN 1-58157-001-5
ISSN: 1056-7968 (series)

Editor: Susan Minnich. Managing Editor: Philip Rich. Text design and typography: Dianne Pinkowitz. Original design for Great Destinations™ series: Janice Lindstrom. Cover design: Jane McWhorter.

Berkshire House books are available at substantial discounts for bulk purchases by corporations and other organizations for promotions and premiums. Special personalized editions can also be produced in large quantities. For more information, contact:

Berkshire House Publishers
480 Pleasant St., Suite 5; Lee, Massachusetts 01238
800-321-8526
E-mail: info@berkshirehouse.com
Website: www.berkshirehouse.com

Manufactured in the United States of America

10  9  8  7  6  5  4  3

*No complimentary meals or lodgings were accepted by the author and reviewers in gathering information for this work.*

Berkshire House Publishers'
**Great Destinations**™ travel guidebook series

*Right on the money.*

— THE NEW YORK TIMES

*. . . a crisp and critical approach, for travelers who want to live like locals.*

— USA TODAY

**Great Destinations**™ guidebooks are known for their comprehensive, critical coverage of regions of extraordinary cultural interest and natural beauty. The authors in this series are professional travel writers who have lived for many years in the regions they describe. Each title in this series is continuously updated with each printing, in order to insure accurate and timely information. All of the books contain over 100 photographs and maps.

**Neither the publisher, the authors, the reviewers, nor other contributors accept complimentary lodgings, meals, or any other consideration (such as advertising) while gathering information for any book in this series.**

Current titles available:
**The Adirondack Book**
**The Berkshire Book**
**The Charleston, Savannah & Coastal Islands Book**
**The Chesapeake Bay Book**
**The Coast of Maine Book**
**The Hamptons Book**
**The Monterey Bay, Big Sur & Gold Coast Wine Country Book**
**The Nantucket Book**
**The Newport & Narragansett Bay Book**
**The Napa & Sonoma Book**
**The Santa Fe & Taos Book**
**The Sarasota, Sanibel Island & Naples Book**
**The Texas Hill Country Book**
**Wineries of the Eastern States**

If you are traveling to, moving to, residing in, or just interested in any (or all!) of these enchanting regions, a **Great Destinations**™ guidebook is a superior companion. Honest and painstakingly critical, full of information only a local can provide, **Great Destinations**™ guidebooks give you all the practical knowledge you need to enjoy the best of each region. Why not own them all?

*To the memory of George McMillan, who first brought me to the Lowcountry and turned my eyes to its subtleties, and to our son, Tom, with whom I continue to love it.*

# Contents

CHAPTER ONE
*"No Fayrer or Fytter Place"*
**HISTORY**
1


CHAPTER TWO
*Getting Here, Getting Around*
**TRANSPORTATION**
27


CHAPTER THREE
*A City of Stories*
**CHARLESTON**
48


CHAPTER FOUR
*An Old City, A Modern City*
**SAVANNAH**
118


CHAPTER FIVE
*Sea Island Gems*
**BEAUFORT, EDISTO, AND BLUFFTON**
161


CHAPTER SIX
*Courts, Courses, Sails, and Sand*
**HILTON HEAD**
204

## CHAPTER SEVEN
*Practical Matters & Seasonal Events*
### INFORMATION
245

# Acknowledgments

A project as large as this one, which gathers together for readers both a sense of Lowcountry history and all the details that make for a successful visit, necessarily requires the efforts of friends and assistants.

In Charleston, Langhorne Howard and Nina McCully compared notes about a city they love and shared their insights, as they have for many years. The same may be said for Wade Spees, whose photographs for this book, like those that have graced other articles of mine, portray the Lowcountry as a place of serene beauty and rich humanity.

In Beaufort and on St. Helena Island, my home, I was helped by Dale Friedman, Susan Graber, Cheryl and Roger Steele, Mary Mack, and Gracie Reddicks.

Beth Scott of Savannah lent her skills in uncounted ways. Steve Wise, author, museum curator, and military historian, kindly critiqued my History chapter.

Cherie Had, at the South Carolina Department of Parks, Recreation and Tourism and Jenny Stacy at the Savannah Area Convention and Visitors Bureau went far beyond their job descriptions in getting information to me, as they have in the past. The staff of the Chambers of Commerce in Beaufort, Hilton Head Island, and Charleston were thorough and prompt in answering my questions. Special thanks goes to the Charleston Museum for the use of archival photos.

Philip Rich at Berkshire House and Susan Minnich, my editor, displayed commendable and consistent good humor and intelligence, even as they were operating under deadlines I made too tight. Their level of commitment to the project would satisfy any writer's expectations; their efforts made this a better, wiser, and clearer book.

Thanks to my friends, and especially to Priscilla Johnson McMillan who continues to nurture my Lowcountry life.

# Introduction

There are some places about which we have such strong impressions that when we finally go there they seem familiar, as if we had known them forever. For many people the Lowcountry is such a place. It seems to have lodged itself so securely in so many imaginations that I often find, when I am asked about it, that what I have to say matters less than the opportunity I may be giving someone to fine-tune the picture they already have.

Where these clustered impressions come from, whether learned in a history lesson on the Civil War, gathered from a friend, understood in a novel, or viewed on a movie screen, seems less important than the fact that they feel fully conceived. This isn't surprising, for in a sense the Lowcountry has earned our permanent attention. It is a compelling world. Like other places that have witnessed tremendous historic upheavals and whose residents have had to adjust to changed circumstances, it evokes a natural sympathy in us for its stories.

I first stepped foot in the Lowcountry late in the summer of 1979, and ever since I have been listening in on its history. I return again and again to places where I feel the presence of the past and its rituals: to the shores of St. Helena Sound, where I catch crabs on a string or dig for oysters much as Native Americans might have done; to Drayton Hall where beds of lilies bloom as they did in Jefferson's Monticello garden; to Penn Center, where descendants of slaves honor their heritage and the strength of their forebears in song; to the squares of Savannah, laid out more than 250 years ago and still possessing a power of geometry that untangles nature and orders the pace of urban life.

The region's physical beauty is just as evocative. The landscape is soft, uninterrupted by hills on land, carpeted with marsh grass and flowing waters at its edges. The air itself seems to press down, weighted by all the humidity, wrapping the Lowcountry like a package. There are distinctive seasons here which bring their own changes in color and light, in bird migrations and blossoms. Every day the shoreline is redefined by the tides.

This book is intended to both introduce you to some of the long-standing pleasures and pastimes found in the Lowcountry and point you in directions where you might discover ones of your own. In individual chapter openings, and in the History chapter, it lays out a broad context into which you may place yourself, as a traveler looking to plan a day or as a reader adjusting the imaginary pictures you arrived with to those you observed first hand.

Sometimes, your efforts may be studious — admiring architecture, exploring sites of historic and cultural significance. At other times, you will be content to satisfy your senses: to feel the beach between your toes, smell the salt marsh, watch a pelican dive, taste fresh shrimp. Don't neglect to listen for old stories, either.

It may turn out that, having come to the Lowcountry for a vacation, you end up joining the ranks of those who return for good. The glossy residential resorts on the developed islands like Kiawah, Seabrook, and Hilton Head have drawn national attention to the area; Beaufort has appeared on so many "Best Small Town" lists and attracted so many new visitors that it is possible, as it was not even ten years ago, to walk down its main street and see only unfamiliar faces. The Spoleto Festival has put Charleston on an international map.

Yet the inexorable need in many of us for community, for a sense of continuity that comes from bringing the past forward, keeps the Lowcountry alive, keeps it from resting solely on the life of its past for vitality. New restaurants, bookstores, jazz and blues clubs, clothing shops, galleries, and B&Bs are embedding themselves in the old Lowcountry places, in its old buildings, enlarging the remnant world as spats fasten on oyster banks and make them grow.

The success that has come to the Lowcountry as a tourist destination has not forced its hand. Not everything is obvious. The ever-willing, eager-to-please personality of the New South it could take on has been held in check by its conservative, deeply ingrained traits of pride and tradition. Achieving such a balance is perhaps the most significant sign that the Lowcountry has come of age.

*Cecily McMillan*
*St. Helena Island, South Carolina*

## THE WAY THIS BOOK WORKS

This book is divided into seven chapters. Several of them cover specific regions of the Lowcountry. But, like a shelf of individual volumes, it encourages browsing: you may want to thumb through the opening sections of individual chapters, for example, to get an overview of the subject. Or you may want to start with the History chapter and pick and choose among the others as your visit unfolds and your needs become apparent.

If you're interested in finding a place to eat or sleep — and during the high season in spring you're encouraged to consider advance planning — look over the restaurant and lodging charts in the *Index* (organized by area and price); then turn to the pages in the general index and read the specific entries for the places that most interest you.

Some entries, most notably those in the **Lodging** and **Dining** sections of chapters, include specific information (telephone, address, hours, etc.) organized for easy reference in blocks in the left-hand column. All such information has been checked for accuracy as close to the time of publication as possible, but details change so it's best to call ahead.

## PRICES

Prices change, too, and for that reason we've avoided listing specific prices in favor of noting their range. Lodging price codes are based on a per-room rate, double-occupancy in the high season months. Low season rates, which may apply in the summer (except at beach resorts) and in December and January, are usually about 20 percent less. In the high season many places, small and large, require a minimum two-night stay and may also have specific rules regarding adequate notice and refunds in the event of cancellation. Check ahead.

You might also confirm information that we've provided about policies in effect concerning such things as handicapped access, off-street parking and rules about smoking.

Restaurant prices indicate the cost of a meal including appetizer, entree, and dessert, but not bar beverages, tax, or tip. Prix-fixe menus are noted. Here again, the season of your visit may bring on special conditions: when there are crowds, most restaurants extend their hours of operation, serving meals both earlier and later. In the winter, they may shut down for a day or two.

### Price Codes

|  | *Lodging* | *Dining* |
| --- | --- | --- |
| Inexpensive | Up to $50 | Up to $10 |
| Moderate | $50 to $110 | $10 to $20 |
| Expensive | $110 to $180 | $20 to $30 |
| Very Expensive | Over $180 | Over $30 |

**Credit cards** are abbreviated as follows:

| AE — American Express | DC — Diner's Card |
| --- | --- |
| CB — Carte Blanche | MC — MasterCard |
| D — Discover Card | V — Visa |

For year-round tourist information see the sources listed on the last page of the Information chapter.

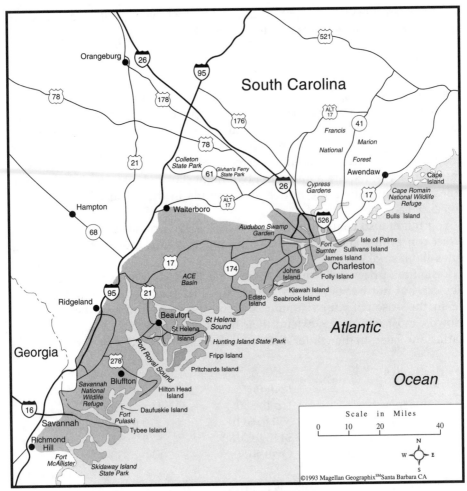

**THE LOWCOUNTRY**

# The
# CHARLESTON, SAVANNAH & COASTAL ISLANDS
## Book
### *A Complete Guide*

# CHAPTER ONE
## *"No Fayrer or Fytter Place"*
## HISTORY

Toward the middle of the 16th century, European adventurers were spreading across the Atlantic Ocean in a wild burst of exploring, hoping to claim for their sovereigns and sponsors vast territories of land and the riches they believed to flourish there. Aboard what now seem to be preposterously small ships and guided by hopeless maps (few of these expeditions ever landed where they intended), they arrived, established forts, and set to their business. One of the places they landed — Spanish, French, and English in succession — was the region we now know as the Lowcountry of South Carolina and Georgia.

Wade Spees

*The vastly rich, tidal world the explorer Ribaut praised: "No fayrer or fytter place."*

The next 150 years was a period of settling and retreating, of establishing colonies and defending them — from one another, from the Native Americans who lived there, and from the twin scourges of disease and deprivation. Motivated by religious zeal and political unrest at home, as well as by the drive to acquire real estate, slaves, or converts to Christianity, the Europeans kept returning to build, to trade, to map, to start life over in new places on which they imposed an Old World order. In the end, it was the English who dominated the Lowcountry.

While the accounts of these years outdo one another in their use of superlatives to describe God and king, they contain even richer praise for the new country. Captain Jean Ribaut, a Frenchman who led a group of 150 Huguenot colonists to the Lowcountry in 1562, claimed in a report (translated into English the following year) that there was "no fayrer or fytter place" than the area of Port Royal Sound, near present-day Beaufort, one of the "goodlyest, best and frutfullest countres that ever was sene"; where egrets were so plentiful the bushes "be all white covered with them"; where there were "so many sortes of fishes that ye may take them without net or angle."

On a site which is now at the edge of a golf course at the Marine Corps Recruit Depot on Parris Island, Ribaut and his settlers built Charlesfort. It was a basic defensive structure measuring 96 feet by 78 feet, barricaded with palisades, and surrounded by a moat. There were gun platforms at its corners and, inside, a rude house with a straw roof. Modest though it may have been, Charlesfort represented the first attempt by the French to establish a colony in what is now the United States. The effort took place three years before the founding of St. Augustine by the Spanish, and 45 years before the English settled Jamestown.

Impressed with the Lowcountry and confident of its potential, Ribaut quickly returned to France, intending to return with supplies and recruits. He never made it back; the colony itself collapsed soon afterwards. The well-situated site did not lie fallow for long, however. In 1566 the Spanish expanded their reach north from St. Augustine and constructed Fort San Felipe on the ruins of Charlesfort. It seemed inevitable that a place so plentifully endowed would not go begging.

To a modern traveler who chances upon a rookery in Hunting Island State Park, or to the youngster throwing a cast net and needing the strength of two to draw it in, perhaps nothing has changed. Today, as centuries ago, the natural resources of the Lowcountry are breathtakingly impressive wherever you

*A typical Lowcountry walk: mild day, sandy road, under the oaks, in the afternoon light.*

Wade Spees

go. There will be schools of dolphin by your boat off Hilton Head, dozens of crabs in the basket you hauled to Kiawah Island, hundreds of eggs in the log-gerhead turtle's nest on Pritchard's Island, and thousands of terns, which — when they rise all at once off Egg Bank in St. Helena Sound — appear as a cloud of smoke on the horizon. There will be late-afternoon light so intense and golden it makes the dun bark of the grayest sycamore shimmer with light.

And remember: when Ribaut called the Lowcountry a place "where nothing lacketh," Charleston, Beaufort, and Savannah had not even been invented.

By 1740, each of these towns had developed the intense self-consciousness — the spirit of place — that is apparent there today. You can find it in the watercolors of a native artist, in the concert of an African-American chorus, in the words of a docent, in the tales of a fisherman. Before the first roads were laid, the wharves constructed, or the means of governance fully conceived, the continuity of culture that characterizes all the Lowcountry was begun. It is the rare American place to have evolved intact, with its monuments and houses and symbols of achievement still pointing to a documented and recognized past.

So overwhelming is the sense of place in the Lowcountry that I have often felt of people I know that, if they ever left the city limits of Charleston — or Beaufort or Savannah — they would vaporize.

There's no doubt, to read from their accounts, that visitors from the earliest days of settlement have shared the feeling that the Lowcountry is a special place, a dramatic place apart. Looking backwards, it is hard to pinpoint pre-cisely when the term "Lowcountry" — or even, as it is sometimes spelled, "Low Country" — became widely used. It is certainly an apt geographical description for an area that is hill-less and hardly above sea level. But to accu-rately define the Lowcountry, to comprehend it at its broadest, you must con-sider that it is many things: a place of dozens of distinctive, interconnected natural communities and ecosystems; a site where historical forces have been converging, sometimes with disastrous consequences, for 400 years; a region whose tiny society influenced national culture; a self-conscious political subdi-vision of the United States.

Technically, the Lowcountry is divided from what is known as the South Carolina Upcountry by the fall line, that feature of geography which bisects the state from the Georgia border at Augusta, approximately 90 miles from the coast, to North Carolina. Upland of the fall line the soil is red clay, and it is hilly; downward the land flattens and spreads, creating broad alluvial plains which meet the sea.

As to its other defining attributes, the Lowcountry that stretches from Charleston to Savannah and encompasses the Sea Islands in between seems to be characterized by a sense of pride that will never leave it. Old families, old houses, old customs, old loyalties remain, if not guiding principles, then ones whose legacy is passed on, as one might give a quilt to the next generation. As the writers of the classic WPA Guide, *South Carolina, A Guide to the Palmetto*

*State,* wrote in 1941, the Lowcountry inhabitant "may live in Charleston, a city that competes with the New Jerusalem in his dreams; or he may live in a drafty Georgian country house" but he "recalls his past glory with a pride that surpasses his ability to appreciate thoroughly the good things of the present."

Of course, the protection of this vital spirit has come at a price. Lowcountry residents were willing to pay it once, to take the drastic measure of firing on Fort Sumter, and they are continuing that commitment. Maintaining Historic Districts, scenic vistas, two-lane island roads, Gullah communities, marine sanctuaries comprising tens of thousands of acres — these are among the accomplishments of present-day preservationists who seek to insure the presence of the past in everyday life. Their victories are for you to savor, too.

## NATURAL HISTORY

The coastline that defines the Lowcountry was, until about 245 million years ago, still more or less attached to the eastern rim of what became present-day Europe and Africa. The shifting of geologic plates that caused the movement of the landmass and created the southern Appalachians, among other mountain ranges, led to the formation of the Atlantic Ocean and the Lowcountry coastal plain.

---

### Sand Hills

I continued through this forest nearly in a direct line towards the sea coast, five or six miles, when the land became uneven, with ridges of sand hills, mixed with sea shells, and covered by almost impenetrable thickets, consisting of Live Oaks, Sweet-bay, Myrica, Ilex, . . . The dark labyrinth is succeeded by a great extent of salt plains, beyond which the boundless ocean is seen. Betwixt the dark forest and the salt plains, I crossed a rivulet of fresh water, where I sat down a while to rest myself, under the shadow of sweet Bays and Oaks; the lively breezes were perfumed by the fragrant breath of the superb Crinum, called by the inhabitants, White Lily. This admirable beauty of the sea-coast islands dwells in the humid shady groves, where the soil is made fertile and mellow by the admixture of sea shells . . . and the texture and whiteness of its flowers at once charmed me.

—From *Travels of William Bartram*
(First published in 1791)

---

In the geologic history of the southeast region, the coastal plain is a rather new development. Long before the present-day coastline obtained its shape, toward the end of the Miocene — third epoch of the Cenozoic Era — the upcountry regions already were well-established. They were formed in an earlier era, the Mesozoic (220–70 million years ago, the time when the dinosaurs came and went), and their ancient mineral formations contrast sharply with those of the coast.

Over time, a cycle was begun. Eroded material from these highland ridges was carried by streams draining the Blue Ridge and Piedmont uplands and deposited, again and again, to the south and east. This Cretaceous material extended the landmass. Periodic inundation by the sea followed, thus covering the sediment and creating distinctive geologic layers of clay, sand, and gravel. At least seven such terraces have been identified, ranging in elevation from 25 feet to 270 feet. Mining activity near Charleston has unearthed fossils of sharks' teeth and mammoth vertebrae.

In short, millions of years ago much of the present-day Lowcountry was under water, while as recently as thousands of years ago, the Native Americans who lived here probably collected oysters and shellfish from beds that, were we to locate them today, would lie some 95 miles out to sea.

Today, well beneath the sandy soil, ranging in thickness from 1000 to 3000 feet, lie the sandstone, silt stones, shale, and limestone that were dumped there. They undergird the land and stretch well beyond it into the ocean to form the continental shelf and the upper slope. The oldest rocks of the coastal plain lie in scattered sections under these layers and it is activity in their faults that can, and has, caused earthquakes, such as the one that damaged Charleston in 1886.

The geologic history of the Lowcountry has given its farmers, residents, and for a time its phosphate-mining industry, some unique advantages. Unlike northern coastal areas such as New England, the area is free of surface rocks. Preparing a field never required the building of a stone wall beside it. The nature of subterranean rock formations has provided some especially good soils for timber cultivation. More important, the deeper layers of rocks serve as aquifers to provide potable water for agriculture, industry, and homes — not an idle resource given the near sea-level elevation of the Lowcountry.

Finally, if the Lowcountry were without the plentiful deposits of easily eroded rock that tumbled from the highlands over the years, the region would have no beaches. The sand you traverse, across miles of coastal and barrier beach, is their legacy.

The phenomenon of rocks-into-sand is one piece of the Lowcountry's geologic history. Another is the transformation of one massive ocean into a landscape of sculptured sounds, estuaries, and marshes. Their evolution has defined the Lowcountry as the site of one of the nation's most productive fisheries, a home to dozens of species of native and migratory birds, and a habitat for mammals small and large. Even the trees and plants of the coast flourish in direct response to these various bodies of water.

## THE MARINE ENVIRONMENT

The Lowcountry marine environment includes several distinctive parts: swamps, estuaries, marshes, maritime forests, dunes and interdune meadows, tidal creeks and sounds, alluvial and blackwater rivers. Their functions are interdependent; to all, tidal action — about six to eight feet throughout the region — is significant. Evidence of the complexity of the marine ecosystem is best seen at any number of points where the land meets the sea, for it is here that some of the most dynamic and subtle dramas of nature are played out. To witness them, a traveler need do no more than lean over a bridge at low tide, step out of the car by a rural creek, or walk the beach.

Perhaps the most common sight of the Lowcountry is the field of smooth cordgrass (*Spartina alterniflora*) that makes up the salt marsh, and the muddy banks and flats that cut through it. Rimmed by wax myrtle and Carolina cherry laurel on its banks, overshadowed by huge live oaks whose limbs are draped with Spanish moss (an air plant, member of the pineapple family) and dotted with resurrection fern, the salt marsh is probably nature's most productive nursery.

What you will see here is this: filter-feeders such as snails, crabs, oysters, shrimp, and mullet ingesting the detritus — a potent mixture of decomposed marsh grass, animal matter, algae, and fungi. Or something larger, a heron, say, or a bottle-nose dolphin (locally called porpoise), or a raccoon eating its smaller prey. The fiddler crabs with their lopsided claws will gather and disperse by the hundreds, a muddy cavalry. Look up and there are the shrimp boats, nets dragging at their sides. Behind them flock the gulls scavenging for cast-off fish. As the tide recedes, you will hear the marsh pop like 100 pricked balloons. The earthy smell of "pluff mud" will fill the air.

---

### A Pleasing Music

A beautiful green frog inhabits the grassy, marshy shores of these large rivers. They are very numerous, and their noise exactly resembles the barking of little dogs, or the yelping of puppies: these likewise make a great clamour, but as their notes are fine, and uttered in chorus, by separate bands or communities, far and near, rising and falling with the gentle breezes, affords a pleasing kind of music.

—From *Travels of William Bartram,* 1791

---

In brackish marshes slightly farther inland, along the tidal rivers, there will be more sediment, flushed from the upland, and greater plant diversity. In the shelter of the vegetation lie the nests of waterfowl; in the highest trees is, perhaps, the nest of a bald eagle. Three of the rivers, the Ashepoo, Combahee, and

*The Lowcountry provides a habitat for the bald eagle and many other endangered species.*

Wade Spees

Edisto, form one of the largest estuarine systems on the East Coast — the ACE Basin, located in and around U.S. Highway 17 south of Charleston. Protection and expansion of the basin is assured by a consortium of federal, state, and private interests. Farther south, the Savannah Wildlife Refuge offers another opportunity to see these natural forces at work.

## THE WORLDS OF ISLANDS AND CITIES

The barrier islands offer another view of the marine ecosystem. Developed or not, they maintain a sense of isolation and fragility at "the edge of the world." Even as they appear solid, they are in fact changing shape all the time, their dunes migrating, growing, eroding, their forests shaped by the unforgiving winds and salt spray. The lives of the birds and mammals that make their homes here are impacted daily by the elements. If the beach has suffered from

---

### *Voluptuous Charm*

Picket life was of course the place to feel the charm of the natural beauty on the Sea Islands. We had a world of profuse and tangled vegetation around us, such as would have been a dream of delight to me, but for the constant sense of responsibility and care which came between. Amid this preoccupation, Nature seemed but a mirage, and not the close and intimate associate I had before known. I pressed no flowers, collected no insects or birds' eggs, made no notes on natural objects, reversing in these respects all previous habits. Yet now, in the retrospect, there seems to have been infused into me through every pore the voluptuous charm of the season and the place; and the slightest corresponding sound or odor now calls back the memory of those delicious days.

—From *Army Life in a Black Regiment*
by Thomas Wentworth Higginson
(First published in 1869)

erosion, oak-tree roots and upended palmettos will obstruct your path. As if to mock this rough beauty, dozens of sanderlings play at the water's edge, while overhead, the big brown pelicans impose an order of their own as they fly in unerring formation.

You may be lucky enough to participate in a late-night "turtle watch" when groups of residents observe the 300-pound loggerhead sea turtles drag themselves up the beach, dig holes, and lay eggs. On several barrier islands, teams of people are charged with marking the nests and moving the eggs to a secure hatchery, away from predators, poachers, and high tides. At the time of release, the hatchlings make their way to the ocean in groups of two and three, and then somehow, miraculously, paddle with their tiny fins to the open sea.

Precisely where these turtles go is not known. From Lowcountry marinas, it takes a big fishing boat several hours to reach the Gulf Stream, where, as every fisherman knows, the big, fighting fish swim — creatures that might eat a turtle in a second. And there are other giants in this marine wildness — the right whales and the manatees.

Coastal refuges show life in abundance; but even in the cities, away from the water's edge, you will be surrounded by natural beauty. In downtown Savannah, the parkways are filled to bursting with azaleas and flowering dogwood in the spring. Honeysuckle, jessamine, wisteria, and trumpet vine tumble wildly over garden walls or race up the trunks of trees. And then there are the birds: the tiny Carolina wren, practically domesticated as it makes its nest in a flower box; mourning doves cooing on telephone wires, and the ever-present mockingbird.

---

### The Mock-Bird

This ancient sublime forest, frequently intersected with extensive avenues, vistas and green lawns, opening to extensive savannas and far distant Rice plantations, agreeably employs the imagination, and captivates the senses by scenes of magnificence and grandeur. The gay mock-bird, vocal and joyous, mounts aloft on silvered wings, rolls over and over, then gently descends, and presides in the choir of the tuneful tribes.

—From *Travels of William Bartram*, 1791

---

Mark Catesby, the naturalist who "discovered" the mockingbird in this region over 250 years ago, noted its fantastic ability to mimic. Today it is said that the bird can imitate 39 songs and 50 call notes, not to mention the cackling of hens, the creak of old gates, and the croaking of frogs. Given the diversity and abundance of Lowcountry life, the mockingbird has songs enough for a lifetime.

# SOCIAL HISTORY

*This sculpture, "Landing Brave" by Peter Toth, stands at Charles Towne Landing. It honors the Native Americans who lived off the area's natural bounty and taught the early settlers of Charles Town to do so.*

Wade Spees

## EARLY HUMAN INHABITANTS

The Native Americans who ranged along the coast from the earliest days — as far back as 10,000 B.C. — have left the merest impression of their lives in patterned pottery shards, woven reed baskets, huge shell middens and shell rings, cypress-log canoes, and the remains of burial or religious sites scattered throughout the region. They also left their names, now anglicized in common usage, to confirm their presence in a dozen Lowcountry places. Some of the most prominent archaeological remains have been found on coastal islands — Hilton Head, Callawassie — suggesting that these early inhabitants possessed both geographic agility and a sense of territorial significance. Their population is thought to have numbered 50,000 at its peak.

The Native Americans of the Lowcountry were divided into loose tribal confederations, each of which may have communicated in its own tongue. They spent the summers along the coast and on the coastal islands, farming and harvesting fish and shellfish; in winter they retreated inland, where they hunted deer and small game. An apparently abundant food supply and an absence of harshness in the climate or geography seem to have helped insure the stability of these native societies. Communal farming produced several crops a year of corn and bounteous harvests of beans, peas, pumpkin, and watermelon. The forests yielded wild fruits, nuts, berries, and plants for food; roots and bark for medicinal drinks. Well-fortified towns, rimmed with circular stockades and enclosing an ever-burning ceremonial fire, established their home base.

The Native Americans' houses had the appearance of rude Quonset huts, long and domed. They were constructed of wooden frames over which mats, woven from palmetto fronds, could be draped, or, during hot weather, removed. Inside, the walls were lined with benches for sleeping. Some houses were grander than others, featuring rooms and pillared platforms usually reserved for a chief or tribe member believed to have unusual wisdom or healing powers.

A larger structure, perhaps 200 feet in diameter, served as a community center for religious and social activities. Early European observers noted devout attention to ritual celebrations in praise of the harvest, accompanied by singing, dancing, and playing of instruments — cane flutes, drums, and rattles made from shells and seed pods. Some Native American games included forms of bowling and lacrosse. They laid their dead to rest, wrapped like swaddled babies, atop high scaffoldings.

## ENCOUNTERS WITH EUROPEANS

By the time of their first encounters with white men, the coastal Native Americans had sorted themselves into various confederacies. From Charleston to the Savannah River lived a group of tribes known collectively as the Cusabo, including the Combahee, Ashepoo, Edisto, Stono, Wando, Kiawah, and Etiwan.

Their responses to the incursion of Europeans were mixed: some were generous and open to trade, teaching the newcomers how to fish and make secure shelter, and in so doing probably saved their lives. Some Native Americans also shared farming techniques. One white settler told of his success in cultivating with one tribe such crops as grape vines, pomegranates, orange and fig trees, barley, onions, and garlic. Some Native Americans and their chiefs, known as *caciques*, helped the Frenchmen of Charlesfort build a ship, caulked with moss, for a return voyage to Europe. Some delivered to English explorers the prime high-bluff settings on which the newcomers laid the cities of Charles Town and Savannah. Some boarded ships and went abroad, or to Barbados.

Other accounts, however, report canoe flotillas fleeing in shock, the villagers hiding for days in the woods. Fighting and massacres were not unknown. Among the Europeans, the toll was largely on French and Spanish settlers, who were the first to land.

If the settlers faced an uneasy alliance with the Cusabo, the Cusabo themselves knew an even stronger enemy in the Westo, a vigorous inland tribe. Over time, the Westo dominated until they in turn were swept out by stronger tribes and the English settlers of early Charles Town.

By the time of persistent English colonization, toward the end of the 17th century, another tribe, the Yemassee, had gained prominence in the region. Once friendly with the Spanish explorers to the south and educated in their ways of civilization, this group shifted its allegiance to the English as its members migrated north. They proved to be loyal supporters of Colonel "Tuscarora Jack" Barnwell, a flamboyant Irishman who had recently come to the Lowcountry, in a campaign to subdue hostile North Carolina tribes. Barnwell, who is buried in St. Helena's Episcopal Churchyard in Beaufort, proved to be a diplomat, as well: in 1719, he was called on by the settlers of Charles Town to represent their grievances to the Lords Proprietors, an action that resulted in the formal establishment of a royal colony.

The Yemassee carried on a healthy deerskin trade with the new Europeans, and there developed over time a far-ranging network of agents, outposts, and agreements. Yet, finally, the very success of the enterprise and the pressure of increased migration onto native lands proved to be the colonists' undoing. Long-simmering resentment of unscrupulous traders, unfair taking of land, and abuse of their people led to a gathering of fifteen Native American nations, who directed an assault from the Yemassee town at Pocotaligo. They attacked on Easter Sunday, 1715, killing as many traders as they could and sending the residents of Beaufort to their ships. The bloody Yemassee War lasted two years. At times, hundreds of warriors were dangerously close to Charles Town, reminding its residents of their isolation and pitiful protection under the crown. Eventually, the Yemassee forces disbanded and moved out of the region for good. By the middle of the 18th century, the last remnant tribes near Savannah had left the area.

## THE SETTLING OF CHARLES TOWN

Carolina was originally known to Europeans as "Carolana," and it was the dream of the kings of Spain and France to have it. Their struggle for domination, played out on lands far distant from their own, and among native inhabitants who had been there for centuries, marked the earliest days of settlement.

The Spanish arrived first, in 1521, under the leadership of Francisco Gordillo: he named the Sea Island area Santa Elena. Further colonization was planned for but never materialized. Five years later, another Spaniard, Vasquez de Ayllon, having heard marvelous stories of the rich, vast land of Santa Elena, gathered 500 settlers and established his party at a point farther north along the coast. Their hopes, too, were to be dashed — by illness, a revolt among the slaves they had brought, attacks by Native Americans, and unusually harsh winter weather.

In 1562, Captain Jean Ribaut established Charlesfort, the first Protestant colony in North America, in the area he named Port Royal. Charlesfort, too, soon petered out, and by 1566, the area belonged to the Spanish, who commenced to build a string of forts along the coast. In 1629, Charles I of England announced his intentions of ownership. In the end, it was the English claim that stuck, although the early residents of Charles Town faced down Spanish, French, and Native forces several times before they were secure.

Time passed, however, before the English pursued their claim by actually settling. It took a monarch pressed to return favors — and a group of men with means, entrepreneurial spirit, and a keen sense of the market — to reap the benefits imagined for so long by so many. The monarch was Charles II, king of England during the Restoration. The group of men was Carolina's Lords Proprietors: Sir John Colleton, the Duke of Albermarle (George Monk), Lord Craven, Lord Berkeley, Sir William Berkeley, Sir George Carteret, the Earl of Clarendon, and Lord Ashley (Anthony Ashley Cooper).

The familiar nursery rhyme that calls Old King Cole a "merry old soul" might aptly have applied to Charles II. By 1663, restored to the throne after the dispatch of Cromwell, Charles found himself short of cash and facing obligations to those who had helped him in the late civil war. As a token of his appreciation, he gave to his loyal friends the territory "described in the parts of America not yet cultivated or planted, and only inhabited by some barbarous people who have no knowledge of Almighty God." This was to be the Carolina Province. Its development, particularly along the lower coast, was to define a society that exists today.

Planning for colonization began immediately. Sir John Colleton, who had lived among the planters in Barbados, convinced his associates of the need for expansion of the society there (already nearly 40 years old) and of the profits to be made in overseeing its relocation. In the summer of 1663, Captain William Hilton sailed the ship *Adventure* into Port Royal Sound, and their project began in earnest.

Hilton's successful foray and contact with friendly natives led to another exploratory trip three years later under the leadership of Captain Robert

*A replica of the* Adventure, *docked in Old Towne Creek. Captain William Hilton's vessel arrived from England in 1663 — a surprisingly small boat to undertake such a journey. It was later used as a coastal trading vessel.*

Wade Spees

Sandford. This time, the English left behind Henry Woodward, a surgeon whose interest in the culture, language, and habits of the Native Americans was to ease the way, several years hence, for the first settlement at Charles Town. That day finally came in 1670 with the arrival of the ship *Carolina*, the only one of three ships to complete the voyage from England via Barbados.

It was at first unclear precisely where to settle — whether in the vicinity of Port Royal Sound, which Hilton had explored, or farther north, along the North Edisto River, where Sandford had ventured. Finally, after further viewing of both sites under the piloting and careful guidance of the *cacique* of the Kiawah tribe, the colonists established a fort at Albermarle Point, in the lands of the Kiawah, at Old Towne Creek up the Ashley River from present-day Charleston.

The earliest years of this colony have been brought to life at Charles Towne Landing which today offers a true sense of the importance of siting —high on a bluff from which unfriendly Spanish ships might be seen — and evidence of agricultural successes and failures. Small-scale farming worked; large cash crops, upon which rested the hopes of the Barbadian planters, didn't as yet.

In 1671, another shipload of colonists arrived, including more from Barbados, accompanied by their slaves; and by the following year the colony consisted of 30 houses and 200 people.

The colonists prospered and gained confidence, such that by 1680 they had removed themselves from Albermarle Point to a site on the peninsula at the mouth of the harbor, where they laid out their city. From this time forward, the development of Charles Town — indeed of the entire Lowcountry of which it was the capital — proceeded rapidly.

## EARLY GROWTH AND PROSPERITY

**B**etween 1690 and 1720, according to the historian Carl Bridenbaugh, the population of Charles Town tripled. New immigrants included French Huguenots and Irish, who established themselves in business and government. Wharves, churches, protective sea walls, defensive bastions, and homes were built. Streets were named (Church, Broad, Meeting, Tradd, and Queen are among those you can see today) and some of them were even paved with oyster shells. Trade with the Native Americans was lively, and exports thrived: deerskins and fur were shipped to England; pork, corn, naval stores, and lumber went to Barbados and the southern islands. The vast natural networks of creeks and rivers opened up the countryside to planters who raised beef and pork, cultivated cotton, rice, and indigo, and harvested lumber. And of course the waterways were crucial to transporting all these goods to Charles Town.

In governance, the influence of the Barbados colony continued to be felt in the key areas of law and representation by parish, and in the adoption of the slave code. The settlers from Barbados also imposed their architecture — the classic design with its raised basement and upstairs piazzas —and their intent to develop plantations outside the city limits. The increasing importation of slaves followed, an absolute essential in making large-scale agriculture a success.

Thus, from the very beginning, Charles Town was a society in which profitability and expansion — not to mention ease of living, even among the less grand — were inextricably tied to slaves and their management by law and custom. The historian Peter Wood estimates that by 1715 the slave population exceeded the European population.

Prosperity did not guarantee security, though. Charles Town faced threats from outsiders: there were skirmishes with Native Americans, Spanish soldiers, even pirates such as Blackbeard (Edward Teach) and Stede Bonnet. In 1718, 49 pirates were hanged.

Success in trade and a growing, more diverse population did, however, embolden the citizens to improve their lot. Prompted by resentment toward England (which refused to help pay for the defense of the city, attempted to enact trade restrictions, and raised the colonists quitrents, among other heavy-handed actions), the citizens challenged the very form of proprietorship under which their colony had been established. In 1721, after much to-and-fro with England, the Carolina Province became a royal colony. By the 1730s, it was referred to by its new name, Charlestown. Only after the Revolution, when it was incorporated as the new state of South Carolina's first city, would it finally adopt the now-familiar spelling as Charleston.

## EXPANSION IN THE COLONIAL LOWCOUNTRY

Once people were settled, once they were safe, once they had established their markets and their means of production in slaves, the Lowcountry around colonial Charlestown started its meteoric climb to achieve what it eventually became: person for person, the wealthiest region in the colonies.

It started with rice; then came indigo, and finally cotton. The fact that all these crops were suited to Lowcountry cultivation, that there was land to support them and slaves to work them, that there was desire abroad for their harvest (in some cases a bounty paid for it), and hefty profit to be made on it, left only a need for a class of men to seize the opportunity to grow rich. As was the case in other colonies, there were plenty of them, and they promptly did so.

The world they began to establish, the ways they embellished it, the physical order they imposed on it, and the choices they made to keep it alive defined Lowcountry culture right up to the Civil War. Even after that, even today, the echoes of those efforts resound in Lowcountry political, social, and economic life. In the deepest way, they form the basis of the stories people tell themselves about who they are.

As planters and their families spread out — and as new colonists continued to arrive from Barbados — they ventured across the Ashley River to Magnolia and Drayton Hall and Middleton Plantation; they went to Goose Creek and

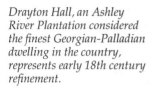

*Drayton Hall, an Ashley River Plantation considered the finest Georgian-Palladian dwelling in the country, represents early 18th century refinement.*

Wade Spees

points inland, to Beaufort, across the Sea Islands of Kiawah, Seabrook, John's, Edisto, St. Helena, Lady's, and Hilton Head. In addition to their main house in the city, they might establish a "big house" on one plantation and then own several others that were far more rustic, run by overseers and a slave crew. Profits were turned to acquire new land and slaves. A merchant, having amassed a fortune in town, would follow a path similar to the one taken by this newly landed gentry. Planters were businessmen, and vice versa.

Thus emerged a small society that was at once far-flung across the Lowcountry but glued together by shared aspirations, tastes, assumptions about plantation life and the treatment of blacks, even by marriage.

The relation between city and country was intimate. Charlestown, already the throbbing commercial heart of this society, came to display all its wealth. There were theatrical performances, clubs of every variety, subscription concerts followed by elaborate balls, racetracks, even a "season" that included "Race Week" in February, which was marked by nonstop celebrations, balls, concerts, and festivities attended by city residents and by planters and their families who would travel in from the country. Thomas Elfe, a magnificent cabinetmaker whose work can be seen at the Heyward-Washington House, set a standard for stylistic elegance. Direct trade with England, estimated to have been six times what it was with the other colonies, delivered the latest in fashionable household goods. Children were sent abroad to be educated.

By 1740, a reliable monthly postal service allowed members of this class to connect with their counterparts throughout the colonies. The hierarchy was in place, as was a concomitant sense of "breeding" and the unique sense of power derived from owning much of the population (the slaves) and determining the lives of most everyone else (the tiny, dependent class of working craftspeople). The vast tidal landscape and the people who inhabited it had been brought under control.

A "single house" of the Georgian period, built of cypress and adorned, as the best houses might be, with a drawing-room mantel by Thomas Elfe.

Wade Spees

Carl Bridenbaugh has written of this period that the first families of Charlestown presented "the unusual spectacle of a class of culture and leisure living on the very edge of the wilderness a life of refinement." In fact, there was still a lot of wilderness. To the south, it was just being tamed. By 1742, when there were nearly 7,000 people living in Charlestown, Savannah's population numbered only in the hundreds.

## THE FOUNDING OF SAVANNAH

**B**y comparison with the settling of Charlestown, the founding of Savannah in 1733 was seen as a far less ambitious enterprise — and perhaps a morally loftier one. The colony began as the idea of a group of twenty Englishmen, who petitioned the Crown for a grant of land. They were known as the Trustees, and they had idealistic, philanthropic goals: land would be held communally, settlers would be selected from "impoverished classes"; Trustees would pay for passage of settlers; there would be no liquor, slavery, or land speculation. The Trustees were given executive and legislative powers for 21 years. They could distribute land to settlers, but land was held in the Trustees' name.

The 114 or so settlers who arrived under the flag of King George were mostly of modest means, and their goal — as outlined by the Trustees — was the development of exports, including wine and silk. They were also supposed to defend the colony from the Spanish, and thus provide a buffer for prosperous Charlestown.

They were led by General James Oglethorpe, a high-minded Englishman with a caretaker's concern for his flock. Many addressed him as "Father." Such was his sense of mission that when the ship *Ann* arrived in Charlestown harbor for consultations with the royal governor, the passengers were required to remain aboard and fish for their supper, so as not to have their heads turned by the glamorous city ashore.

Continuing south, the *Ann* stopped at tiny Beaufort. Here passengers *were* allowed to fraternize with the residents, whose standard of living probably appeared to be more in line with what the newcomers, in the best of circumstances, might hope to accomplish. General Oglethorpe chose as his site for Savannah a place where "the river forms a half-moon, along the south side of which the banks are about 40 feet high, and on the top a flat, which they call a bluff." He was assisted by Colonel William Bull, a engineer from Charlestown with local surveying experience, and guided by Tomochichi, a friendly Yamacraw chief. The site was about 18 miles from the river's mouth on the Atlantic, on water sufficiently deep for ships drawing up to 12 feet to navigate within 10 yards of the shore.

Oglethorpe and Bull immediately set themselves to the task of planning the city, and it is the legacy of their inspired effort that distinguishes Savannah today. The city was, and is, a meticulously planned urban environment stretching back from the river in a series of squares and boulevards which, then as now, are landscaped focal points. The basic form consisted of blocks of five symmetrical 60 by 90 foot lots encompassing 20 squares. Space was designated for public buildings and market areas, as well as for secure retreats, in which settlers living outside the city limits could take cover in the event of Native American uprisings. The plan has been designated a National Historic Civil Engineering Landmark.

As things turned out, relations with the Native Americans remained friendly. Tomochichi supported the colonists' work throughout his life and was instrumental in winning the trust of tribes in the area. He was also willing to support Oglethorpe in battles with the Spanish, which were to occur sporadically over the next 10 years. The existence of a trading post nearby — run by John Musgrove, from South Carolina and his wife, Mary, who was part Creek — also smoothed the way for natural contact.

Given such a propitious start, it was up to the settlers to dig in, to clear and build, hunt and farm, and establish the Trustees' Garden. This they did, on the grants of 50 acres received by heads of families (five acres in the city, 45 outside it for farming). The settlers were also the beneficiaries of hundreds of head of livestock from their South Carolina neighbors, as well as rice and horses. For quite some time, even after Savannah got on its feet, South Carolina, and the port of Charlestown in particular, was to dominate the commercial life of the southern coast.

More settlers, including Irish, Scots, Swiss, Germans, and Italians, came very quickly. Jews and Protestant Salzburgers from the German-Austrian border area sought refuge from religious persecution. By 1741, there were 142 houses, a courthouse, jail, storehouse, market building, and a 10-acre, fenced public garden. By 1742, the liquor ban was repealed due to popular demand.

Soon enough the settlers found that some of the original restrictions intended to guide development were hampering it. By 1749, the ban on slavery was repealed because settlers felt they could not compete with South Carolina's productivity and overseas trade. In 1750, the Trustees relinquished their hold on land (again, by popular demand): private property ownership ensued.

In 1752, when the original Trustee Charter was up for review, Parliament refused further aid. As a result, in 1754, the colony became a royal province with governance by a royal council appointed by the King. As such, the province was subject to all the taxes, levies, duties, etc. that the other American colonies endured.

Thus in a sense released from Oglethorpe's idealism, the colonists proceeded to develop plantations as their neighbors had. However, it took until the close of the French and Indian War in 1763 (when Florida was ceded to England) for Savannah to begin to flourish as a colonial city and primary port serving the Georgia backcountry. By the time of the Revolution, the South Carolina and Georgia colonies had settled lingering border disputes, were engaging freely in trade, and were communicating through four Lowcountry newspapers. The region had pulled together, united by shared commercial and social goals, and a culture deeply affected by slavery.

In 1775, a Provincial Congress was called because Savannah residents were as fed up with English governance and taxation as the rest of the colonies. In a show of solidarity and goodwill, the colony joined the Revolution.

## THE AMERICAN REVOLUTION

Ten years before reports of the battles of Lexington and Concord reached the Lowcountry, its residents were taking independent action to defy British rule, especially its methods of colonial governance and taxation. By the time of the Stamp Act in 1765, they had become wealthy, self-confident and better-organized in their own military defense. Having built their cities from scratch, they were in no mood to be further subjugated, and their responses were violent. In Charlestown, long-festering political disagreements between the colonists and the royal governor burst to the surface. They bitterly resented his order to move the Assembly and center of government to Beaufort, a day's journey by boat. In Savannah, where relations between colonists and governor had been more cordial, groups of Liberty Boys nevertheless were openly challenging loyalists and destroying British property.

By 1774, many colonists had become defiant. The merchants of Charlestown

*Fear of fire in homes relegated cooking to nearby "kitchen houses" like this one behind the Heyward-Washington House. Thomas Heyward, Jr. signed the Declaration of Independence.*

Wade Spees

refused to buy tea that had been taxed, preferring to let it mold in the Exchange Building, which you can see today at the foot of Broad Street. British products were boycotted. Five delegates were sent to the First Continental Congress. In Savannah, leaders gathered at Tondee's Tavern to sign a petition denouncing the acts Parliament had passed in response to the Boston Tea Party (the Intolerable Acts) and insisting on their independent rights.

At this point, war seemed inevitable, even though there were loyalists throughout the Lowcountry who urged negotiation and reconsideration of non-importation policies. In 1776, four South Carolinians and three Georgians signed the Declaration of Independence. Colonial rule was over, but the fighting had just begun.

In the first significant victory of the Revolution (June 28, 1776, a day that is still celebrated in Charleston), General William Moultrie, outnumbered and outgunned, defeated an invading fleet of 50 British warships from his position on Sullivan's Island, in a fort built of palmetto logs. Visitors to the site today are impressed by the degree of risk and bravery that battle entailed.

But the Lowcountry was not yet secure. In December 1778, the British captured Savannah, and in May 1780, after a one-month siege, they finally subdued Charlestown. The British wreaked vengeance on the colonists by imprisoning and executing patriots. When they finally left the Lowcountry, in 1782, they were loaded down with war booty.

The American Revolution had a profound effect on the heretofore stable Lowcountry society. It was nothing less than a civil war dividing families and generations. According to Robert Rosen in *A Short History of Charleston*, William Bull was for the king; his nephews for the revolutionaries. Daniel Heyward was a Tory, but his son Thomas signed the Declaration of Independence. Similar clashes of ideals and politics occurred in other promi-

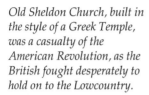

*Old Sheldon Church, built in the style of a Greek Temple, was a casualty of the American Revolution, as the British fought desperately to hold on to the Lowcountry.*

Wade Spees

nent Lowcountry families such as the Draytons, Pinckneys, Manigaults, Horrys, and Hugers.

The political questions raised by the conflict sensitized new classes of people to their own self-interest. The governments that came into place afterwards reflected these diverse new motivations. No longer were mechanics and other artisans — "the little people" — satisfied with government dominated by the planter class, especially when planters' slaves soaked up most of the available work. As for the wealthy, they were forced to read the handwriting on the wall; fortunately, some of the Lowcountry's planters were themselves ardent patriots, and they adjusted to democratic government, though their influence remained out of proportion to their numbers.

The years following the Revolution saw a fantastic boom in population, in building, and in commerce. Many of the houses of the Lowcountry date from this Federal period, in which new fortunes were made and old ones even further enhanced. If the architecture of the Lowcountry can be read as a book, this is its first great chapter.

Entrepreneurs, ship captains, military people, and merchants from New England came to the cities and the Sea Islands to build their plantations. While the bounty on indigo was a casualty of war and led to a decline in that crop, the invention in 1793 of the cotton gin, on a plantation near Savannah, meant that the process of removing seeds from cotton could occur with greater ease and speed. Slaves working in the ginhouses still plucked by hand seeds from the most highly prized strain then being grown: Sea Island cotton, whose long, silky fibers would be broken by the action of the gin. These seeds were saved, talked about, compared, and the best of them used for the following crop. Despite ups and downs in the cotton market and competition from the rest of the new American republic, for most of the next 60 years the Lowcountry flourished.

*In March, a broad hillside of flowering azaleas borders the rice mill pond at Middleton Place; the formal gardens were built by slaves in the middle of the 18th century.*

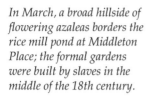

Wade Spees

## PLANTATION LIFE AND GULLAH CULTURE

The first African-American slave came to the Lowcountry to stay in 1670. Ever since then, slaves, freedmen, and their heirs have defined in the most essential way imaginable the politics, growth, lifestyle, culture, language, and habits of the Lowcountry. The complexity of relations between blacks and whites — who, in city or country, lived in close quarters and experienced daily contact but were governed by strict social codes enforced by penalties — has informed all Lowcountry history. Fear of black uprising, especially after the ill-fated Denmark Vesey rebellion in 1822, made for a regulation of life unknown outside the South.

For the best overview of slave life, visit The Charleston Museum. Or drive to Middleton Place, another site which, with its landscaped gardens and farm-yard, offers splendid evidence of the world the slaves built. Imagine the daily bustle of slaves around what is now Charleston's Market Area, or in Savannah's waterfront warehouses, now restored.

When you are out and about in the Lowcountry, probably the two most significant things to ponder, when thinking about its past, are the immense *enterprise* that characterized plantations (where they now may be silent and grand, they were once fantastically busy places with dozens of buildings) and the *isolation* the slaves endured there.

The world of the plantation was self-sufficient, marked by dozens of specific activities taking place according to the season: gathering marsh hay for fertilizer, harvesting, clearing and burning the fields, building and repairing, growing food crops, moting and ginning cotton, packing it in the cotton house, taking it to the landing to be shipped on barges. Within that world of action, and responding to its often crushing demands, there arose a culture among slaves, now generally called the Gullah culture, which included elements of their

African past. Scholars have identified these remnant "Africanisms" in religious and mythical beliefs, in patterns of speech and dress, in basketry, art, dance, and song. In its totality, Gullah is a way of life that informed — and still informs — the manner in which slaves and their descendants managed their relationship toward white people and kept intact some expression of their own identity.

From the earliest days, black slaves from certain rice-growing regions of the West African coast were prized for their knowledge of that crop's cultivation. Rice-growing is a tricky business. It requires periodic flooding of fields, the design, building, and maintenance of a dike-and-gate system, and hundreds of people, including children, to protect the rice plants from birds, gather it in, separate the grain from the chaff by means of sea-grass "fanner baskets," and clean it with mortar and pestle. In all of these areas, black people were experienced, and they taught what they knew.

Indigo and cotton crops demanded other kinds of hard labor — in preparing the fields with usually nothing more than a hoe and a plow-dragging ox, in building pits to soak the indigo or in chopping weeds to free the cotton plants, in extracting the dye or picking tufts from spiky bolls. Labor was apportioned by "tasks" of land, a task being about a quarter of an acre, for which slaves were responsible. Plantation ledgers were organized around work completed according to this system. In addition, slaves were used as carpenters, blacksmiths, cooks, loggers, boat-builders, butchers, and house-servants. While planters left at the onset of "the sickly season" to escape malaria, blacks were immune to this fever and worked through the miasmic heat of summer.

A caste system grew up within the population that served the needs of the plantation master: slaves associated with domestic life were at the top, and field hands were at the bottom. Becoming a black "driver" meant that a slave would work with an overseer to direct crews; it also meant meting out punishment and whippings to fellow slaves. With blacks outnumbering whites by vast majorities, keeping order through work and brutality was essential to the plantation system.

The treatment of slaves varied widely in the Lowcountry. It is important to remember that while the majority of white people in the city and the country owned slaves, only a very small portion of them owned more than a dozen. Some planters bought and sold families; some kept them together, some did not. Some allowed friendships or marriage to occur between plantations; some took skilled slaves to the city and hired them out. Some planters allowed slaves to hunt and fish, keep gardens, raise fowl, and sell eggs. Some gave them staples — molasses, cloth, tobacco, shoes — on a periodic basis.

Slaves lived in cabins or slave rows that shared a common wall and had dirt floors. On the plantations they worshipped at praise houses — usually small, clapboard buildings lined with benches — where services were marked by recitations of the gospel, praying, and the singing of spirituals in which an elder "deaconed out" a line and the worshippers responded in unison. They buried their dead in separate slave cemeteries, dozens of which are in still in use today.

*Slaves who were skilled craftsmen or domestic servants sometimes lived in cabins like these at Boone Hall Plantation.*

Wade Spees

Whatever the specific case, a slaves' identity (and that of his family) was tied to one place, which he might never leave during his lifetime. If ever he did travel it was under a strict pass or ticket system. His fortunes were often tied to one white family, and his heirs to its heirs. Education of slaves was either haphazard or strictly forbidden.

It is not possible to overestimate the way in which the Civil War disrupted the order imposed by the plantation world and the society it held in check. When recovery was to come to the Lowcountry, it would come to the countryside last.

## THE CIVIL WAR AND THE YEARS OF POVERTY

If the Lowcountry is seen by visitors as a place rich in references to the Civil War, both physical and spiritual, perhaps it is because there was such a difference in the "before" and "after." The cataclysmic changes wrought by that great conflict are well known.

Perhaps less well known is the fact that even before the Civil War, the Lowcountry already had been undergoing a slow transformation. Historians point to a definite drift of the Lowcountry after the 1820s, from occupying a place at the center of colonial and post-Revolutionary commerce to becoming just one of many prosperous regions in the South.

The Lowcountry's golden age was, in fact, the now-distant time of relative innocence and optimism long before the antebellum era, a time of cosmopolitan outlook and quiet accommodation with the rest of the country that was lost during the overheated days immediately prior to the Civil War. (It has only been in the later years of the 20th century — some might say as recently as the great resort booms, the "second Yankee invasion" — that the Lowcountry has been able to consider itself as reentering the mainstream of American culture.) The nostalgia for long-lost days, which most every visitor to the Lowcountry feels, is probably for a time more nearly 200 years ago than 140.

*The artistry — and the wealth — that produced the graceful "flying staircase" at the Nathaniel Russell House in Charleston was never to be matched after the Civil War.*

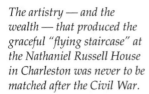

Wade Spees

By the 1850s, due to a number of factors, including the price and availability of cotton elsewhere, protective tariffs for new industries in the north, and the emergence of the abolitionist movement, the Lowcountry had lost its position of national preeminence. As a result, its outlook became more narrowly regional. Political positions hardened; tolerance for a national view of things receded. The institution of slavery was viewed less as a necessary evil — possibly temporary — and more as a positive benefit, one from which Southerners could not turn back. And there were politicians, like John C. Calhoun, who made an eloquent case for this vision. As Mary Boykin Chesnut wrote in her diary at the time of secession: "South Carolina had been rampant for years. She was the torment of herself and everyone else. Nobody could live in this state unless he were a fire-eater."

Of course, life did go on, populations increased, profits were made. Charleston and Savannah grew, with the addition of magnificent mansions in the Greek Revival style — such as Charleston's Edmondston-Alston House — or the Regency style — such as the William Scarbrough House in Savannah. Small towns like Beaufort raised their own gentry. Nonetheless, planters' societies that might, in the past, have discussed nothing more ominous than crop yields, seed types, and the accounting practices of their agents and cotton factors, now found their attentions turned to defensive matters concerning their slaves, their fortunes, and their state's rights.

---

S ecession is the fashion here. Young ladies sing for it; old ladies pray for it; young men are dying to fight for it; old men are ready to demonstrate it.

—From a dispatch to the London *Times*, April 1861, sent from Charleston by an English journalist

In December 1860, led by Lowcountry Secessionists, South Carolina separated itself from the Union. The following year, Georgia followed suit. Soon, the harbor forts that watched over both cities — Fort Sumter and Fort Pulaski — were battle sites. Both of the forts can be visited today, and the story of their defense is a dramatic one.

Additional glimpses of the Civil War period are poignantly on display at the Confederate Museum in Charleston, with its frayed uniforms and flags, and in the Green-Meldrim House in Savannah, headquarters of General Sherman, who, having completed his victorious March To the Sea in 1864, not only celebrated Christmas in Savannah but also offered the city itself as a gift to President Lincoln.

A less well known chapter of Civil War history, having Beaufort as its center, concerns the efforts on the part of Northern abolitionists to live among the newly freed slaves and prepare them for full "citizenship." The enterprise followed by several months the Union invasion of Port Royal in November 1861. Over the next several years, a hundred or so men and women took up residence in the abandoned plantation houses, managed the plantations for the government, which looked to cotton crops for revenue, and set up schools for slaves young and old in front parlors and cotton houses.

After the Civil War, the Lowcountry, now impoverished, turned in upon itself. It was as if people simply went home and stayed there, hoarding their gentility in their city homes as they might their last pennies, taking in sewing, teaching, and boarding guests. In the country they concentrated on making a living again as farmers, albeit far more modest ones. People were thrown back on their resources — their fishing and hunting and farming — and they made do. For every "Porgy" there were hundreds more: only small numbers of freedmen actually received, and were able to hang on to, land they had been promised.

Although phosphate mining, timbering, and shipyards emerged as centers of postwar activity, the economy was slow to repair itself. An idea of just how poor conditions were, right up until World War II, can be glimpsed in the work of Walker Evans, Marion Post Wolcott, and other photographers sent by the Farm Security Administration to document Lowcountry life.

As it turns out, the legacy of poverty was just as crucial in preserving the built environment of the Lowcountry as prosperity had been, in the early years, for bringing it to life. As early as the 1920s, Charlestonians were organizing to save their old buildings. In 1931, the city passed the nation's first Historic District zoning; some 20 years later, the Historic Savannah Foundation was founded to oppose the demolition of the Isaiah Davenport House.

Ever since, these cities' Historic Districts and properties in the country nearby have been central attractions to generations of tourists. They have provided architects, landscape gardeners, historians — even novelists — with material for inspiration. It is a remarkable testament to the Lowcountry's enduring legacy and powers of regeneration that, despite all this intellectual trawling, the region doesn't seem fished out.

## THE LOWCOUNTRY LEGACY

Through all its changes, the Lowcountry landscape has retained its immense allure for those who have lived and traveled here, from roving early settlers to today's nomads of the bus tour. Perhaps this is because a sense of history and a sense of place intersect at so many points in the Lowcountry. There is no high ground here. History itself provides the only vantage point, the only way to detach oneself from an insular sense of place that is always responding to forces — of wind and tide, of society and war — greater than itself.

It was and is a place to be desired. Whether your quest is satisfied by filling a bucket with oysters, or paddling a canoe in the marsh, or visiting an old home accompanied by nothing more than your imagination, the Lowcountry offers a rare chance to enact and to observe the subtle rituals of the past, and to take from them, for yourself, the pleasures they've delivered for so long to so many.

---

To describe our growing up in the lowcountry of South Carolina, I would have to take you to the marsh on a spring day, flush the great blue heron from its silent occupation, scatter marsh hens as we sink to our knees in the mud, open you an oyster with a pocketknife and feed it to you from the shell and say, 'There. That taste. That's the taste of my childhood.' I would say, 'Breathe deeply,' and you would breathe and remember that smell for the rest of your life, the bold, fecund aroma of the tidal marsh, exquisite and sensual, the smell of the South in heat, a smell like new milk, semen, and spilled wine, all perfumed with seawater.

—From *The Prince of Tides* by Pat Conroy
(Boston: Houghton Mifflin Company)
©1986 by Pat Conroy

---

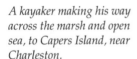

*A kayaker making his way across the marsh and open sea, to Capers Island, near Charleston.*

Wade Spees

# CHAPTER TWO

# Getting Here, Getting Around

## TRANSPORTATION

The first and most important fact about the Lowcountry is that it is mostly water. Land is an illusion, an accident, nothing to count on. Perhaps this is why the old houses of the region's cities and towns — and the dense feeling of permanence they exude — are so wildly venerated, above and beyond their architectural and historic status. While they certainly represented the values of an elite planter class up until the Civil War, they also appear — now, as in the past —

Courtesy of The Charleston Museum, Charleston, SC

*The men of Charleston's "Mosquito Fleet" rowed bateaux and collected oysters while running with the tide.*

literally to triumph over their surroundings, as if daring wind, water, and the harsh storms of hurricane season to teach them the lessons of frailty.

In September 1989, Hurricane Hugo did just that. Walls of water pushed 40-foot boats onto the downtown streets of Charleston. For weeks the drinking water tasted of turpentine, resinous and tannic, as fallen trees decomposed into rivers and leached into the water table, which in the best of times has never been more than a few feet away from the salty sea.

And that was just one storm. Day in and day out, water defines the Lowcountry, its aesthetics, its cuisine, its recreation, the siting of its houses, its economy, its history, its means of transportation. The way people get from place to place today still is determined by a force Lowcountry residents know they can never control, no matter how high bridges are built to accommodate the boat traffic beneath, nor how wide the causeway across the marsh. It takes but one glance at a boat stranded on a mud bar at low tide — as often happens — to realize how dependent the region is on the good graces of the tides.

The tides, which cast the riches of sea life toward shore and offered the first planters the possibility of harnessed power, bestowed on the Lowcountry a

natural abundance of marine and bird life and brought vast wealth in the cultivation of rice. The settlements that clustered around what we know today as
peninsular Charleston, flanked by the Ashley and Cooper Rivers, grew up
there to take advantage of the tidal watercourses. Flat-bottomed plantation
barges loaded with rice and, later on, bales of cotton, plied the rivers and
creeks to the city harbor. Throughout the Lowcountry, eight-oared bateaux,
made on the plantations and navigated by slaves, clove the marsh from one
plantation to another, carrying news, goods, and passengers. In Savannah, the
river offered both protection to an English colony in the Southern wilderness
and a commercial means by which its first English citizens — many of them
destitute or castaway — could start their new lives.

For nearly 200 years, water was the best highway in the Lowcountry. Quite
often, what roads existed were hardly distinguishable from the water. In 1784,
a traveler noted a "common highway" that "as lonely and desolate as this part
of the road is, without shade and with no dwellings in sight, it is by no means
a tedious road. The number of shells washed up, sponges, corals, sea grasses
and weeds, medusae, and many other ocean products which strew the beach,
engage and excite the attention."

As time went on, people of the Lowcountry took nature one step further:
they made roadbeds of oyster shell, fashioning a crown at the "center line" to
facilitate drainage. These were the best roads around, and in some towns like
Beaufort they were in use well into the 20th century. An unimproved road,
such as you'd find — and still find today — on the Sea Islands, was plowed
through fine sand, perhaps a foot deep, rutted and banked. More than one
elderly Lowcountry resident can tell a tale of pushing a Model T Ford through
this sand, or of watching the ice melt through the sawdust when the iceman
got stuck.

Perhaps as a result of the reliance on water travel, as well as the sheer isolation of the plantations and their rural dependencies, a thickly veined series of
land transportation routes never really developed in the Lowcountry. Instead
of trains and roads and bridges with soaring arcs, there evolved a fleet of small
packet steamers that made their way from island to island, picking up passengers, mail, produce, and cotton to deliver in Charleston and Savannah. And
ox-drawn carts, or horses, or marsh "tackies" (diminutive horses, something
like a Shetland pony) serviced them! When, in 1894, the historian Henry
Adams visited St. Helena Island, he traveled first by train, then by carriage
over a sand road, then on a shell road, then by foot to the ferry crossing, then
over the river to board the steamer *Flora*, which carried him to his destination.

These days, your car will take you almost anywhere you want to go in the
Lowcountry (which, for the purposes of this book, comprises the coastal plain
from Charleston to Savannah, from the Atlantic inland about 40 miles).
Driving here is convenient, of course, but the seamless experience of transportation provided by the automobile has displaced an older, deeper feeling —
that of reliance on the tides, the whimsy of weather, and navigators who mea-

### *Swamps*

Nearly one-third of this vast plain is what the inhabitants call swamps, which are the sources of numerous small rivers and their branches: these they call salt rivers, because the tides flow near to their sources, and generally carry a good depth and breadth of water for small craft, twenty or thirty miles upwards from the sea, when they branch and spread abroad like an open hand, interlocking with each other, and forming a chain of swamps across the Carolinas and Georgia, several miles parallel with the sea coast. These swamps are fed and replenished constantly by an infinite number of rivulets and rills, which spring out of the first bank or ascent.

—From *Travels of William Bartram*, 1791

sured the desire to move against what was possible. It might be said that the rhythm of life in the Lowcountry, dubbed the "Slowcountry" by some, was nurtured in those enforced waiting moments; sometimes it seemed wiser to stay put.

Fortunately, the growth of travel services has produced options to help a modern visitor reclaim this feeling of "down-time," during which you can, in a most modern way, observe your surroundings closely and well. The choices are outlined in this chapter. These days, the boat that takes you in the creek may be a Boston Whaler with a powerful outboard engine, but once you get out on the water, eye-level with the fiddler crabs scudding along the bank, you may as well be riding in an old Lowcountry bateau.

Finally, if you're coming to the Lowcountry from a city, or from someplace where water only runs from the tap, and if you're coming in by plane, take all the time you can to look out the window as the pilot descends. If the plane is circling low, as it often does, notice the watery necklace of islands and savannas, linked by tidal creeks, that make up the Lowcountry. As an abstraction at 10,000 feet, they seem mere daubs of color, surrounded and embraced by water. The truth is, that's the way they really are at ground level, too.

## GETTING TO THE LOWCOUNTRY

### BY CAR

Unless your visit to the Lowcountry is limited strictly to Charleston or Savannah or to a self-contained Hilton Head resort — and many delightfully complete visits are — you might consider this trip to be one where having your own car really pays off. The Lowcountry is decentralized; a lot of

*Savannah's newest bridge
spans the river between
Georgia and South Carolina.*

space separates those "points of interest." What's more, appreciating that very space by finding yourself in it lies at the heart of the Lowcountry experience. That's where you'll find some of the region's subtle treasures: the view of a marsh at sunset, the sight of feeding pelicans as they hit the water, the faded impression of an abandoned oyster-shell road strewn with wildflowers. It is in these very open spaces, in their linked geography, that the sense of times passed and lives abundantly lived will catch up with you and shape your awareness of what the Lowcountry is all about.

*From Washington and points north:* Travelers from the north can reach the Lowcountry by approaching it on I-95, which roughly parallels the coast. From there, well-marked exits direct you to downtown Charleston (via I-26), to Beaufort (via Highway 21), to Hilton Head (via Highway 46, then 278) and Savannah (via I-16). The coastal destinations beyond the big cities, such as Kiawah Island, Edisto Island, Beaufort, and Hilton Head, lie approximately an hour east of I-95. Distance from Washington to Charleston: 512 miles; to Savannah: 616 miles.

*From Jacksonville and points south:* Like visitors from the north, drivers from the south approach on I-95 and then turn east to the coast. Distance from Jacksonville to Charleston: 241 miles; to Savannah: 139 miles.

*From Asheville and points northwest:* Take I-40 to I-26, then follow I-26 toward Spartanburg and Columbia. About an hour out of Columbia, you meet I-95. At that point either continue east to Charleston or turn south. Distance from Asheville to Charleston: 265 miles; to Savannah: 297 miles.

*From Charlotte:* Take I-77 south to I-20 at Columbia; follow I-20 for a few exits to link up with I-26 east. Distance to Charleston: 200 miles; to Savannah: 240 miles.

*From Atlanta:* Take I-75 to I-16. When it crosses I-95 go north for Charleston, or continue directly to Savannah. Distance to Charleston: 286 miles; to Savannah: 259 miles.

Once you're in the Lowcountry, you will discover **U.S. Highway 17**, one of the region's oldest roads and still perhaps the most direct, a two-lane ribbon of blacktop that threads its way from above Charleston to Savannah (and beyond) through marshes, old rice fields, and bottomland forests. It's worth cutting off I-95 to get there, or to use it exclusively as your north-south highway. Turnoffs that access the Sea Islands to the east (Kiawah, Seabrook, Edisto, Port Royal, St. Helena, Hilton Head) and the Ashley River plantations to the west (along Hwy. 61) are well marked, as are historic sites, parks, and picnic grounds.

## BY BUS

*G reyhound* serves Charleston, Beaufort, and Savannah and maintains stations in those cities. It also serves points in between, but here the stops are less formal — perhaps as simple as a crossroads store. As a result, if you're planning to do a substantial amount of traveling by bus, you should consult both a detailed map and the bus schedule. Don't expect to find a taxi or rental-car stand — or even a working pay telephone — at every stop.

The service and price to Charleston and to Savannah from various points are roughly equal; in many cases the same bus goes to both cities. Travel times on longer trips may vary up to three hours, according to the number of stops and the specific route, so it's wise to ask about arrival times and whether or not it's a direct trip. (Usually there's at least one "express" trip per day.) Sample listings of weekday prices and frequency of service (both subject to change) from several cities follow. In general, once you purchase your ticket, it is only refundable at 85% of face value; that is, should your plans change and you wish to redeem your ticket, you will be charged a 15% cancellation fee.

To the *Savannah Greyhound Bus Terminal*, 610 W. Oglethorpe Ave. (912-232-2135):

*From New York* (16–22 hours): *Greyhound* (800-231-2222) runs five buses daily from the Port Authority at 625 8th Ave. (at 42nd St.). The 1998 one-way fare was $83, round-trip $145.

*From Washington D.C.* (11–16 hours): *Greyhound* (202-289-5154) has eight buses departing daily from the terminal at 1005 First St. N.E. The 1998 one-way fare was $100, round-trip $200.

*From Jacksonville* (3 hours): *Greyhound* (904-356-1841) departs ten times daily from the station at 10 N. Pearl St. The 1998 one-way fare was $18, round-trip $36.

*From Columbia* (4 hours): *Greyhound* (803-256-6465) has four buses departing daily from the station at 2015 Gervais St. The 1998 one-way fare was $27, round-trip $52.

*From Charlotte* (6 hours): Three *Greyhound* buses (704-375-9536) depart from the station at 601 W. Trade St. daily. The 1998 one-way fare was $45, round-trip $89.

*From Atlanta* (6 hours): Four *Greyhound* buses (404-522-6300) depart from the terminal at 232 Forsythe St. daily. The 1998 one-way fare was $37.45, round-trip $74.90.


## BY TRAIN

Amtrak travels the north-south corridor, making daily stops at North Charleston (the only station stop for Charleston, it's about 25 minutes from downtown), Yemassee (about 30 miles west of Beaufort), and Savannah. On the long hauls from major cities like New York, Washington, and Miami, there are generally two trains a day, departing morning and evening and arriving either late the same day or early the following morning. Traveling by night is a nice option for these 8- to 13-hour trips: when you awaken, you're there.

The rates for sleeping accommodations (economy or first-class, which includes meals) are usually tacked on to the lowest coach fare — and that fare varies depending on how far in advance you make your reservations and the availability on specific days. Call Amtrak (800-872-7245) or your travel agent for rates and schedules. Special packages with airlines might be available, as well as discounts if you can restrict your travel to certain days. Reduced fares for families or children are usually offered for summer travel.

If you're staying near Beaufort, Yemassee is your station stop. Make prior arrangements to be picked up; it's a country crossroads with minimum through traffic. The *Beaufort Cab Company* (843-524-4940), the *Yellow Cab Company of Beaufort* (843-522-1121), and *The Point Tours* (843-522-3576) can carry you to town. The 1998 fare was $35.

Some 1998 Amtrak fares from selected cities follow.

*From Washington:* Trains depart Union Station twice daily for North Charleston, a trip that lasts about 8.5 hours. Coach fares run between $144 and $286 round-trip. With sleeping accommodations the round-trip fares start at $410. Round-trip coach fares to Savannah range from $148 to $366; from $380 to $600 including sleeping accommodations.

*From New York*: One train departs Penn Station for North Charleston for the 13-hour ride. Coach fares range from $148 to $354 round-trip; with sleeping accommodations, from $480 to $680. There are two trains daily for Savannah. The round-trip coach fares are $148 to $356; starting at $460 for sleeping accommodations.

*From Chicago*: Travel includes layover and switching trains. One train daily to North Charleston, a 36-hour ride. Coach fares range from $224 to $440 round trip, $440 to $820 for sleeping accommodations. To Savannah, a 30-hour ride, coach fares range from $222 to $444 round-trip; from $640 to $1,120 with sleeping accommodations.

*From Jacksonville*: Trains depart once a day to North Charleston, twice a day to Savannah. A round-trip coach fare to North Charleston costs between $86 and $150; to Savannah it's $56 to $92.

*From Miami*: The morning train to North Charleston arrives 13 hours later and costs between $112 and $288, round-trip. There are two trains to Savannah. A round-trip fare costs between $114 and $228.

## BY COMMERCIAL AIRLINE

*Savannah's new airport celebrates the students and artists who have enriched the city in the last decade by bringing restaurants, galleries, and scores of old buildings to life.*

Wade Spees

Travelers bound for the Lowcountry can arrive and depart from *Charleston International Airport* or *Savannah International Airport*. Or they can use *Hilton Head Airport*, which is smaller and handles private planes and commuter shuttle service.

Numerous domestic and international carriers serve the Lowcountry cities, either with nonstop flights or connecting service through the regional hubs of Charlotte, NC, Raleigh/Durham, or Atlanta. The recent rebuilding of Charleston International and Savannah International into spacious, good-looking and easy-to-navigate airports has simplified the travel process, especially if you're traveling with golf clubs, "boogie" boards for body surfing, or a large family.

Once you're at the airport, you may want to pick up a rental car (best reserved in advance). For complete information, see the section on rental cars under "Getting Around the Lowcountry."

## BY PRIVATE PLANE

**I**f you're flying on your own, contact the following county or regional airports or services:

| | |
|---|---|
| **Beaufort County Airport** | 843-525-7647 |
| **East Cooper Airport** | 843-884-8837 |
| **Hilton Head Airport** | 843-681-6386 |
| **John's Island Airport** | 843-559-2401 |
| **Savannah Aviation** | 912-964-1022 |
| **Signature Flight Support** | 912-964-1557 |

## BY BOAT

**T**he *Intracoastal Waterway* winds through creek and river, ocean and sound, from one end of the Lowcountry to the other, making for some of the finest and most sublime cruising on the East Coast. The region's history of reliance on water travel, plus the recent development of marinas affiliated with the new resorts, have conspired to produce facilities of top quality and convenient location. If you're planning a water-based trip, it's best to judge the local options according to your particular needs — the size of your boat, availability of on-site repair services, proximity to sightseeing or restaurants or shopping, length of your stay, your price range, etc.

If you want to make use of the recreational services based at marinas, see the **Recreation** section in the appropriate chapter for some ideas. If your main

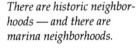

*There are historic neighbor-hoods — and there are marina neighborhoods.*

Wade Spees

mode of transportation is by boat, check the listings for details on berthing facilities and services. You should also consider word-of-mouth recommendations along the way.

## GETTING AROUND THE LOWCOUNTRY

This section will help you decide how you want to travel within the Lowcountry, for as you plan your trip, the kind of vacation you desire will really depend on how mobile you wish to be. For example, driving a rental car in the Lowcountry can be fun: the landscape is dead flat, and what hazards there are — ground fog that hangs about headlight-height, wild and brief summer showers — are local phenomena so site-specific that you may come upon them and then pass through them wondering all the time why it's not raining "over there."

On the other hand, if your destination is Charleston or Beaufort or Savannah, their *Historic Districts* are best savored on foot or bicycle, or by joining any one of the dozens of tours offered by city-licensed operators. While these guides offer their commentary on cultural, historic, military, and architectural sites, you can be riding in a horse-drawn carriage, a tour boat, a mini-van, a motorized trolley, a bus — even a surrey with the fringe on top. Knowing the breadth and variety of these services should help you make your transportation choices. These touring options available follow at the end of this chapter.

---

### The Shell Road

The only thoroughfare by land between Beaufort and Charleston is the 'Shell Road,' a beautiful avenue, which, about nine miles from Beaufort, strikes a ferry across the Coosaw River. War abolished the ferry, and made the river the permanent barrier between the opposing picket lines. For ten miles, right and left, these lines extended, marked by well-worn footpaths, following the endless windings of the stream; and they never varied until nearly the end of the war. Upon their maintenance depended our whole foothold on the Sea Islands; and upon that again finally depended the whole campaign of Sherman.

—From *Army Life in a Black Regiment*, 1869
by Thomas Wentworth Higginson

## LOWCOUNTRY ACCESS

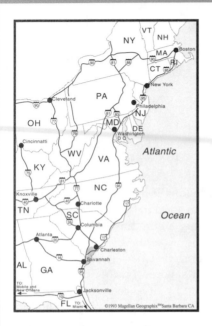

The approximate distances and driving times to Charleston and selected cities are given in the charts below. The distance between Charleston and Savannah is 114 miles, so depending on the direction from which you are travelling, you should adjust accordingly. If you're touring within the Lowcountry, however, stopping along the way between Charleston and Savannah in places like Beaufort, Hilton Head, Bluffton, Edisto, or Walterboro, this trip easily may take a day. In general, traveling to specific Sea Island destinations located to the east of the major cities can add up to an hour to your trip.

To Charleston from:

| CITY | MILES | HOURS |
|------|-------|-------|
| Atlanta | 291 | 5 |
| Boston | 1012 | 17 |
| Charlotte | 219 | 4 |
| Chicago | 906 | 15.5 |
| Knoxville | 395 | 7 |
| Miami | 590 | 10.5 |
| New Orleans | 784 | 13 |
| New York | 768 | 13 |
| Washington, D.C. | 532 | 8.5 |

## BY BUS

*Greyhound* is your carrier between Savannah and the North Charleston station at 3610 Dorchester Rd. (800-231-2222; 843-744-4247) with a stop in Beaufort (843-524-4646) at 1307 Boundary St. Buses run several times daily and the trip takes about two hours and 45 minutes. In 1998, the one-way weekday fare between Savannah and Charleston was $22, round-trip $43. The fare to Beaufort was $11 one-way, $22 round-trip. From Beaufort to Charleston costs $20 one-way, $40 round trip. There is no service to Hilton Head.

In *Charleston,* the attractive trolley-like *Downtown Area Shuttle (D.A.S.H.)* (843-724-7420) makes regular stops along five routes in the Historic District and greater downtown area. Board at the Visitor Center at 375 Meeting St., where you are encouraged to park your car. The D.A.S.H. maps and schedules are easy to follow and color-coded by route. All-day shuttle passes cost $2; a three-day pass is $5; single rides are $0.75. Fares for adults over 55 and disabled passengers are $0.25, except at rush hours, and children age six and under ride free. Exact change is required.

In *Savannah,* there's *C.A.T. — Chatham Area Transit* (912-233-5767). Fares are $0.50 per ride; $1.50 for a day pass; $4 for a three-day pass. The 22-passenger electric-powered shuttle bus makes 32 stops throughout downtown. C.A.T. also provides specialized door-to-door service for disabled passengers, but you should call to arrange the specifics before your visit.

## BY TRAIN

*Amtrak* (843-744-8264) runs two trains daily — one in the morning, one in the evening — between Charleston and Savannah, a trip of about 90 minutes. 1998 coach fares were $16–32 one-way, between $31 and $50 round-trip.

## BY PLANE

The quickest way between points in the Lowcountry is by plane; and if you charter one you can treat yourself to grand sightseeing as well. The following companies offer a variety of charter, touring, aircraft rental, and emergency services, some of which operate 24 hours a day:

### *Charleston*

| | |
|---|---|
| **Flying High Over Charleston, Inc.** | 843-569-6148 |
| **Million Air Charleston Executive at John's Island** | 843- 559-2401 |
| **Million Air at Charleston International** | 843-744-2581 |

*Beaufort*

**Mac Air**                                                     843-522-0748

*Savannah*

| | |
|---|---|
| **Aeroborne Enterprises** | 912-857-3220 |
| **Diamond Aviation** | 800-476-9181 |
| **DMS Aviation** | 912-644-5118 |
| **Savannah Aviation** | 800-544-8032 |

*Hilton Head*

**Executive Air Ltd.**                                         843-689-5300

In 1998, the average round-trip cost between Charleston and Savannah for a twin-engine plane (pilot plus eight passengers) was $850, based on an hourly-rate. Sightseeing tours over the Charleston area in a 4-seater plane cost $125–$150. They last a little over an hour and accommodate three passengers. You may be able to make arrangements for a single-engine plane, a jet, and even for one-way service, depending on your needs.

## BY TAXI OR LIMOUSINE

*Alternative transportation in Charleston includes rickshaws, bicycles, and buggies. Can wings be far behind?*

Wade Spees

In the heat of the summer the ice-cold interior of a plush limousine will deliver heavenly relief; or, if modesty suits you better, you may want simply to hire a car and driver for a day. Whether you're touring by the hour or desire longer service, here are some options:

## Charleston

| | |
|---|---|
| Carey Limousine | 843-723-2383 / 800-336-4646 |
| The Charleston Connection | 843-556-5752 |
| Low Country Limousine | 843-760-6060 / 800-968-1707 |

## Beaufort/Hilton Head

| | |
|---|---|
| Allen Limousine | 843-846-4242 |
| At Your Service Transportation | 843-837-3783 |
| Camelot Limousine & Tours | 843-842-7777 |
| Lowcountry Adventures Ltd. | 800-845-5582 |

## Savannah

| | |
|---|---|
| A & E Luxury Limousine | 912-354-2982 |
| Atlantic Coast Limousine Service | 912-232-9988 |
| Southern Knights | 912-920-0828 |

In addition, there are taxi, van, and limousine services at both the Charleston and Savannah airport terminals; you can use these if transportation is not provided by your hotel or resort area. If you're staying in a B&B, the proprietor may be able to make an arrangement for you or suggest a service. The 1998 one-way taxi fare from Charleston International to the city was $15; to the resort islands, $30. From the Savannah Airport to downtown costs $18. The rates are based on one passenger traveling; group rates are available. If your destination is somewhat further afield, say from Savannah to Beaufort (a 60-minute ride), expect to pay between $60 and $75. Within the cities, taxis should be called well in advance, for they are sometimes slow to respond, and street pickup is limited.

## BY BUS, MINIVAN, OR TROLLEY

After all is said and done, the emergence of the "New South" has just as much to do with economics and enlightenment as with air-conditioning. There's no doubt that the comfort and cool of a minivan or bus tour — in which the guide is like your favorite classroom teacher and the atmosphere as fresh as a fine hotel room — has its virtues. The audio is high-quality, and many companies provide vehicles with extra-large windows which offer great views. These tours also travel to sites out of the city limits, such as historic forts and plantations.

But remember that comfort comes at a sacrifice — larger vehicles may not be able to navigate the old, sometimes alley-width streets of Historic Districts, and the pace is swiftly modern. They are a good choice for handicapped pas-

*Riding a trolley leaves time for observing city life in all directions — down the receding street, framed by live oaks, or ahead to landscaped squares.*

Wade Spees

sengers, the eager visitor who wants to cover a lot of ground in a day, and those with a taste for the deluxe. Tours range from one to 2.5 hours, longer for out-of-town sites. In 1998, the price per person ranged from $13 to $26, with reduced rates for children.

### *Charleston*

| | |
|---|---|
| **Doin' The Charleston** | 843-763-1233 / 800-647-0087 |
| **Living History Tours** | 843-207-9000 |
| **Sites and Insight Tours by Al Miller** | 843-762-0051 |
| **Sweet Grass Tours** | 843-556-0664 |
| **Talk of the Town** | 843-795-8199 |
| **Taylored Tours** | 843-763-5747 |

### *Beaufort*

| | |
|---|---|
| **Gullah & Geechie Mahn Tours** | 843-838-7516 |
| **The Point Tours** | 843-522-3576 / 800-774-8288 |
| **Spirit of Old Beaufort** | 843-525-0459 |

### *Hilton Head Area:*

| | |
|---|---|
| **Camelot Limousine and Tours** | 843-842-7777 |
| **Gullah Heritage Trail Tours** | 843-689-9317 |
| **Low Country Adventures** | 843-681-8212 / 800-845-5582 |

### Savannah

| | |
|---|---|
| **Gray Line Trolley Tours** | 912-234-8687 |
| **Hospitality Tours** | 912-233-0119 |
| **Negro Heritage Tour** | 912-234-8000 |
| **Old Savannah Tours** | 912-234-8128 / 800-517-9007 |
| **Old Town Trolley Tours** | 912-233-0083 |
| **Tapestry Tours** | 912-233-7770 / 800-794-7770 |

## BY RENTED CAR

A rriving by air and then renting a car during your stay is your best option if you plan to explore the Lowcountry. However, if you are planning to stay in one city or resort, a car might not be necessary. In any event, it is imperative, if you are traveling in the spring — high season throughout the Lowcountry — that you make reservations early.

Get a map to anticipate your turns (the kind the rental agency gives is fine); it's not that there are so many, it's just that there may be but one sign — miss it and you'll find yourself 10 miles out of your way.

Most of the major car rental companies have cars available at the airport terminals as well as in Charleston, Savannah, Beaufort, and Hilton Head. They include:

*Visitors approaching Hunting Island State Park are reminded of what residents know from experience.*

Wade Spees

**Alamo**: 800-327-9633 (Charleston International, 843-767-4417; Savannah International, 912-964-7364).

**Avis**: 800-831-2847 (Savannah International, 912-964-1781; Hilton Head, 843-681-4216).

**Budget**: 800-527-0700 (Charleston International, 843-760-9025; Savannah International, 912-966-1771; Hilton Head, 843-689-4040).

**Enterprise**: 800-736-8222 (Beaufort, 843-524-0494; Savannah, 912-920-0050; Hilton Head, 843-689-9910).

**Hertz**: 800-654-3131 (Charleston, 843-767-4552; Savannah, 912-964-9595).

**Thrifty**: 800-367-2277 (Charleston, 843-552-7531; Beaufort, 843-522-9996; Savannah International, 912-966-2277).

*From Charleston International Airport:* Follow the airport access road to I-26 into Charleston. Any downtown exit will take you to the peninsula. If you're traveling to Sullivan's Island or Isle of Palms, exit at I-526 east. If you're heading to the Ashley River plantations or Folly Beach, take I-526 west. For Edisto or Beaufort, take I-526 west and, when it intersects with Highway 17, go south. Turns for individual Sea Islands are marked.

Miles: 15 to downtown Charleston; 30 to Sullivan's Island and Isle of Palms; 30 to Kiawah and Seabrook; 40 to Edisto; 70 to Beaufort.

Time: 25 minutes to downtown; 40 to Sullivan's Island; 60 to Edisto, 80–90 to Beaufort.

*From Savannah International Airport:* Follow the access road to I-95, then to I-16 downtown. Hilton Head is about a 45-minute drive from I-95. Get on I-95 northbound. Take Exit 5 at Hardeeville. Follow Hwy. 46 to Hwy. 278, which is the main road on Hilton Head. For Beaufort, take Hwy. 307 to Hwy. 21. At I-95 turn north. Take Exit 8 to Beaufort along State Rd. 88. At the intersection of Hwy. 278 turn left, and then take the next right. Follow this road, Hwy. 170, directly into Beaufort.

Miles: 11 to Savannah's Historic District; 35 to Hilton Head; 40 to Beaufort.

Time: 25 minutes to Savannah, 50 to Beaufort and Hilton Head.

*From Hilton Head Airport:* Exit the airport and travel south on William Hilton Parkway, Highway 278. Exits for individual plantations are clearly marked.

## BY BOAT

Keep in mind that the Lowcountry is mostly water. If you can tear yourself away from the authentic seductions of what has come to be called by planners and preservationists "the built environment," you will be rewarded by views of marshes and marine life that exist in such a pristine state in only a few places in the United States. Even better, you may be overcome by a feeling

*You can still take in the view from a schooner, as passengers did 350 years ago.*

Wade Spees

of wondrous detachment as you see the skylines — and, at dusk, the twinkling lights — of the Historic Districts fade from view.

Whether you're kayaking or canoeing on your own, or joining a cruise, an excellent area map is available from Coastal Expeditions, Inc. (843-884-7684; P.O. Box 556, Sullivan's Island, SC 29482; $8.95). Some options for harbor and tour-boat cruises, and rides aboard sailboats and pontoon boats, follow. (Other options — for example, "Nature Cruises" — appear in the **Recreation** sections of individual chapters.) The trips generally last two hours, but longer excursions can be arranged. The 1998 per-person fares ranged from $12 to $25; reduced rates for children.

### Charleston

**Bohicket Charters/Rentals**      843-768-7294
**Charleston Explorer**      843-853-4386

| | |
|---|---|
| **Fort Sumter Tours/Charleston Harbor Tour** | 843-722-1691 |
| **Gray Line Water Tours** | 843-722-1112 |
| **Schooner Pride** (84' tall ship) | 843-571-2486 |

*Hilton Head Area*

| | |
|---|---|
| **Adventure Cruises** | 843-785-4558 |
| **Calibogue Cruises** | 843-681-7925 |
| **Vagabond Cruises** | 843-842-7179 |

*Beaufort*

| | |
|---|---|
| **ACE Basin Tours, Inc.** | 843-521-3099 |
| **Blackstone's Barge River Tours** | 843-524-4330 |
| **Coastal Excursions** | 843-770-0107 |

*Savannah*

| | |
|---|---|
| **Lowcountry River Excursions** | 912-898-9222 |
| **Old South Ducks, Inc.** | 912-232-3859 |
| **River Street Riverboat Co.** | 912-232-6404 |

## TOURING WITHIN THE HISTORIC DISTRICTS

### BY BICYCLE OR ON FOOT

The Historic Districts of Charleston, Beaufort, and Savannah are absolutely manageable under your own steam, and discovering their nooks and crannies independently reproduces in a nearly magical way the scale and rhythm of the past. Furthermore, even though their homes, churches, and ballast-stone streets have been preserved impeccably, they are still neighborhoods, not museums. Getting out from under the windshield or behind the tinted glass will help you understand the real, living context of these places, in which so much has occurred over time. Besides, it's probably dangerous to smell the jasmine and make a left turn at the same time.

There are many types of conveyances to choose from: bicycles, tandems (for two), and pedal carriages (for two or three people). Rentals are available by the hour, the half-day, the day, or the week. In 1998, the common hourly rate was $4 for a bicycle, $5 for a tandem, and $15 for a pedal carriage. Additional services by arrangement might include a two-hour personalized tour with a picnic.

## *Charleston*

| | |
|---|---|
| The Bicycle Shoppe | 843-722-8168 |
| Mike's Bikes | 843-795-3322 |

## *Beaufort*

| | |
|---|---|
| Lowcountry Bicycles | 843-524-9585 |

## *Savannah*

| | |
|---|---|
| Cycle Logical | 912-233-9401 |

Walking tours have come of age in the Lowcountry. Extolling the virtues of one's city in lacy prose is what most old-time residents do naturally, and at the drop of a hat. There are many stories to tell, and an abundance of people to tell them.

As guiding has evolved, so have tours tailored to specific interests: architecture, gardening, Civil War history, African-American culture, Jewish heritage, the real-life sites of films or novels set in the Lowcountry, significant religious buildings, and the success stories of the historic preservation movement. With sufficient advance notice, some private guides will craft a unique tour for your group, or offer bilingual service.

For travelers who wish to explore on their own, the Visitors Centers in Charleston, Beaufort, and Savannah offer guidebooks and maps outlining walking tours in the Historic Districts. (These are useful for bicyclists, too.) Narrated tours on cassette tape (for your car or, with a portable unit and headphones, for walkers and cyclists) are also available for rent.

Walking tours generally last up to two hours and are scheduled in both morning and afternoon. Reservations are recommended. In the summer, you are advised to wear a hat and sunscreen. In 1998, the price per person ranged from $9 to $20, with children under 12 free or at a reduced cost. Since some tours may operate from private homes, you may encounter answering machines, not always with the name of the tour identified. If you leave a message, your call will most likely be returned; or, you can try another tour.

Here are some ideas.

## *Charleston*

| | |
|---|---|
| Architectural Walking Tours | 843-893-2327 |
| Chai Y'All Tours | 843-556-0664 |
| Charleston Tea Party Tour | 843-577-5896 / 843-722-1779 |
| Charleston Walks | 843-577-3800 |
| Civil War Walking Tour | 843-722-7033 |
| Gullah Tours, Inc. | 843-763-7551 |
| Written in Time | 843-577-5931 |

### Beaufort

| | |
|---|---|
| The Spirit of Old Beaufort | 843-525-0459 |

### Savannah

| | |
|---|---|
| Ghost Talk, Ghost Walk | 912-233-3896 |
| Historic Walking Tours | 912-355-1740 |
| Hospitality Tours | 912-233-0119 |
| Square Routes | 912-232-6866 |
| Tours by BJ | 912-233-2335 |
| Victorian Lady Tours | 912-236-1886 |

## BY CARRIAGE

**B**oard a refurbished, horse- or mule-drawn carriage, and find yourself imagining the past at a leisurely pace while your guide tells colorful tales. The companies listed below are some among several. Tours generally last one hour and are scheduled throughout the day and evening. In 1996, the price per person ranged between $10 and $16; children ride free or at a reduced rate. Discounted rates and customized or private tours are often available if you book in advance. In Charleston and Savannah, tours depart from either the company stables or make stops at pre-arranged pick-up sites. In Beaufort, tours leave from the Visitors Center at 1006 Bay Street. Call for reservations and meeting sites.

### Charleston

| | |
|---|---|
| Charleston Carriage Co. | 843-577-0042 |
| Classic Carriage Tours | 843-853-3747 |
| Old South Carriage Co. | 843-723-9712 |
| Olde Towne Carriage Co. | 843-722-1315 |
| Palmetto Carriage Works | 843-723-8145 |

### Beaufort

| | |
|---|---|
| Beaufort Tour Service | 843-525-1300 |
| Carriage Tours of Beaufort | 843-521-1651 |

### Savannah

| | |
|---|---|
| Carriage Tours of Savannah | 912-236-6756 / 800-442-5933 |
| Magnolia Carriage Co. | 912-232-7727 |

The carriages haven't changed much, and neither have the mules.

Wade Spees

## "In A Sulky"

I ride right through the morning, from nine 'til four, without suffering from the heat so much as in one trip to town and back on one of our warm, still days at home. I have my white umbrella, there is usually some breeze, often a very cool one; the motion of the sulky puts me to sleep, but the heat of the sun has not been oppressive more than once or twice on this island. If I had attempted to follow all the directions I received before leaving, concerning my health, I should have been by this time a lunatic.

—Charles Ware to his family in Massachusetts, from St. Helena Island, July 30, 1862

*From* Letters From Port Royal, 1862–1868, *Elizabeth Ware Pearson, Editor — letters from the Northern abolitionists who went to the Beaufort area in early 1862 to teach the newly freed slaves.*

# CHAPTER THREE
# *A City of Stories*
# CHARLESTON

Charleston is one of the nation's oldest urban environments. It has been the site of some of the most dramatic and significant events in American history, and it has an architectural inventory that is more varied and abundant than any other city in America. As a colonial city, and then as a regional capital for more than 300 years, it has a continuity of culture.

To a visitor, awareness of this cultural

Wade Spees

*The beach is a naturally dramatic stage for performers from the Anonymity Dance Company.*

legacy may seem quaint or idiosyncratic. It is, in fact, a meaningful and pervasive sentiment, one that informs the smallest turn of phrase and the largest civic hopes of people who have long viewed their city as a place apart, a place with values so closely held that residents would, and did, die for them. In such a world (Charlestonians have called their home "The Holy City" with only a trace of irony) it is not surprising that when residents talk with visitors about Charleston's history — about its essence — they begin by talking about relationships: those between the races, between and among individuals and families, between the region and the rest of the country.

Compounding this sense of intense intimacy with the past is its indisputable physical expression in the city's man-made and natural landscape. For while it is one thing to tell a story of times gone by, it is quite another to be able to locate that narrative, and to read it, in an urban setting that still exists and reverberates with meaning. This quality is at the core of the city's cultural identity, more important than buildings or objects, although are plenty of them, too. Charleston is a city of culture because people still believe that a sense of history and of place distinguishes their lives.

Charleston has stayed small — some might say defiantly so — in a way different from any other region in the United States. Unlike many other American

Courtesy of The Charleston Trident Convention & Visitors Bureau (used by permission)

**CHARLESTON**

places, it was not compelled to reinvent itself over time. The traditional cultural pleasures to be had in dress balls, small concerts, the cultivation of gardens, card playing, church picnics, and literary societies continued for generations. The life of the plantation, in which families would be absent from the city except in seasonal bursts, heightened the importance of domestic culture: it has been said that without the plantations, set at some distance from each other, there would have been no tradition of Southern hospitality, nor the development of the domestic art of "visiting," so significant to this day.

Most obviously, Charleston stayed the same for so long because it liked what it was. It preferred its provincial insularity to what it perceived as vulgarity elsewhere. Especially in the early years of this century, it was too worn down to do much but carry on in the old ways, its people too habituated to the familiar social roles they inherited long after the society which had assigned those roles had been wiped out. They couldn't step out of their skins, and, for the most part, didn't want to.

But when the time came to protect the life they knew and valued, Charlestonians acted. They did not do so violently, of course, as in the case of Fort Sumter, but by means of political talent, hard work, and a potent sense of what mattered, residents were able to enact the country's first historic preservation ordinance to protect buildings and sites that might have otherwise been destroyed in the name of "progress."

The success of preservation efforts in the ensuing 70 years has meant that the past has been brought forward for all to see: in individual houses, in neighborhoods, and in whole districts. The city has become a colorful tapestry and a magnificent backdrop for all sorts of cultural activities.

Like the historic sections of the city, cultural activities keep brushing themselves up, reinvestigating the old, and cultivating the new. For every historic house there seems to be an art gallery; for every plantation tour, a presentation on slave life. Where blossoming gardens were once celebrated informally, now programs and walks guide a visitor's appreciation. The spirituals of the praise houses and the blues of the cotton fields are performed for bigger audiences. Modest sailing regattas have become Water Festivals.

Perhaps no event showcases Charleston like the annual Spoleto Festival, held for several weeks in May and June (for information see the Spoleto entry in the **Culture** section). Dozens of operatic, theatrical, dance, and musical performances transform the city. Exhibits of fine art and lecture series proliferate. Performers and artists with international reputations take up residence and flock to restaurants and parks.

Putting aside all of the activity that enlivens Charleston, it is enough to say that it is a marvelous city because it has escaped the trend that architectural critic Ada Louise Huxtable calls the "theming of America" in which "authentic reproductions" of the past are constructed selectively from scratch, squeaky clean: Charleston has no need to be replaced by a neater version of itself to be understood.

# LODGING

*George Washington didn't sleep here, but he came to visit.*

Wade Spees

When President George Washington toured the states of the new nation in 1791, he was determined to observe life as it was lived on all levels of society. In the Lowcountry, he accepted the hospitality and enthusiastic graciousness of the planters — he was rowed in their barges by slaves dressed in finery, and took meals in their mansions — but he preferred to spend the night in the "public houses" that existed along the main highways, in the simple places frequented by messengers and mail-carriers, small farmers and merchants. He even paid his own way, when he was permitted.

The public houses of Washington's day are long gone, of course, but the modest style of overnight lodging they offered, of clean rooms, shared bathrooms and perhaps communal meals, existed well into the 20th century. It was a custom, like most, that had its roots in necessity: during the years of poverty following the Civil War, taking in guests provided income for families or Confederate widows, who still lived in the commodious old houses.

These days, if you stay in an old home that has been transformed into a glossy bed-and-breakfast — and they are among the most romantic lodging options — the only Confederate widow in evidence will be in a portrait on the wall. They are elegant places, with Jacuzzi tubs and fireplaces: you are likely to hang your clothes in an antique armoire or view from your window walled gardens rimmed with flower beds and dense with camellias and azaleas.

Charleston also has first-rate luxury hotels; several inns and hotels renovated from larger commercial buildings; modest chain hotels; and, on its outskirts, dazzling beach resorts. The lodgings included here represent offerings in all of these categories. The list is by no means complete — there are new places springing up all the time. Rental agents, who might help you locate a house or villa in a quiet beach neighborhood, or in a private beach resort, have also been included.

Each option carries with it unique possibilities for you to consider. Although the distance between Charleston and the beach is not great, if you intend to spend most of your time in the city, to shop and eat out and take part in cultural life, you may not want to travel some distance to the beach for a night's sleep. Alternatively, if golf, tennis, boating, and being on the ocean are at the center of your vacation, or especially if you're travelling with children, it might be wise to make a resort or rental home your base, and travel to Charleston by day. Of course, for trips lasting several days, many combinations of lodging are possible.

Given the highly evolved level of tourist hospitality, some generalizations can be made. The services and facilities in the large hotels — including valet and room service, access/facilities for handicapped persons and children — compare favorably to those in other cities. The luxury inns, for their part, seem to be outdoing each other in their touches of detail: decanters of sherry and fruit baskets in your room; evening turn-down service complete with chocolates on the pillows; daily newspapers delivered with your breakfast; afternoon tea or refreshments served gratis in gardens, parlors, or courtyards. Even the bed and breakfast units, where a home's owner is your host, may offer helpful extras like jogger's maps, a selection of restaurant menus, and tips on great places to walk or sights to see.

If you're traveling with children, some hotels and inns can recommend on-site baby-sitting services. You should inquire and make specific arrangements in advance. Some places discourage guests traveling with children, but the rules are not always hard and fast, and can depend on a child's age, the number in your group, or the season. You will usually be charged for an extra person in the room; additional bedding can be provided. At the resorts, well-staffed activity programs occupy the younger set. If you have other special needs, you should ask to see if they can be accommodated. Pets, for example, are sometimes allowed, but few places really like to advertise the fact; most have regulations regarding smoking. Off-street parking is usually provided by the hotel, or other arrangements are included in your tariff, but you should confirm the arrangement. For more information, see the *Introduction*.

## *Rates*

| Inexpensive | Up to $50 |
| Moderate | $50 to $110 |
| Expensive | $110 to $180 |
| Very Expensive | $180 and up |

These rates do not include room taxes or special service charges that might apply during your stay.

### Credit cards

AE — American Express
CB — Carte Blanche
D — Discover Card

DC — Diner's Club
MC — MasterCard
V — Visa

## HOTELS AND LARGER INNS

*The grand tradition of Charleston architecture, New World style, at the Charleston Place.*

Wade Spees

**CHARLESTON PLACE**
843-722-4900 /
   800-611-5545.
130 Market St., Charleston,
   SC 29401.
Price: Expensive to Very
   Expensive.
Credit Cards: AE, D, DC,
   MC, V.

The building of this luxury hotel and the elegant shopping complex around it signaled a change in the look and feel of downtown Charleston — as if the city had finally hit the commercial big-time. The hotel's huge, glossy, presence (443 rooms) overshadows the small scale of King Street and has brought bigger stores, like Saks Fifth Ave., in its wake. It hums by day and night with tourists and convention guests. There are two restaurants, a popular bar, an Olympic-sized pool, and a complete fitness center on site. For all its size and dramatic appointments — a grand staircase, a huge chandelier, massive pots of flowers, shiny marble floors, and rooms of polished furniture — it's not off-putting, just more like its own village within the city. Special rate packages, which include tickets to Spoleto performances, are worth looking into.

**FRANCIS MARION
  HOTEL**
843-722-0600 /
  800-433-3733.
387 King St., Charleston, SC
  29403.
Price: Expensive to Very
  Expensive.
Credit Cards: AE, D, DC,
  MC, V.

Newly restored and reopened in mid-1996, it was a solid 1920s hotel to begin with: wide stairs and hallways, wood-paneling, plaster moldings covered in gold-leaf, a lobby with big windows and club chairs, and high ceilings. Today there are 226 guest rooms, including 66 suites of various configurations for extended families. It overlooks Calhoun Square, (with great views of Charleston from rooms on the upper floors) in the upbeat, College of Charleston neighborhood.

**KING CHARLES INN**
A Best Western Property.
843-723-7451 /
  800-528-1234.
237 Meeting St., Charleston,
  SC 29401.
Price: Moderate.
Credit Cards: AE, D, DC,
  MC, V.

A clean, convenient, place for visitors on a budget. There are 91 rooms, including some for non-smokers and some with French doors that open onto small balconies. The outdoor pool is located on an elevated, screened terrace, affording good privacy for an establishment that's in the heart of downtown. It may be modest but the service is attentive and the location unbeatable at the price.

**LODGE ALLEY INN**
843-722-1611 /
  800-845-1004.
195 E. Bay St., Charleston,
  SC 29401.
Price: Expensive to Very
  Expensive.
Credit Cards: AE, MC, V.

Lodge Alley was one of the first top-notch inns to emerge when the old warehouses on East Bay St. were renovated. It's a place of highly-polished, well-designed spaces, including a big outdoor courtyard where there is often live jazz at night. The original massive beams and brick walls have been left exposed in many rooms. The solid feeling is augmented by heavy doors, thick bedspreads, armoires, ample club chairs and, in some rooms, big sofas. There are 93 rooms which run the gamut from modest in size (mostly in the main inn building) to big, plush, private, and adorned with fireplaces and refrigerators. One- and two-bedroom suites offer completely furnished kitchens and can be rented by the night or, in the winter and summer, by the month. A one-night deposit is required to secure reservations.

**THE MILLS HOUSE**
A Holiday Inn Hotel.
843-577-2400 /
  800-874-9600.
115 Meeting St., Charleston,
  SC 29401.
Price: Expensive to Very
  Expensive.
Credit Cards: AE, D, DC,
  MC, V.

This is a big, bustling hotel with marble floors and glittering chandeliers where you can relax and people-watch from the cozy "Best Friend Bar," or sitting on a banquette in the lobby. (Nightly entertainment increases the foot traffic.) There are 214 guest rooms, tastefully outfitted with reproduction furniture, and 19 suites which have spacious areas for relaxing or meeting friends. After a day of walking, you may want to take a few laps in the pool or stretch out on the deck with the newspaper.

## SMALLER LUXURY INNS

**THE ANCHORAGE INN**
Innkeeper: Barry Hutto.
843-723-8300 /
  800-421-2952.
26 Vendue Range,
  Charleston, SC 29401.
Price: Moderate to
  Expensive.
Credit Cards: AE, MC, V.

This inn has distinguished itself by taking on a 17th-century English "coaching" theme: stucco finish on the walls, tapestries, painted furniture, muslin curtains, and beams exposed as they would be in a cottage of Shakespeare's time. There are 19 rooms and suites, some with Jacuzzi tubs and big sofas or handy card tables for writing all the postcards you promised to send. Continental breakfast is served buffet-style; wine and cheese is offered in the late afternoon.

**ANSONBOROUGH INN**
Innkeeper: Kevin Eichman.
843-723-1655 /
  800-522-2073.
21 Hasell St., Charleston,
  SC 29401.
Price: Moderate to
  Expensive.
Credit Cards: AE, D, MC, V.
A non-smoking inn.

The Ansonborough is a good example of how tasteful renovation, in this case of a circa-1900 stationer's warehouse near the Market, can infuse new life (and modern amenities) in old buildings. It's hard to believe that the airy lobby you see today — crisscrossed by massive exposed beams, dramatically lit, adorned with wildlife prints — and the spacious rooms above, were at one time probably no more than dark cubbyholes accessed by drafty passageways. Each of the 37 suites has a kitchen facility for light meals or snacks — you can request basic cookware — and varieties of bed sizes so that your suite can accommodate comfortably everyone in your party. Continental breakfast is served in the lobby.

**BARKSDALE HOUSE INN**
Innkeeper: Merritt
  Galifianakis.
843-577-4800.
27 George St., Charleston,
  SC 29401.
Price: Moderate to
  Expensive.
Credit Cards: MC, V.

This inn and its rear carriage house are set on a side street in the center of Charleston's shopping district, just blocks from the Market and the Gaillard Auditorium. You can leave your car here and make several forays in a day, returning to freshen up between expeditions in the air-conditioning, in a whirlpool tub (five rooms have them), or by the mellow light of a gas-log fire. Formal decorating touches, such as patterned valances and drapes, Scalamandre borders, and tall armoires that hide the television, add to the sense of settled-down privacy. There's a courtyard for Continental breakfast and a back porch where you can review the day's doings over a glass of lemonade.

**BATTERY CARRIAGE HOUSE INN**
Innkeepers: Katharine and Drayton Hastie.
843-727-3100 /
800-775-5575.
20 South Battery, Charleston, SC 29401.
Price: Expensive.
Credit Cards: AE, MC, V.

The main house at Number 20 South Battery was built in 1843, and today's visitors stay in rooms beneath and behind it, in the old carriage house. South Battery defines the edge of the historic residential district known as "South of Broad." This is the neighborhood that comes to mind when most people think of Charleston, a place of iron gates entwined with jasmine, columned houses set on high foundations, and narrow streets. There are 10 small rooms. Rush rugs offset pencil-post beds; hanging pots full of fragrant flowers soften the classic lines of the balcony. Continental breakfast and the newspaper arrive at your door, or you can start your day under the rose arbor.

**FULTON LANE INN**
Innkeeper: Reg Smith.
843-720-2600 /
800-720-2688.
202 King St., Charleston, SC 29401.
Price: Moderate to Very Expensive.
Credit Cards: MC, V.
Handicap Access: Two rooms.
A non-smoking inn.

This inn is located between King and Meeting Streets amidst the downtown antique and gallery district. The 27 rooms have a refreshing, airy, look: sisal, wicker, and muslin decorating accents; louvered shutters; wall-coverings and paint in soft, liquid colors like celadon, pale peach, and lemon. The feel is summer in the Lowcountry — all year long. You can go simple or go deluxe, with canopied beds and fireplaces, kitchens, and cathedral ceilings; all rooms have either one king-sized bed or two queen-sized beds.

**JOHN RUTLEDGE HOUSE INN**
Innkeeper: Linda Bishop.
843-723-7999 /
800-476-9741.
116 Broad St., Charleston SC 29401.
Price: Expensive to Very Expensive.
Credit Cards: AE, D, MC, V.

Tradition has it that John Rutledge (who later signed the U.S. Constitution) built this imposing house in the heart of Charleston around 1763 for his bride, Elizabeth Grimke. The antique furnishings, parquet floors, high ceilings, carved mantelpieces, and rich fabrics that characterize the house today suggest its original opulence, such as might have impressed President George Washington. Nineteen rooms (17 non-smoking) are offered to guests, either in the main house or in two carriage houses, and each one includes color television and mini-refrigerator. Suites are even more deluxe: additional sitting room, Jacuzzi tub, fireplaces. Continental breakfast is included and full breakfast is available. The huge upstairs sitting room, where you will find scrapbooks on the house's history and a collection of antique firearms, is a wonderful place to take tea or sherry. A first-night's deposit is required one month in advance, with a 72-hour cancellation policy.

*Tea in the courtyard at Maison DuPre, taken at most any season.*

Wade Spees

**MAISON DU PRE**
Innkeepers: Lucille and
    Bob Mulholland.
843-723-8691 /
    800-844-4667.
317 East Bay St.,
    Charleston, SC 29401.
Price: Moderate to
    Expensive.
Credit Cards: D, MC, V.

Three restored "single houses" and two carriage houses make up the inn, which is a short walk from the Gaillard Auditorium. There are 15 guest rooms spread throughout, some with private balconies that overlook the garden and courtyard, which are, themselves, among the inn's best features. Here you may imagine yourself sitting at a table as the light fades and the crepe myrtle blossoms float to the ground, sipping a glass of French wine, indulging yourself in a good novel or book on Charleston's history. Mrs. Mulholland is a painter and her work, as well as that of other artists, graces the walls. The feeling is at once European and elegant, but very cozy. Continental breakfast is complimentary, as is a wonderful afternoon tea party.

**PLANTER'S INN**
Innkeeper: Larry Spelts.
843-722-2345 /
    800-845-7082.
112 N. Market St.,
    Charleston, SC 29401.
Price: Moderate to
    Expensive.
Credit Cards: AE, D, DC,
    MC, V.
Handicap Access: Two
    rooms.

A location at the intersection of N. Market St. and Meeting St. makes this 62-room inn superbly convenient to nightlife, shopping, the Gibbes Art Gallery, and the historic residential areas. You can walk in any direction and find something going on. On weekend evenings, especially, the sidewalks will be crowded — the closest Charleston comes to having a "big city" feel. The rooms are elegant, with big bathrooms, and many have gas fireplaces and four-poster beds. Non-smoking rooms are available; Continental breakfast is included. A courtyard garden and rooftop terrace, as well as 1997 renovations, make this a top choice.

*Rooms in the shadows of an oak tree, piazzas to catch the breeze at Two Meeting Street Inn.*

Wade Spees

**TWO MEETING STREET INN**
Innkeepers: Jean and Pete Spell; Karen Spell-Shaw.
843-723-7322.
2 Meeting St., Charleston, SC 29401.
Price: Expensive to Very Expensive.
Credit Cards: None.
A non-smoking inn.

This Queen Anne mansion, with its wrap-around porches and rocking chairs, Tiffany stained-glass windows, and carved oak paneling, recently turned 100 years old, but probably has never looked better. Its public sitting rooms and guest rooms are filled with Oriental rugs and period accessories, and highlighted by fabrics and wall-coverings in rich, deep colors. There are nine rooms on three floors, all with private baths, most with ceiling fans, some with private balcony access. Honeymooners and couples celebrating a special anniversary often book rooms here a year in advance — especially those rooms with canopied four-poster beds so big that a special set of stairs is needed to climb into them. Continental breakfast is served in the dining room or on the patio. There is no smoking. Reservations are accepted with one night's tariff as a deposit; on weekends, a two-day reservation is required; a three-day minimum stay on holidays. Children over 12 are welcomed.

**VENDUE INN**
Innkeeper: Coyne Edmison.
843-577-7970 /
800-845-7900.
19 Vendue Range, Charleston, SC 29401.

The inn and adjacent West building are located immediately behind Charleston's waterfront park — a great place for a walk — and the inn's rooftop terrace and informal bar has a grand view of the harbor. The old complex of buildings offers a range of accommodations, 45 in all, from small rooms off narrow hallways to sumptuous suites

Moderate to Very Expensive.
Credit Cards: D, DC, MC, V.
Handicap Access: Available on first-floor rooms.

that feature fireplaces, marble tubs with Jacuzzis, well-stocked wet bars, even bathroom telephones. If you're traveling with another couple, or with family, or if you intend to entertain during your visit, such a suite arrangement might be a good idea. There are period furnishings throughout, and some light touches: a working player piano with several hundred piano rolls, shelves of books you are free to read, informal chamber music performances in the courtyard, and afternoon wine and cheese.

**VICTORIA HOUSE INN**
Innkeeper: Beth Babcock.
843-720-2944 /
800-933-5464.
208 King St., Charleston, SC 29401.
Price: Expensive to Very Expensive.
Credit Cards: D, DC, MC, V.

**B**uilt in 1889 in the Romanesque style, this inn offers 18 luxurious guest rooms and suites in a lush Victorian setting. There's lots of light and space, and even the less-grand rooms have handy, well-stocked refrigerators; the petite suites have whirlpool baths and fireplaces. The garden and lobby are convivial places to eat breakfast, meet other guests, or collapse with a refreshment at the end of the day. Continental breakfast is delivered to your room.

*A private entrance to your B&B takes you behind the garden walls.*

Wade Spees

A central reservation service, *Historic Charleston Bed and Breakfast* (843-722-6606 / 800-743-3583 / 843-722-9589 fax; 57 Broad St., Charleston, SC 29401) provides listings of rooms with private baths in the Historic District, in old homes, or in larger, self-contained buildings like carriage houses. There are some bargains, but most rates fall into the Moderate to Very Expensive range (Credit Cards: MC, V). Staying in such accommodations offers you the chance to feel like a local and to have privacy; some are well-suited to larger parties, families, or couples traveling together, and they may also have their own kitchen facilities, gardens, and bicycles for you to use. Most have telephones and televisions, but if it's important, you should confirm. Smoking is usually not permitted, and there are strict deposit and cancellation policies.

Another way to get behind the garden walls is to contact individual homeowners who rent "dependencies" attached to their property, such as kitchen buildings and carriage houses, or rooms in their own houses. Yet another possibility is to stay in lodgings which are not owner-occupied but not exactly commercial, either. Places of this sort tend to be as large as, say, four rooms and may be quite private. Contact the owners directly for rates, availability, lodging policies, and directions. Credit cards that are accepted are noted. Otherwise, cash, personal check, or traveler's check are acceptable. Here are some ideas:

**1837 BED AND BREAKFAST** (843-723-7166; 126 Wentworth St., Charleston, SC 29401) Eight guestrooms and a carriage house, verandas with rockers, full breakfast. Moderate. AE, MC, V.

**27 STATE STREET** (843-722-4243; 27 State St., Charleston, SC 29401) Enter your private suite through the courtyard of a four-square, circa 1800 house in Charleston's "French Quarter," a block off East Bay St. Expensive to Very Expensive.

**36 MEETING STREET BED AND BREAKFAST** (843-722-1034; 36 Meeting St., Charleston, SC 29401) Three guest suites in an 18th-century "single house," each with private bath and kitchenette. Two of them are two-bedroom units; one is a one-bedroom. Children welcome. Moderate. MC, V.

**BRASINGTON HOUSE** (843-722-1274; 328 East Bay St., Charleston, SC 29401) Four rooms in a Charleston single house furnished with antiques, king-sized beds, cable television. Breakfast included. MC, V.

**CAPERS-MOTTE HOUSE** (843-722-2263; 69 Church St., Charleston, SC 29401) Four rooms with private baths in a circa 1730 house listed on the National Register of Historic Places. Moderate. MC, V.

**THE KITCHEN HOUSE** (843-577-6362; 126 Tradd St., Charleston, SC 29401) Two guest rooms with private baths located in a charming restored outbuilding (circa 1731) next to a Colonial herb garden. Expensive. MC, V.

### Charleston Environs

If you prefer to stay outside Charleston, near a plantation or one of the Sea Islands, you'll find plenty to choose from. Here are some possibilities, arranged by locale, with separate sections on resort and rental accommodations and beach rental agents.

**MIDDLETON INN**
Manager: Doyle Gray.
843-556-0500 /
800-543-4774.
4290 Ashley River Road,
Charleston SC 29414.
Price: Moderate to
Expensive.
Credit Cards: AE, MC, V.
Handicap Access: Some
rooms.

The Middleton Inn is located on a bluff adjacent to the beautiful gardens at Middleton Place, about 25 minutes from downtown Charleston. If you want to enjoy utter serenity and privacy, or to take long walks along the Ashley River or at the Middleton Place Gardens (admission waived for inn guests), this is for you. The inn was designed by W.G. Clark, completed in 1985, and it's handsomely modern on the outside, splendidly understated on the inside. There are working log fireplaces, custom-made furniture, soft colors, and large bathrooms. Floor-to-ceiling windows with louvered shutters filter the light and air. There are 55 rooms in the four-building complex, each with a refrigerator. Continental breakfast is included. The restaurant at Middleton Place serves lunch daily, and dinner on Friday and Saturday.

## *Folly Beach*

**HOLLIDAY INN OF FOLLY BEACH** (843-588-2191 / 800-792-5270; 116 W. Ashley Ave., Folly Beach, SC 29439) This modest motel, one block from the beach, is as reliable as the chain hotel with the similar name, but it's much more inviting. Inexpensive to Expensive. AE, D, MC, V.

**CHARLESTON ON THE BEACH** (843-588-6464 / 800-290-0001; 1 Center St., Folly Beach, SC 29439) A big (132-room) oceanfront hotel (part of the Holiday Inn chain) with game room, pool, restaurant, and bar. Handicap access and non-smoking rooms available. Moderate to Expensive. AE, D, DC, MC, V.

## *Isle of Palms*

**SEA CABINS** (843-886-8144 / 800-476-0400; 1300 Ocean Front Blvd., Isle of Palms, SC 29451) There are 138 units here, clean and spare, each one with a bedroom, bath, kitchenette, living room, and balcony. Room for up to four adults. Moderate to Expensive. AE, MC, V.

## RESORTS AND RENTALS —CHARLESTON AREA SEA ISLANDS

The Sea Island resort areas around Charleston are approximately 35 minutes away from downtown. They are, by themselves, fully self-contained destinations from which you can travel to the city by day to sightsee and shop, and to which you can return for recreation, dining, and relaxation. In the summer, the islands provide unsurpassed beach access, ample opportunities for tennis and golf, and organized activities for children and adults.

What follows here is a list of the *resorts* and an outline of their lodgings. If you are interested in longer stays of a week or more, you may also want to contact some of the *rental agents* who specialize in rental of private beach properties, including villas and houses located both within the resorts and outside of them.

Rental accommodations are usually fully furnished, including washer and dryer, but you should check to see if you need to bring anything, if there are special features like handicap access, or if a fee for cleaning after your departure is included. Deposits are necessary, and if you need to cancel, you must often do so up to three weeks in advance to have your deposit returned. During summer months, minimum stays of three days (in a villa) to a week (in a house) are often required.

The 1998 summer rental prices for a two-bedroom, oceanfront house ranged from $1,200 to $1,250 per week. Of course, the farther you are from the beach — by a lagoon, say, or the marsh — the less expensive the rate. Prices are generally lower in the winter months, when many resorts offer discounted accommodations packages.

**KIAWAH ISLAND GOLF & TENNIS RESORT**
843-768-2121 / 800-654-2924 / 803-768-9339 fax.
www.kiawah-island.com.
12 Kiawah Beach Drive, Kiawah Island, SC 29455.
Price: Expensive to Very Expensive.
Credit Cards: AE, D, DC, MC, V.

The 150 guest-room inn is a big, rambling building with wooden decks and breezeways, ceiling fans, and plenty of places to sit in the shade. Youngsters have fun exploring its nooks, and adults appreciate the sense of privacy and quiet corners. Non-smoking rooms are available. Villa accommodations with kitchens (some 300 units) come in many sizes and are located throughout the resort. The beach is private and 10 miles long; there's an oceanfront pool, several smaller recreation areas, excellent golf and tennis facilities, six restaurants, and some nice resort shops. One of the best ways to get around is by bicycle along the 16 miles of paved trails. Kiawah remains the best-groomed, best-planned resort in the Lowcountry, and the most-desired site for new, extravagant "beach houses."

**SEABROOK ISLAND RESORT**
843-768-1000 / 800-845-2475 / 803-768-4922 fax.
1002 Landfall Way, Seabrook Island, SC 29455.
Price: Expensive to Very Expensive.
Credit Cards: AE, D, MC, V.

Guests at Seabrook, a 2,200-acre private country club community, are accommodated in one-, two-, and three-bedroom villas with kitchens. It's very low-key here: you can be left alone to wander the beach, ride bikes or horses, play golf or tennis, swim, lie in the sun, or catch crabs off a dock.

**WILD DUNES RESORT**
843-886-6000 /
  800-845-8880.
5757 Palm Blvd., Isle of
  Palms, SC 29451.
Price: Expensive to Very
  Expensive.
Credit Cards: AE, D, DC,
  MC, V.

Wild Dunes is just 15 miles north of Charleston, a convenient place to stay if you want to savor both beach and resort life, and the night-time excitement of the city. The 93-room Boardwalk Inn is new and there are dozens of units of varying sizes, with kitchens. At your doorstep, all the golf, tennis, and water sports you could want. Nearly three miles of beach lie within the resort; outside it, Isle of Palms has a commercial strip with restaurants and shops.

## BEACH RENTAL AGENTS

**Beachwalker Rentals** (843-768-1777 / 800-334-6308; 3690 Bohicket Rd., Johns Island, SC 29455) Accommodations on Kiawah Island.

**Benchmark Rentals, Inc.** (843-768-9800 / 800-992-9666; P.O. Box 773, Johns Island, SC 29457) Kiawah homes and villas. www.lfoa.com/benchmark.

**Carroll Realty** (843-886-9600 / 800-845-7718; 103 Palm Blvd., Isle of Palms, SC 29451) Homes and villas by the week, month, or year on Isle of Palms, Wild Dunes, and Sullivan's Island.

**Dunes Properties** (843-886-5600 / 800-843-2322; 1400 Palm Blvd., Isle of Palms, SC 29451) Vacation rentals throughout the year on Sullivan's Island, Isle of Palms, Seabrook, Dewees Island, Folly Beach, and at Wild Dunes.

**Folly Island Realty** (843-588-9653; P.O. Box 946, Folly Beach, SC 29439).

**Great Beach Vacations** Rentals at Kiawah (800-845-3911); Seabrook (800-845-2233); Wild Dunes (800-346-0606); Isle of Palms (800-344-5105); Sullivan's Island (800-247-5050); 2 Beachwalker Drive, Kiawah Island, SC 29455. A free 32-page guide to all the beach resorts is available.

**Pam Harrington Exclusives, Inc.** (843-768-0273 / 800-845-6966; 3690 Bohicket Rd., Suite 2-C, Johns Island, SC 29455) Homes and villas on Kiawah. http://www.kiawahexclusives.com.

# DINING

Dining is one Lowcountry ritual that remained important, even through hard times. Schoolchildren released for an hour from class and fathers home from the office gathered daily at the midday meal. It honored family, tradition, the art of conversation, and the resourcefulness of the cook. As the extraordinary Southern chef Edna Lewis has said: "The birds are just the beginning. In the South you put everything you have on the table."

Indeed, accounts tell of hunting and fishing parties that delivered marsh hens, dove, quail, and crab by the dozens; that brought in pigeons and deer hunted by torchlight; that landed huge drum, a beast of a fish that pulled at hook and line and dragged a bateau as a whale might. Add to these hunters' trophies the harvest from garden and field — okra, corn, peas and beans, turnips, beets, greens and, of course, rice, first introduced to the Lowcountry in the late 1600s — and you had, and have to this day, a traditional Southern meal, flavored as always with meat marked by "a streak of lean and a streak of fat."

It was not only the natural bounty of the land and the availability of labor to harvest several crops each season that led to sumptuous, uniquely prepared Lowcountry meals. The sheer management of the plantation and its physical layout — including individual kitchens and smokehouses — gave rise to a separate world of cooking. It was one managed by slaves who contributed to recipes their own sense of spicing, texture, ingredients, and method. The influence of their African and West Indian heritages, combined with European preferences, produced a distinctive regional style that is being redefined by chefs like Edna Lewis and food historians and writers like John Martin Taylor. The sense that Charleston has truly come of age is nowhere more in evidence than in its many excellent, and a few superbly inventive, restaurants.

Here are some suggestions. The general price range we list is meant to reflect the cost of a single meal, usually dinner, featuring an appetizer, entree, dessert, and coffee. Cocktails, beer, wine, gratuity, and tax are not included in the estimated price.

### Dining Price Code

| | |
|---|---|
| Inexpensive | Up to $10 |
| Moderate | $10 to $20 |
| Expensive | $20 to $30 |
| Very Expensive | $30 or more |

### Credit Cards

| | |
|---|---|
| AE — American Express | DC — Diner's Club |
| CB — Carte Blanche | MC — MasterCard |
| D — Discover Card | V — Visa |

During Spoleto, most Charleston restaurants relax their hours, serving lunch as late as 3 p.m., early supper at 5:30 p.m., and full meals at midnight. The crowds pile up, so make reservations. If you're rushing between performances, enjoy a picnic in the open-air pavilions at the Waterfront Park at the foot of Queen Street, in the shady grove of Washington Square, or on a bench at the Battery.

Wade Spees

*Sightseers on a carriage tour admire Anson's, where the freshest ingredients are lightly sautéed moments before they reach your table.*

**ANSON**
843-577-0551.
12 Anson St.
Open daily.
Price: Expensive.
Cuisine: American.
Serving: D.
Credit Cards: AE, CB, D, DC, MC, V.

Anson practically glows from the street. Run by longtime Lowcountry restaurateurs, the cooking technique here is last-minute sautéing: the dish arrives at your table sizzling hot, with crispy vegetables, meat, fish, or fowl glistening with juice. The produce comes from local farms growing Charleston "heirloom" vegetables that were cultivated in the area during the 19th-century; the rice is "Carolina Gold," growing again after a 100-year hiatus; the lamb, duck, quail, and squab are free-range. The meticulous presentation matches the decor — lots of attention to the tiniest detail of color and contrast. There are comfy banquettes and lots of smaller tables for four or six, done up in heavy linens. The fish entrees are fresh from the boat, and the she-crab soup laced with sherry probably the best you'll taste. Dinner starts at 5:30.

**BAKER'S CAFE**
843-577-2694.
214 King St.
Open daily.
Price: Inexpensive.
Cuisine: American.
Serving: B, L.
Credit Cards: AE, DC, MC, V.
Special Features: Take-out bakery items.

If you're bracing for a day of window shopping and antiquing along King St., stop in here first for breakfast, including delicious croissants. It's bigger than a bakery, but hasn't lost the early-morning freshness that makes such places so cheerful. Classical music plays in the background, the light pours in the storefront-style display windows, and watercolors, prints, and posters enliven the pale walls. Weekend brunch is very popular, but you'll find your wait to be a friendly one, among others who may be relaxing with the newspaper on a outdoor bench or strolling until some tables clear.

**BEAUMONT'S**
843-577-5500.
12 Cumberland St.
Open daily.
Price: Expensive.
Cuisine: French.
Serving: L, D, Sun. brunch.
Credit Cards: AE, D, MC, V.

**B**eaumont's is Charleston's version of a restaurant in the Provence region of France. The cuisine and the portions are hearty; the ell-shaped interior is distinguished by exposed brick walls, adorned by family portraits; the tables are inviting and comfortable. It's as if it were Sunday afternoon in the country — every day. Brunch is a favorite, and not just eggs, either: try the calf liver, filet mignon, or creamy pate.

**BOOKSTORE CAFE**
843-720-8843.
412 King St.
Open daily.
Price: Inexpensive.
Cuisine: American.
Serving: B, L, D.
Credit Cards: MC, V.

**J**ust as the name has it, this is a place where you can eat and read and have that extra cup of coffee. Fried oysters, roasted half-chicken, fried green tomatoes, and solid ham-and-eggs make this a top local choice. It may seem a bit out of the way if you're staying downtown, but it's right near the Visitors Center and would be a good place to drop in if you're headed back to your car, or on your way to the Manigault House or Charleston Museum.

**CAROLINA'S**
843-724-3800.
10 Exchange St.
Open daily.
Price: Expensive to Very Expensive.
Cuisine: American.
Serving: D.
Credit Cards: AE, DC, MC, V.

**L**ate-night crowds converge at Carolina's, at the two-dozen tables lining the main passageway or in back by the bar, amidst oversized antique French posters and crowded banquettes. You could have a light meal of omelets or pasta, more substantial local delicacies like grilled smoked Carolina quail with spicy greens and tasso grits, or sit at the bar. The juicy baby back ribs are not for the meek. The restaurant occupies the site of the former Perdita's, in its day the best formal, old-fashioned — and many would say only — place to eat in Charleston for many years. If there's one place that shows how far the city has come toward a vision of itself as a sophisticated enclave, a place to see and be seen, this is it.

**CELIA'S PORTA VIA**
843-722-9003.
49 Archdale St.
Open daily.
Price: Inexpensive to Expensive.
Cuisine: Italian, Sicilian.
Serving: L, D.
Credit Cards: AE, D, DC, MC, V.

**A** family heritage of four Italian grandparents — and quite a few of their paintings and lighting fixtures — has bestowed a cozy, old-world feeling here. You will often see local chefs on a busman's holiday, as well as downtown regulars, sitting down to a meal or chatting over a glass of wine in the small adjacent deli. Fresh homemade mozzarella is a big draw; the pasta dishes are inventive; the wine list is broad and deep. Spoleto performers

Reservations suggested.
Special Features: Order an
elegant picnic or
purchase condiments,
pastas, beer, and wine
from the deli (open
daily).

often drop by to play, and sometimes there's a jazz
pianist.

*Enter the courtyard to Fulton Five and imagine you're in an
intimate family restaurant in sunny Italy.*

Wade Spees

**FULTON FIVE**
843-853-5555.
5 Fulton St.
Closed Sunday.
Price: Moderate to
  Expensive.
Cuisine: Italian.
Serving: D.
Credit Cards: AE, CB, DC,
  MC, V.

It's said that one reason Gian Carlo Menotti chose
Charleston as the site for his Spoleto Festival
USA is that the city had a Mediterranean feel, a
serene charm as easy to appreciate and as softly
worn as stucco walls in a seaside village. Fulton
Five wasn't open then, but it fits the description
better than any place in Charleston. Sylvia Meier's
small restaurant exudes quiet confidence and lack
of pretension. The appetizers are the finest around,
among them field greens with fennel, carpaccio,
calamari with peppers. The pasta dishes, usually
three, are simply adorned or just tossed with excellent olive oil and herbs. The
decor is both sumptuous and comfortable: green walls that seem murky and
lustrous, recessed windows set off by dark brown shutters, brocade fabrics.
Dinner starts at 5:30.

**GARIBALDI'S**
843-723-7153.
49 S. Market St.
Open daily.
Price: Moderate to
  Expensive.

Garibaldi's established itself in Charleston at a
time when the city was first feeling its oats as
a result of downtown restoration projects and the
Spoleto festival. As patrons entered from busy
Market Street, which was itself just beginning to

Cuisine: Italian; seafood.
Serving: D.
Credit Cards: AE, MC, V.

boom with fancy ice-cream shops and streetside cafes, you could read on their faces a look of surprise that seemed to say: Charleston, suddenly hip! The murals, outdoor courtyard, and clusters of interesting-looking people endowed the simplest dinner — fettucine Alfredo, say, with salad and a glass of wine — with a sweet giddiness. Even as Charleston has grown up, Garibaldi's doesn't seem jaded.

**GAULART & MALICLET**
843-577-9797.
98½ Broad St.
Closed Sunday.
Price: Inexpensive to
  Moderate.
Cuisine: French.
Serving: B, L, D.
Credit Cards: AE, D, DC,
  MC, V.

Not big enough to be called a bistro, much more pleasant than a bar, "Fast and French" as it is nicknamed is unlike any eatery in town. You sit on high chairs at a black-topped counter that juts out into tiny bays, and your neighbors are as likely to be Broad St. lawyers as local artists. Platters of pate, sausages, selections of cheeses, and French bread are served; hearty soups; fondues; excellent wine. The smoked salmon is great, finished off with fruit. The menu is full of variety, and it's available at wonderfully odd times, late at night, for example, as well as if you're hungry at 5:30 and want to make an early theater performance.

**LOUIS'S**
843-853-2550.
200 Meeting St.
Open daily.
Price: Expensive
Cuisine: American.
Serving: D.
Credit Cards: All major

At his first restaurant in Charleston, chef Louis Osteen made a big splash: when he was in the kitchen he brought a subtle touch and wonderful sense of companion tastes to the most obvious entrees. His new menu, and his new place, remain ambitious and learned, even though he could, with his popularity secured, rest on his laurels. The setting, by New York designer Adam Tihany, is cool and restrained; the marvelous, wide-ranging menu (including "little extras" like mashed lima beans and mint) is definitely not. The food is good and so are Osteen's ideas.

**MAGNOLIA'S UPTOWN/
  DOWN SOUTH**
843-577-7771.
185 E. Bay St.
Open daily.
Price: Moderate to
  Expensive.
Cuisine: "Nouvelle"
  Southern.
Serving: L, D.
Credit Cards: AE, MC, V.

This big and breezy place epitomizes the willing-to-please personality of the New South. It's energetic, with a menu that sticks to basic Southern foodstuffs — greens, black-eyed peas, grits, and shrimp — and dresses them up in unusual ways. It's very popular, more visitors than locals during the high season.

*The contemporary decorative ironwork that graces the Market East Bistro recalls the craftsmanship of the city's 19th century artisans.*

Wade Spees

**MARKET EAST BISTRO**
843-577-5080.
14 Market St.
Open daily.
Price: Moderate to
  Expensive.
Cuisine: European/
  American bistro.
Serving: L, D, Sun. brunch.
Credit Cards: AE, D, DC,
  MC, V.

Located at the foot of the Market area, just across E. Bay St., the Bistro is a small, bright, two-level restaurant, serving a bit more formally upstairs (where there are table linens, shiny wood floors, paintings, and sparkling glassware), and a little more loosely below (tile floors, a comfortable, open bar, small tables). Contemporary decorative ironwork adorns the windows and entrance passageway, the creation of local artist Nick Hentosh. Specialities include lobster ravioli and smoked salmon tartar, both big favorites among the local crowd.

**PINCKNEY CAFE AND ESPRESSO**
843-577-0961.
18 Pinckney St.
Closed Sun. and Mon.
Price: Inexpensive to
  Moderate.
Cuisine: American eclectic.
Serving: L, D.
Credit Cards: None.
Special Features: Take-out
  available.

A pale yellow, flower-bordered cottage with a porch full of tables and chairs would be an inviting site even if it were a dress shop. As it is, the cafe attracts crowds of young booksellers, artists, students, lawyers, and families who come for the casual atmosphere and fresh, unaffected food. The antipasto salad is great for lunch, but the regulars may talk you into the black bean burrito — order both from the kitchen counter. Dinner is full-service and grilled fish, flavored with mint or pecan butters, a favorite. Loads of coffee selections and a variety of sweet desserts to go with them.

**PENINSULA GRILL**
843-723-0700.
112 N. Market St. (at the
  Planter's Inn).

Located in the loveliest new setting in Charleston, the light in the dining area is suffused with soft gold overtones, as if the color had been rubbed on

Open daily.
Price: Expensive.
Cuisine: American.
Serving: D; Sun. brunch.
Credit Cards: All major.

the air. The room has a great geometry, a square place punctuated by pillars and further softened by the wall and floor treatments (velvet and tightly woven rush). Jello would taste good here. Order local items (clams, crabs, vegetables, and greens), experiment with the dozen or so sauces, or really have fun and select from the Champagne Bar menu. (The bar is in a kind of foyer, tiny and splendid.) The chef is Robert Carter, who has been recognized as a big talent.

**RESTAURANT MILLION**
843-577-7472.
2 Unity Alley.
Closed Sunday.
Price: Very Expensive.
Cuisine: French.
Serving: D.
Credit Cards: AE, DC, MC, V.
Reservations required.

Luxury and formality of the sort found here, combined with superb French haute cuisine, is rare: the prestigious French guide to international dining, *Relais & Chateaux,* cites Million among its 18 United States listings. You can chose from two *prix fixe* dinners ($45–$70 per person) or select individual dishes which might include squab enriched with goose liver and truffles, duckling with juniper berries, rack of lamb with fennel mousse, or medallions of peppered tuna. The dining room is hung with antique tapestries; the tables are large and set at a generous distance from one another; the service is impeccable.

**SARACEN**
843-723-6242.
141 E. Bay St.

Saracen is located in a building that would be considered elegantly unusual for a restaurant, but when it was established as the Farmers and

*Ornate Moorish-influenced architecture, unique in Charleston, provides a dramatic setting at Saracen's.*

Wade Spees

Closed Sunday and Monday.
Price: Expensive.
Cuisine: French.
Serving: L, D.
Credit Cards: AE, DC, MC, V.

Exchange Bank in 1853, it must have been positively shocking. Huge arched windows held in place by massive decorated woodwork reflect architectural styles that have been called, all at once, Moorish, Gothic, Hindu, and Persian. The menu changes according to season and the availability of fresh market ingredients, but the style is basically French and the results, especially the soups, are sublime. Charlie's Little Bar, a wonderful place upstairs, is where Charleston's own *jeunesse d'or* start their eventful evenings.

**SERMET'S CORNER**
843-853-7775.
276 King St.
Open daily.
Price: Moderate.
Cuisine: North African, Mediterranean.
Serving: L, D.
Credit Cards: All major.

This restaurant looks and acts like a real bistro, where students, children, grandparents, couples, and solo types feel at home. It's simple and open: big plate-glass windows open onto a busy intersection just north of the Omni and Saks. The salads are imaginative, many garnished with wonderful fruit relish and there are plain choices for kids and the less-adventurous: a bowl of pasta, sandwich, soup. Kind, friendly waitstaff, original art on the walls, and loyal, local patrons.

**SLIGHTLY NORTH OF BROAD**
843-723-3424.
192 E. Bay St.
Open daily.
Price: Expensive to Very Expensive.
Cuisine: Contemporary Southern.
Serving: L, D.
Credit Cards: AE, D, DC, MC, V.

This restaurant has received great press, for the cooking and because it combines the classy best of the old — comfort, stability, self-confidence — with the unpredictable whimsy of the new. Its name (S.N.O.B.) is a riff on the Establishment, as wickedly precise as any social definition in Nancy Mitford's lexicon, for it's not, as they say in Charleston, "S.O.B." (located "South of Broad" in the city's prestigious old-family neighborhood) and it's glad of it. The newest-minted Southerners (formerly known as retired Yankees) come here a lot, and long-time locals count it among the best. An old-fashioned, polished bar with stools (and a bartender who'll ask how you are, fetch you water or light your cigarette) greets you on the right. The menu includes fresh sautéed vegetables, fish and meat entrees, sauces with a Southern flair, and great desserts.

**SPIRIT OF CHARLESTON DINNER CRUISE**
843-722-2628.
City Marina, 17 Lockwood Drive.

You can extend your touring day and take advantage of the warm evening breezes by eating and relaxing aboard a 102-foot cruise boat that motors around the harbor and scenic rivers. A

Tues.–Sat. except in winter
  months.
Price: Expensive.
Cuisine: American.
Serving: D.
Credit Cards: AE, D, DC,
  MC, V.
Reservations required.

four-course meal is served and there is dancing
and live entertainment. The cruise lasts three
hours.

**VICKERY'S**
843-577-5300.
15 Beaufain St.
Open daily.
Price: Inexpensive to
  Moderate.
Cuisine: American; Cuban.
Serving: L, D.
Credit Cards: AE, D, MC,
  V.

A popular place for young, local up-and-comers, with tables and banquettes surrounding a horseshoe-shaped bar, and walls decorated with ... stuff. Outdoor dining under the umbrellas is cherished; inside it's noisy and friendly. You will probably see the guide who just led your tour (or mother of guide) eating at the next table. If there's a not-too-self-conscious "post-Spoleto" Charleston, Vickery's describes it. Cuban and Caribbean spices warm up burgers, chicken, and pork; black beans and rice, with hot sausage, is the choice of regulars; three-dozen varieties of beer wash it all down.

## Charleston Area and the Sea Islands

If you are staying at a Sea Island resort, you will find a variety of dining choices offered in a range of prices and styles; but most of them, like the resorts themselves, are characterized by a sense of unsurprising order and solid predictability. If you are more adventurous and want to eat with local people, you might try some of the following restaurants.

**BOWEN'S ISLAND
  RESTAURANT**
843-795-2757.
Bowen's Island Rd. (Turn
  right off S.C. 171, 1.6
  miles before Folly Beach.)
Open Mon.–Sat.
Price: Inexpensive to
  Moderate.
Cuisine: Lowcountry
  seafood.
Serving: D.
Credit Cards: None.

If Huck Finn lived in the Lowcountry this is where he'd eat. He'd feel at home — newspapers for tablecloths, soda or beer straight from the cooler, barely any silverware, wooden tables scarred with penknifed initials, walls covered with autographed scrawls. He'd appreciate the food, too, for it's the real thing: hushpuppies, fried shrimp, and the house specialty, roasted oysters. Lowcountry oysters are so sweet and small they make other oysters look fat and vulgar by comparison. Here, they're prepared the old-fashioned way — dug from the marsh flats, thrown across a piece of sheet metal above an open fire, then covered with wet rags. When they've steamed open the cook will shovel a smoking load onto your table. The restaurant has been open some 50 years and seems so far to have resisted, as Huck might, any banal attempt at self-improvement.

**EDISTO MOTEL RESTAURANT**
843-893-2270.
Hwy. 17 at Jacksonboro.
Open: Thurs., Fri., Sat.
Price: Inexpensive to Moderate.
Cuisine: Southern.
Serving: D.
Credit Cards: No.

The restaurant is not on Edisto Island, but part of a plain old motel complex on Hwy. 17, like dozens of others that serviced travelers heading south before the days of I-95 and national lodging chains. The reason customers line up outside to wait for a table is a Lowcountry legend: the shad-roe served in the spring, taken from locally caught shad, is creamy-delicious. Call ahead to make sure it's on the menu.

**ROSEBANK FARMS CAFE**
843-768-1807.
Bohicket Marina Village, Seabrook Island.
Open daily.
Price: Inexpensive to Expensive.
Cuisine: Seafood; Southern.
Serving: L, D.
Credit Cards: AE, D, MC, V.

Tucked among the shops of the marina village, and overlooking the berthed boats, Rosebank is worth a trip if you're exploring the rural or resort Sea Islands. The seafood is fresh and seasonal, topped with sauces like mango or encrusted with peanuts. The vegetables are local, and some of the best, like fried green tomatoes, can be ordered as sides. There are large murals — scenes from nature, portraits — that would look sensational in a down-town restaurant, and make for a soft, modern feel. A blue-plate special, ordered at the bar, is a terrific way to start an evening or end a day of touring.

**SHEM CREEK BAR AND GRILL**
843-884-8102.
508 Mill St., Mt. Pleasant.
Open daily.
Price: Moderate to Expensive.
Cuisine: American, seafood.
Serving: L, D, B (Sat., Sun.).
Credit Cards: AE, D, MC, V.

This place draws a big boating crowd, especially on summer nights. There's a bar at the dock, a very popular raw bar inside, and views aplenty. It's very much a local scene: beer-in-the-bottle, casual, noisy, and fun.

**SLIGHTLY UP THE CREEK**
843-884-5005.
130 Mill St., Mt. Pleasant.
Open daily.
Price: Expensive.

Among the many places to eat right at the dock, this is the best. The sunset, and the views of Charleston and the skyline are terrific, and the atmosphere is like its Charleston cousin, Slightly North of Broad. Friendly and casual, easy for chil-

Cuisine: Seafood, Southern regional.
Serving: D, Sun. brunch.
Credit Cards: AE, D, DC, MC, V.

dren, who will love to watch all the marina-related activity.

## FOOD PURVEYORS

### BAKERIES/COFFEE HOUSES

**Cafe Brio** (843-853-8275; 129 Meeting St.) Great big sandwiches and a local crowd make for a busy, cheerful spot.

**Fulford & Egan Coffee and Tea House** (843-723-4374; 190 King St.) Stop in practically all day (to 11 p.m.) every day for Belgian waffles, homemade muffins and breads, and specialty beverages, including Italian sodas, and hot and cold coffee concoctions.

**Saffron** (843-722-5588; 333 E. Bay St.) The glass cases filled to brimming with pastries and the racks of fresh bread should promote thoughts of a gourmet picnic; or you can eat here, three meals a day, in the sleek cafe with a checkerboard floor. A small gourmet grocery features vinegars, cheeses, jellies, and other treats.

### CANDY AND ICE CREAM

**Charleston Chocolates** (843-577-4491; 190 East Bay St.) It's Valentine's Day year-round here with hand-dipped chocolates and fancy trimmings.

**Haagen-Dazs** (843-723-9326; 43 S. Market St.) Sometimes it's even too hot in the Lowcountry for ice cream — it's a melted mess after a few licks — but this old favorite stays open after the sun goes down.

**Lucas Neuhaus** (843-722-0461; 73 State St.) If you're in the Market area and overwhelmed by all the shops and all the merchandise for sale, drop in for one fabulous Belgian chocolate or confection.

### DELIS AND FAST FOOD

**Andolini's** (843-722-7437; 82 Wentworth St.) The place for pizza in Charleston. Informal patio dining.

**Doe's Pita Plus** (843-577-3179; 334 E. Bay St.) A small, bustling place offering sandwiches of chopped vegetables, chicken, or meat stuffed in soft pita bread pockets and seasoned with dressing or light sauces. Side orders of tabouli, hummus, and potato salad.

**Mediterranean Deli** (843-766-0323; 90 Folly Rd., South Windermere Shopping Center) Cases of imported beers and wines divide the room; the tables are covered in white butcher paper; the chairs and booths are upholstered in vinyl. Many people who know the fancy places still call this their favorite for lunch. A classic, friendly deli.

**Mike Calders Deli and Pub** (843-577-0123; 288 King St.) Feast on Dagwood Bumstead-style sandwiches filled with premium deli fare like liverwurst and corn beef. Top it off with ale and beer from the British Isles. Popular college hangout.

**Sticky Fingers** (843-853-7427; 235 Meeting St.) Ribs, barbecue, and dozens of sides.

## CULTURE

*Charleston's French Huguenot Church, first established in 1687, still offers a French liturgy service every spring.*

Wade Spees

## ARCHITECTURE

If you have more than a passing interest in architecture, you might well approach the riches of Charleston and the immediate area with a game plan and spend your time playing it out. Is it small rooms and thickly-carved mantels of the Colonial Period you like? The fine lightness of touch and classical decoration introduced by the Adam brothers? Do open-air living spaces afforded by piazzas and walled gardens appeal? Ironwork? Brick or clap-board? Small country churches or city steeples? Interiors or exteriors? Grand plantations or modest rowhouses? Rooms adorned with 18th-century furni-ture or ones that remain bare, objects in and of themselves? For suggestions on buildings which express these aesthetic considerations, see the **Historic House** listing later in this chapter.

If you're a generalist, start your day (and park your car) at the ***Charleston Visitors Center*** (375 Meeting St.) where there are lots of maps, helpful docents, and an audio-visual presentation that presents an excellent introduction to the city. From here, you may select a guided tour (for suggestions, see the *Transportation* Chapter): carriage tours, city shuttle buses, mini-van tours, and guides generally collect and discharge passengers at this site. Sometimes a motorized tour is the most efficient way to review the city's deep inventory of houses — from the famous "single house" (one room wide, standing endways with its door to the street) to double-piazzaed mansions dominating their har-borside sites. Or you may head out on your own. Any way you choose, you won't be disappointed.

## DANCE

D ance performances take place through most of the year, especially during the springtime *Spoleto Festival*. Call ahead for schedules and ticket infor-mation.

**Charleston Ballet Theatre** (843-723-7334; 281 Meeting St.).
**Robert Ivey Ballet** (843-556-1343; 1910 Savannah Hwy.).

## FILM

F irst-run movie houses tend to be located in malls away from downtown, and they account for most of the region's audiences. In Charleston, there are one or two theaters left — the *Roxy Theater & Cafe* is a gem, with extra-special beverages and snacks — but from time to time, especially during Spoleto, special film series are scheduled in college auditoriums or libraries. Check local newspaper listings or look for handbills posted around town.

**Ashley Landing Cinema I II and III** (843-571-2380; Ashley Landing Mall).
**Aviation Avenue Cinemas** (843-747-4800; 2390 Aviation Ave., North Charleston).
**Citadel Mall Cinema I-IV** (843-763-7052; Citadel Mall).
**James Island Cinema Theatre** (843-795-9499; 1743 Central Park Rd.).

**Mount Pleasant Cinema 1 2 & 3** (843-884-3614; 1001 Johnnie Dodds Blvd.).
**Northwoods Mall Cinema** (843-569-6794; Northwoods Mall).
**Roxy Theater & Cafe** (843-853-7699; 245 East Bay Street).
**South Windermere Cinemas** (843-766-7336; South Windemere Shopping Center).
**Ultravision 1 & 2 Theatres** (843-556-4200; 1812 Sam Rittenberg Blvd.)

## GALLERIES

Many of the galleries featuring the best work of Lowcountry artists are listed in the **Shopping** section. A visit to any of the ones listed below would enhance your appreciation of the region; the works on exhibit may or may not be for sale.

**Elizabeth O'Neill Verner Studio and Museum** (843-722-4246; 38 Tradd St.) The artist, who was in her 90s when she died in 1979, produced etchings, pastels, and pencil drawings of a Charleston life that seems long past. Visiting her studio is like a step back in time. Also home of the Tradd Street Press, which publishes the work of Mrs. Verner, her daughter, Elizabeth Verner Hamilton, and other books of Lowcountry poetry, stories, and local history.

**Gibbes Museum of Art** (843-722-2706; 135 Meeting St.) The permanent collection includes views of Charleston from the 18th century to the present. Not to be missed are Charles Fraser's exquisite miniatures of the most prominent citizens during the city's early days and Alice Ravenel Huger Smith's water-colors of 20th-century plantation and rural life. Also, a fine museum shop. Open Tues.–Sat. 10–5; Sun. and Mon. 1–5. Adults/$5, Children/$3.

## HISTORIC HOMES, GARDENS & RELIGIOUS SITES

Whether or not you visit a historic site, and how much time you spend there will, of course, depend on your interest and schedule, whether you're traveling with children, and whether you have your own car. It may be preferable, for example, to do just one *big* thing in a single day (a boat ride to Fort Sumter, a visit to a plantation garden) plus two *smaller* ones (see a house museum or church, take a walking tour, picnic in a park).

Distances are not great: to gardens and lighthouses and island sites from Charleston takes about 30 minutes. The sites in the following list are open all year, unless otherwise noted. Admission fees and hours are as of 1998; for the purpose of admission, children are defined as being 12 and under; younger than age five, they're usually free. Keep in mind that the last tours of the day start approximately 30 minutes before closing time. Visitors generally are welcome to enter religious sites, but are asked to observe the worship schedule and related courtesies of visitation as few of the sites offer regular tour services.

**AIKEN-RHETT HOUSE**
843-724-8481.
48 Elizabeth St.
Mon.– Sat., 10–5, Sun. 2– 5.
Admission: Adults $6;
    reduced admission with
    combination tickets to
    other selected historic
    properties.

**B**uilt in 1817, representing high-style Greek Revival and Rococo interiors, the Aiken-Rhett House is preserved in a somewhat less formal way than other houses. It's full of atmosphere, a little worn at the edges. During the fiercest shelling of Charleston in the Civil War, it was the headquarters of Confederate General P.G.T. Beauregard, a purpose for which it was well suited by virtue of its scale, design, and location off the Battery. The intact workyard helps understanding of African-American urban life.

**AUDUBON SWAMP GARDEN**
See "Nature Preserves" in **Recreation** section.

**BOONE HALL
    PLANTATION**
843-884-4371.
Hwy. 17, 8 miles N of
    Charleston.
April 1–Labor Day,
    Mon.–Sat. 8:30–6:30;
    Sunday 1–5; in low
    season Mon.–Sat. 9–5;
    Sunday 1–4.
Admission: Adults $10;
    children $5.

**O**f particular interest at this plantation are the nine mid-18th century slave cabins (these housed house slaves and skilled craftsmen, not the field hands), the Gin House, used for processing cotton, and the magnificent avenue of oaks, which runs three-quarters of a mile.

**CALHOUN MANSION**
843-722-8205.
16 Meeting St.
Thurs.–Sun. 10–4.
Admission: Adults $10;
    children $5.

**V**ictoriania in all its glory: ornate plaster and woodwork, etched glass, and a ballroom. A rarity in Charleston, it was built in 1876, a time when few people had the means to build 25-room mansions.

**CONGREGATION BETH
    ELOHIM**
843-723-1090.
90 Hasell St.
Mon.– Fri. 10–12.

**T**he country's oldest synagogue in continuous use, built in 1840 to replace one that burned, it is a superb example of Greek Revival architecture.

**CYPRESS GARDENS**
See "Nature Preserves" in **Recreation** section.

**DRAYTON HALL**
843-766-0188.
Hwy. 61, 9 miles NW of
Charleston.
Mar.– Oct., 10–4;
Nov.–Feb., 10–3.
Admission: Adults $8;
children $4; teens $6; free
to members of the
National Trust for
Historic Preservation.

It's a measure of the stunning greatness of this 18th-century Georgian-Palladian dwelling that it exists in an architectural class by itself — interior and exterior — even as it remains unfurnished, unrestored, largely unchanged (just stabilized), bare, and magnificent. Built in 1738 and set on a lovely Ashley River site, it is often called one of the most architecturally significant dwellings in America. It is now owned and managed by the National Trust for Historic Preservation. Tours are on the hour; written tours in French, German, and English available. The tour guides are superior — not to be missed even in the pouring rain.

**EDMONDSTON-
   ALSTON HOUSE**
843-722-7171.
21 East Battery.
Tues.–Sat. 10–4; Sun. &
Mon. 1:30–4:40.
Admission: Adults $7; $12
with combination ticket
to the Nathaniel Russell
House.

First built in 1828 by one wealthy man, later enlarged by another, it reveals — in architecture, lavish decoration, documents, family furnishings, silver, and china — the best of what money could buy. You get a sense that, when the Civil War came, this is the life that was lost. An incomparable harbor view.

**EXCHANGE BUILDING/
   PROVOST DUNGEON**
843-727-2165
122 East Bay St.
Daily 9–5.
Admission: Adults $3;
children $1.50.

Even before 1771, when this building was completed, the site on which it stands was used for a variety of public purposes in the young colony. Its commanding location, at the foot of Broad Street, defined both an end boundary for the city, and also, from the water, its point of arrival. In terms of sheer geography it looms large. It's the kind of outsized place that was, and still is, used for huge receptions. During the Revolution the British held political and military prisoners in the basement.

**FRENCH PROTESTANT
   (HUGUENOT)
   CHURCH**
843-722-4385.
136 Church St.

French Huguenots fleeing religious persecution worshipped in Charleston as early as 1687. This church, built on the site of earlier ones, dates from 1845.

## HEYWARD-WASHINGTON HOUSE

843-722-0354.
87 Church St.
Mon.–Sat. 10–5, Sun. 1–5.
Last tour at 4:30.
Admission: Adults $5; children $3. Discounted admission with combination ticket to other Charleston Museum properties.

Built in 1772 by a rice planter whose son, Thomas Heyward, Jr., signed the Declaration of Independence, this house was also the headquarters of George Washington during his visit to the Lowcountry in 1791. Its collection of furniture, including several 18th-century Charleston-made pieces and the magnificent Holmes bookcase, is unmatched. The back courtyard still features its dependencies, open to view, and a small garden.

## JOSEPH MANIGAULT HOUSE

843-723-2926.
350 Meeting St.
Mon.–Sat. 10–5; Sun. 1–5.
Last tour at 4:30.
Admission: Adults $5; children $3. Discounted admission with a combination ticket to other Charleston Museum properties.

The outside of this structure is three stories of brick; the inside is something like shaped light. Designed by native son Gabriel Manigault for his brother and completed in 1803, this house, exuding both formality of plan and spontaneity in gesture, shows the nature of beauty and taste favored by elite planters who may have been, as Gabriel Manigault was, educated in Europe and exposed there to sophisticated design ideas and decorating schemes. The grounds, marked out according to their original uses, make for a cohesive site.

*Growing interest in the Lowcountry's African-American culture is sparking a rediscovery of its historic sites and community leaders.*

Wade Spees

## MAGNOLIA PLANTATION AND GARDENS

843-571-1266.
Hwy. 61, 10 miles NW of Charleston.
Daily 8–5:30; shorter hours in winter.
Admission to the Plantation and Gardens: Adults $9; children 6–12 $4; teenagers $7. Admission to the house costs an additional $5. Admission to the Swamp Garden is $4 adult; $3 teens, $2 for kids.

The current building was floated here by barge in 1873, but the entire tract dates back to the time of the Barbadian planters who relocated on the Ashley River. The legacy here is gardens, acres of them, reflecting (in layout and specimen planting) two centuries of horticulture. The gardens include 250 varieties of *Azalea Indica* and 900 varieties of *Camellia Japonica*; there are bike and walking paths, a petting zoo, a canoe trail, and picnic areas.

## MIDDLETON PLACE

843-556-6020 / 800-782-3608.
Hwy. 61, 14 miles NW of Charleston.
Daily 9–5.
Admission: Mar.–June; Oct. and Nov. Adults $14; children $7; July–Sept., Dec.–Feb., adults $12, children $6. House tours always cost an additional $7 per person.

The formal gardens, laid out in 1741 and constructed by 100 slaves over a period of a decade, feature terraces, camellia allées, butterfly lakes, hillside drifts of azaleas, and acres of landscaped paths. The site is so grand in conception that it can be appreciated even when little is in bloom: the geometry of the original plan itself is breathtaking. The main house was sacked by Union forces; tours of a remaining wing evoke Revolutionary and antebellum life, as do the working stable yard and outbuildings. A gift shop and restaurant are on the premises.

## NATHANIEL RUSSELL HOUSE

843-724-8481.
51 Meeting St.
Mon.–Sat. 10–5, Sun. 2–5.
Admission: $6; $10 with combination ticket to the Edmondston-Alston House.

People have no doubt been admiring this house from the day it was completed (ca. 1808) and with good reason. It represents the high point of the Adam style in the city — its stairway appears to float, a lovely combination of function and fantasy — and it is one of the most thoroughly conceived and exquisitely executed neoclassical dwellings in the nation. A property of the Historic Charleston Foundation.

## ST. MICHAEL'S EPISCOPAL CHURCH

843-723-0603.
Meeting St. at Broad St.
Daily 9–4:30.

This church is still the center of many Charlestonians' lives, as it has been since 1761. With its old bells and gleaming steeple, it is part of the famous "Four Corners of Law" in downtown Charleston, an intersection that represents, in religious, civic, judicial, and federal buildings, the order imposed on society. There is a tranquil walled graveyard to explore, too.

**ST. PHILIP'S EPISCOPAL CHURCH**
843-722-7734.
146 Church St.

Constructed in 1835–1838, facing a central park, and flanked by its graveyard, St. Philip's seems out of the Old World of Europe. The building is sheathed in a mottled, tan stucco material that reflects the gradual shifting in light over the course of a day. The church is open for services Sundays, Wednesdays, and selected Fridays.

**THOMAS ELFE HOUSE**
843-722-9161.
54 Queen St.
Tours Mon.–Fri., 10–12.
Admission: $5.

A meticulously restored, classic Charleston "single house," this dwelling was built before 1760 by the renowned cabinetmaker, who came to Charleston from England in the mid-18th century and left his mark in homes and furniture throughout the city. The carved fretwork that embellishes mahogany tables and chairs makes his work artistically distinctive; his abundant record-keeping has enabled historians to understand his life and times. The small house shows signs of his craftsmanship and knack for fitting things in. The cypress panelling brings a soft glow to the interior.

## MILITARY SITES

The presence of the military — invaders and defenders — has enriched the history of the Lowcountry since the time of the American Revolution, and it is still felt today at military bases, schools, and training centers. You needn't be a veteran, or even a Civil War buff, to enjoy the installations, monuments, forts, and military museums that are so plentiful in the region. Children — with their innate appreciation of danger and adventure, their love of costume and accessories, and their highly developed sense of winning, losing, and just causes — especially seem to twig to these sites and installations.

**AMERICAN MILITARY MUSEUM**
843-723-9620.
40 Pinckney St.
Mon.–Sat. 10–6; Sun. 1–6.
Admission: Adults $5;
    children $1. No fee for
    military in uniform.

Hundreds of artifacts, uniforms, and documents detailing the contribution of members of all branches of the armed forces, from the Revolution to Vietnam.

**THE CITADEL MUSEUM**
843-953-6726.
171 Moultrie St.
Sun.–Fri. 2–5; Sat. 12–5.
Free admission.

Located on the campus of the Military College of South Carolina, founded in 1842, it tells the history of the school and the Corps of Cadets through documents, photographs, and uniforms. Dress parades take place most Fridays at 3:45 p.m. during the academic year.

**THE CONFEDERATE
MUSEUM**
843-723-1541.
188 Meeting St.
(currently under repair; call
for information. Limited
tours of the collection,
relocated to 34 Pitt St.,
Sat. and Sun. 12–4).

There's a Gullah expression in the Lowcountry that sums up this museum: when you ask someone on the telephone "Is that you?" the person may reply, in a weary tone laced with irony, "That's what's leff' of me." This may be what's left of the old Confederacy: uniforms, tattered flags, documents, artifacts, and a fragrant sense of the Lost Cause.

*Fort Sumter, where the stark choices faced by a splintered Union were played out in bloodshed in April 1861.*

Wade Spees

**FORT SUMTER
NATIONAL
MONUMENT**
843-883-3121.
Departure points at the City
Marina on Lockwood
Drive (handicapped
access) and Patriots Point.
Daily trips year round
except Christmas Day;
five or six trips
Mar.–Nov.; fewer in
winter months.
Admission: Adults $10;
children $5.

A relaxing ferry trip, which offers splendid views of the harbor and peninsula, takes you to the place where the Civil War began. Rangers are on hand at the fort to answer your questions; there are gun emplacements to explore, and a museum with artifacts to help you imagine scenes of the siege, which lasted approximately two years and ended in the abandonment of the fort by Confederate soldiers. The entire tour lasts just over two hours.

**FORT MOULTRIE**
843-883-3123.
West Middle St., Sullivan's
 Island; 10 miles E. of
 Charleston.
Daily 9–5.
Free admission.

The primary site of Charleston's seacoast defense system, from its first test in the American Revolution to 1947. The palmetto-log fort that repelled the British fleet is gone, but buildings and earthworks dating from 1809 convey the sense of fragility and isolation the early patriots must have felt. A 20-minute film in the Visitor Center provides an excellent introduction to military life over the years. Operated by the National Park Service.

**PATRIOTS POINT**
843-884-2727.
Hwy. 17 in Mt. Pleasant,
 just over the Cooper
 River Bridge.
Daily 9–5, to 6 in summer
 months.
Admission: Adults $9;
 children $4.

The big ones are berthed here — the aircraft carrier *Yorktown*, the nuclear merchant ship *Savannah*, the World War II sub *Clamagore*, the destroyer *Laffey*, and the cutter *Ingham* — and on self-guided tours you can see their aircraft, guns, and missiles, as well as views of how their personnel lived and worked on board. The view of peninsular Charleston from the signal bridge and platform of the *Yorktown* is unbeatable. Snack bar and gift shop, seating areas for the rest and air you'll need: there's a lot of walking and close quarters.

## MUSEUMS

**AVERY RESEARCH
 CENTER FOR
 AFRICAN-AMERICAN
 HISTORY AND
 CULTURE**
843-953-7609.
125 Bull St.
Tours Mon.– Fri., 2–4; Sat.
 12–5.

Housed in one of the first schools dedicated to educating freed slaves, the center is today a repository of printed and picture materials and objects related to the heritage of the region's African-Americans. It was built by the Freedman's Bureau at the end of the Civil War to meet the needs of 1,000 eager students who had been receiving instruction from teachers sent by the American Missionary Association and other organizations. The reading room of the Center's archives and library is open Mon.–Sat., 12–5.

**CHARLESTON MUSEUM**
843-722-2996.
360 Meeting St.
Mon.–Sat. 9–5; Sun. 1–5.
Admission: Adults $6,
 children $3; combination

The museum, founded in 1773, is the oldest in America. This means that both the ideas that gave the collection its intellectual underpinnings and the very objects themselves, many from Charleston's oldest families, reflect more than two

tickets to Museum and its historic properties available at a discount.

centuries of the city's self-consciousness. Exhibits interpreting subjects as diverse as flora and fauna, fashion, the art of silversmithing, Native American life, and plantation life, come together to provide a seamless image of a special place. The section on African-American slavery — texts, artifacts, photographs, charts — is superb. There is a wonderful "hands-on" room especially for children.

*Reenactments of candlemaking at Charles Towne Landing show the self-sufficiency of early settlers.*

Wade Spees

**CHARLES TOWNE LANDING 1670**
843-852-4200.
Hwy. 171 between I-26 and Hwy. 17.
Daily 9–5, to 6 in summer months.
Admission: Adults $5; children $2.50. Free to handicapped.
Rental bicycles $2/hour with $1.50 deposit. Tram Tour $1.

Consider this 80-acre park an outdoor museum, where the lives of the Lowcountry's earliest European settlers are interpreted in several ways: in an village setting, on a 17th-century replica of a typical coastal trading vessel; and in "wilderness," as found in the Animal Forest, where birds and beasts common to the area in 1670 roam in a secured habitat.

## MUSIC

Charleston has a symphony orchestra and chamber groups that play regularly throughout the year, and, of course, it has *Spoleto*, which brings boys' choirs, operatic soloists, and instrumentalists to the city each May and June. The region is rich in indigenous music, too: blues, jazz, spirituals, gospel. As new audiences for these styles develop, concerts to showcase them are emerging. The *Charleston Blues and Heritage Festival* in April and the *MOJA*

*Arts Festival* in September are two of them. Often, concerts of gospel music and spirituals take place in conjunction with spring and fall house tours and may be held at a historic site. You should check local newspapers for schedules or, once you arrive in Charleston, contact the organizations below for information.

**Charleston Symphony Orchestra** (843-723-7528; 14 George St.) Performances in the Gaillard Auditorium (77 Calhoun St.) throughout the year under the direction of David Stahl. In any season, concert series might include selections from the classical repertoire, pops, and chamber works.

**Lowcountry Blues Society** (843-722-3263; at Erwin Music, 52$^1/_2$ Wentworth St.) The Society's main event — *The Lowcountry Blues Bash* — runs for about 10 days every February and features performances at sites all over the city, from small clubs to larger theaters. The shows are first rate — musicians come from Chicago, North and South Carolina, anywhere the blues are played. You have a range of styles among which to choose, from guitar soloists playing traditional Mississippi Delta blues to bands fronted by harp players.

**MOJA Arts Festival** (843-724-7305; 135 Church St.) The 16-day festival, whose name is Swahili for "one" or "unity," takes place in the fall and celebrates the African and Caribbean cultural influences on the Lowcountry. It includes many musical performances. Administered by the city's Office of Cultural Affairs.

## NIGHTLIFE

The after-supper activities of music, dancing, and general schmoozing in a crowded bar take place in the *Market Area* and *East Bay St.*, where you are as likely to find a ice-cream parlor open late, or an indefatigable tee-shirt vendor still selling his wares, as you are to find a jazz club. Farther afield, on the resort-oriented islands, restaurants and bars often feature bands in the summer: remember, this is the land of the "shag", the highly stylized dance set to beach music that originated in South Carolina. What follows is a list of the better known or easily accessible spots for night owls to enjoy. Cover charges vary widely, depending on the entertainment. Check local newspaper listings when you're in town for special shows.

**Acme-Downtown** (843-577-7383; 5 Faber St.) It calls itself a "neighborhood" dance club which means it's loose, loud, and local.

**Blues House of Wings** (843-881-1858; 1039 Johnnie Dodds Blvd., Mt. Pleasant) Food and the blues in a casual setting.

**Charleston Grill at Charleston Place** (843-571-2265; 224 King St.) Jazz trios nightly in a sophisticated, laid-back setting.

**Chef & Clef** (843-722-0732; 102 N. Market St.) Live jazz and blues nightly to about 1 a.m.; full meals or simple burgers served until midnight.

**Cumberland's** (843-577-9469; 26 Cumberland St.) Band music that's live and loud.

**Dunleavy's Pub** (843-883-9646; 2213-B Middle St., Sullivan's Island) A small place on the corner with a half-dozen or so imported beers and ales on tap and music (acoustic, Irish, small bands) on the weekends.

**Fulford-Egan** (843-577-4553; 231 Meeting St.) The culture of beatniks is coming back into fashion — poetry readings, "designer" leather sandals, acoustic music — and you'll find its expression here. No alcohol served, but coffees, teas, and desserts. Blues performances are especially good.

**Horse & Cart Cafe** (843-722-0797; 347 King St.) Cafe food, dozens of types of beer and weekly poetry slams, when you may take the mike.

**Mills House** (843-577-2400; 115 Meeting St.) Two lounges, one with a piano bar where you can relax and visit. Good place to gather for an after-dinner drink. Look for Big Band tunes or jazzy guitar.

**Music Farm** (843-853-3276; 32 Ann St.) Where the young crowd swarms to dance and mosh.

**Pusser's Landing** (843-853-1000; 17 Lockwood Blvd.) Sensational view of the City Marina from the deck. Excellent food; music Thurs.–Sun.

**Tobacco, Teas & Spirits** (843-577-0027; 364 King St.) Jam sessions and bourbon are what the regulars go for. Excellent tobacco shop.

## SPOLETO

It is said that the first professional dramatic production in America of a play written here was performed in Charleston in the 18th century by a ship-wrecked poet, who was washed ashore, as he put it, "full of lice, shame, poverty, nakedness and hunger."

No such description could conceivably apply to the outstanding performers who come to the city for Charleston's most famous festival (though perhaps some might allow that, like many artists, they are not as well off as they could wish!)

For 18 days at the end of spring, a time of budding oleander, fading azalea, and unapologetically fragrant magnolias, *Spoleto* comes to Charleston and Charleston becomes the city it has long imagined itself to be: an artistic mecca

*Spoleto roars into Charleston like a hurricane — but a nice one.*

Wade Spees

where expressions of high culture find their setting among people who believe they understand the meaning of civilized life.

Spoleto gave Charlestonians a chance to prove their culture and sophistication, and prove it they have. Emboldened by the artistic vision of Gian Carlo Menotti (who fell in love with Charleston and organized the first festival in 1977), and egged on by an indefatigable mayor, Joe Riley, Charleston's cultural and business communities have consistently — and with full attention — adapted themselves and their city to the idea that first-class art of many kinds can inhabit, enrich, and be enriched by the lively, unique qualities of this old city. Spoleto instilled new vigor into the town, giving rise to building projects and renovations, new restaurants, and shops: it linked the pride of the Lowcountry's past to confidence in its future. Perhaps more than anything, it opened the doors of Charleston to the nation.

Spoleto took its name from the town in Italy where, in the 1950s, Mr. Menotti had organized another festival. Spoleto in Charleston was conceived as the counterpart to that venture, though now it stands on its own artistic direction and traditions. In any one season, it offers more than 100 scheduled events, including premieres of opera and dance as well as dozens of chamber music, choral, jazz, and orchestral performances. Performances take place indoors and out — in parks, plantation gardens, amphitheaters, and auditoriums.

If that's not enough, the regular Spoleto events are augmented by some 600 *Piccolo Spoleto* performances (often free), organized by the city's Office of Cultural Affairs (843-724-7305; 133 Church St.). These events can include organ, choral, and madrigal recitals in churches; mime shows, outdoor concerts, and numerous theater productions. (Tickets and schedules for Piccolo

Spoleto are available in Charleston at the Spoleto Box Office, 14 George St., and at the Gaillard Auditorium, 77 Calhoun Street.)

There are several ways to purchase tickets to Spoleto. The first thing to do is request, by mail or telephone, the festival ticket brochure, a near-tabloid size schedule of events with a pre-printed order form. Contact:

**Spoleto Festival U.S.A.**
**P.O. Box 157**
**Charleston, S.C. 29402-0157**
**843 -722-2764 / Fax 843-723-6383.**
**Website: www.spoletousa.org**

If you want to order a pre-designed "ticket package" which might include a dance performance, a play, an opera, and a chamber music event spread over several days, order the brochure *by mid-November or December*. If you're not sure of your schedule, you can order tickets to individual events beginning in *January*. There is a $6 handling charge for ticket orders.

The variety and number of events can be overwhelming, but poring over the brochure and making plans offers the same pleasurable anticipation that stirs avid gardeners as they read beautiful seed catalogues. Of course, the earlier you can confirm travel arrangements and lodging, the better.

If April 1st comes and you are without tickets but want to attend to Spoleto, you can still do it. With basic Spoleto Festival ticket brochure in hand (see above address) you may order tickets by telephone from 9 a.m.–9 p.m. until the festival's end. Call 843-723-0402 (a South Carolina Ticket Agency line dedicated to Spoleto tickets) to order. You may charge to Discover, Visa, or MasterCard. There's a handling charge levied per ticket.

In person, visit the *Spoleto Office* at 14 George St., which is open year round but extends its hours from April until the festival closes. There are also box offices at all Spoleto venues which handle tickets for the events held there. They are generally open daily during the festival from 10 a.m. until thirty minutes after the final performance of the day.

You can even arrive without tickets, and get lucky. Tickets can be purchased up to one hour before curtain time; remaining tickets go on sale at performance sites 30 minutes before curtain. Chairs or standing room for sold out performances at the *Dock Street Theater* and the *Garden Theater* go on sale at 10 a.m. on the day of performance.


**THEATER**


By the middle of the 18th century, theatrical performances were well established in the cultural life of Charleston. In the ante-bellum years theater was but one jewel in the crown of culture, offset by the brilliant setting provided by a society that lived for pleasure and sought it in balls, concerts, seasonal celebrations, and lavish home entertaining.

In this century, it wasn't until 1927 — when DuBose Heyward's novel *Porgy*, the story of a lame Charleston street vendor and his love for Bess, was adapted and performed on the Broadway stage — that drama native to Charleston came alive. Theatrical performances in the Lowcountry still reflect their indigenous stories — they are often showcased during Piccolo Spoleto — but a growing audience also supports new works from nationally known dramatists and selections from the classical repertory. When visiting, call ahead for performance schedules and tickets.

**Charleston Stage Company** (843-965-4032; 800-454-7093; 133 Church St.) Productions that provide special enjoyment for families, plays like *Cheaper By the Dozen* or *A Christmas Carol*; original work, children's theater, and workshops.

**Dock Street Theater** (843-720-3968; 135 Church St.) This is a lovely interpretation of a Georgian-style theater, of the sort 18th-century Charlestonians may have patronized. Rebuilt during the Depression within the old Planters Hotel (circa 1809) as a project of the Federal Works Progress Administration, the theater's cypress interiors, intimate box seats, and terrific acoustics make it a wonderful place to attend performances. It's the site of the immensely popular Chamber Music Series during Spoleto and festival plays, as well as a stage for roving companies.

**Footlight Players** (843-722-4487; 20 Queen St.) An old, established theater company dedicated to community-theater repertory.

## RECREATION

While guessing what a novelist had in mind in his work can be a risky business, perhaps when DuBose Heyward wrote "It is always Sunday on the Sea Islands," he was thinking that there is, in every day, a piece of Sunday here, a piece of time as yet unplanned and unscheduled, in which to enjoy the best of your surroundings both naturally and simply, with as few complications as possible. This is the definition of recreation in the Lowcountry.

### BASEBALL

*Charleston RiverDogs*, a Class A team, plays at Joe Riley, Jr. Park. For tickets and information call 843-723-7241.

## BEACH ACCESS

There are hundreds of miles of coastline between Charleston and Savannah and on the barrier islands. At many points the public can reach the coast at designated access sites. Some of these offer changing areas, restrooms, showers, and picnic tables. Others are mere paths in the sand. Some, like the beaches on pristine barrier islands, are accessible only by boat.

The beaches on this coast are flat and wide, without rocks, overlooked by dunes or maritime forest. The surf ranges from placid to roiling (the Washout at Folly Beach is considered a top surfing spot). Lifeguards are *not* on duty at every beach access point, and swimming may be extremely hazardous in their absence. It is not wise to swim in unmonitored areas. Walking on the dunes, picking the sea oats, and driving on the beach are forbidden.

A few suggestions follow for reaching the beach by land or water. For more detailed information about specific access points, contact the chambers of commerce or tourism commissions listed at the end of the Chapter Seven, *Information*.

*Second graders collect Lowcountry treasures while enjoying a school field trip together.*

Wade Spees

**Sullivan's Island** and **Isle of Palms** are located north of the city on Hwy. 17 and S.C. 703. The beach at Sullivan's is marked by walkways. You may park along the side of streets. At Isle of Palms, the new county park (843-886-3863; Ocean Blvd.) offers pay parking, restrooms, and changing facilities. Located to the south, off Hwy. 17 on S.C. 171, is **Folly Beach**, where, in addition to simple dune walkovers, you can enjoy the fully-outfitted **Folly Beach County Park** (843-588-2426) which offers 4,000 feet of oceanfront access, lifeguards, changing rooms, showers, and pay parking. A bit farther south off Hwy. 17, at the entrance to Kiawah Island, is **Beachwalker Park** (843-768-2395) another well-developed public beach destination with facilities, lifeguards, and limited pay parking.

## SHORE REFUGES

**B**y water, and with advance arrangements, you may visit *Cape Romain National Wildlife Refuge* (843-928-3368; 390 Bulls Island Rd., Awendaw, SC 29429) a 64,229-acre site managed by the U.S. Fish and Wildlife Service. The refuge consists of four parts: *Bulls Island*, a 5,000-acre barrier island; *Cape Island*, a favorite spot for loggerhead turtles to nest; *Moore's Landing*, the site of ferry services, and an observation pier just right for birders; and *Raccoon Key Island*, a popular spot for shelling.

*Coastal Expeditions, Inc.* (843-881-4582; ferry information) offers exclusive ferry service to Bull Island, weather permitting. The 1998 ticket prices were $20 for adults and $10 for children under 12. From Mar.–Nov., the ferry makes two round-trips daily every Tuesday, Friday, and Saturday, and one all-day trip on Thursdays. From Dec.–Feb. there's one trip only, on Saturdays. The company also offers pontoon charters throughout the refuge for larger groups.

Another refuge is *Capers Island* — a classic, undisturbed barrier island managed by the *South Carolina Department of Natural Resources*. Contact them (843-762-5076; P.O. Box 12559, Charleston, SC 29412) regarding public use restrictions, instructions for anchoring and beaching boats, and camping permits. One way to get there is in a sea kayak, on a guided tour (single day or overnight) offered by *Coastal Expeditions, Inc.* (843-884-7684; 514-B Mill St., Mt. Pleasant, SC 29464).

## BIRD WATCHING

*Sharp eyes and enthusiasm are rewarded with sightings of egret, heron, woodpecker, deer, maybe even eagles at Magnolia Plantation's Audubon Swamp Garden.*

Wade Spees

**T**he barrier islands mentioned above provide the least-disturbed habitats for birds and wildlife you're likely to find in the Lowcountry; if you're a serious birder, a visit to any one of them should be included in your trip.

But even if you can't make it to the islands, you will not be disappointed in what you can find in more accessible places. Because of its situation on the North American flyway and its diverse natural environment, the Lowcountry attracts scores of wading, shore, and songbirds, some of them as unusual as the roseate spoonbill and parasitic jaeger. Woodcocks flock in plowed fields, owls hover in roadside forests, and hawks soar over open grassland. In February, you are likely to see thousands of robins and cedar waxwings swarming in country yards, picking the cherry laurel trees clean.

Local Audubon societies, conducting the annual Christmas count, have reported over 200 types of birds from scrub areas to shorefront. Visitor-friendly sites for birding — where you may find boardwalks, observation areas, and informational slide shows or displays, are listed under **Nature Preserves** later in this chapter.

More informal birding sites recommended by local birders include the following:

**I'on Swamp,** 15 miles north of Mt. Pleasant off Hwy. 17 on U.S. Forest Service Rd. 228. Here spring brings warblers — possibly even the shy Bachman's — and the resident upland birds, including red-cockaded woodpeckers, who make their homes here.

**Mt. Pleasant:** the area leading to the old **Pitt St. Bridge.** Here sightings of marbled godwits, oystercatchers, grebes, and mergansers have been reported. Activity is best at half tide, especially in fall and winter. A spotting scope is useful here.

**Sullivan's Island:** around the beach and groins behind **Fort Moultrie.** Here, in fall and winter, you might see peeps or an occasional purple sandpiper.

**U.S. Hwy. 17** by the **Ashepoo and Combahee River crossings.** Anhinga, rails, and gallinules nest in the remnant rice fields.

## BOATING

### CANOEING AND KAYAKING

Interest in these activities has exploded. Guides will lead you along miles of creeks and down rivers; adventurous instructors can teach you how to get beyond the breaking waves into the ocean. Here are some popular locations and names of outfitters:

The *Edisto River,* thought to be the nation's longest free-flowing blackwater stream, offers calm waters and great bird and wildlife observation. As you meander along, you're likely to see great blue herons wading by the oak-lined riverbank, or hummingbirds feeding at wildflowers. The trail follows an ancient waterway used by Native Americans and early settlers. *Colleton State Park* (843-538-8206; Canadys, SC; U.S. Rte. 15, 12 miles north of Walterboro, I-95 exit 68) and *Givhan's Ferry State Park* (843-873-0692; Hwy. 61 and S.C. 30) are along the route. You can put in there, and also camp and picnic.

To inquire about conditions (canoeing and kayaking are not recommended on the Edisto River when the water level is above 7.5 feet) call 843-538-3659. *The Walterboro-Colleton Chamber of Commerce* (843-549-9595; P.O. Box 426, Walterboro, SC 29488) can assist you in renting canoes or kayaks, or securing a guide at certain times of the year.

Canoeing is also permitted at *Magnolia Gardens* (843-571-1266; Hwy. 61) and *Palmetto Islands County Park* (843-884-0832; 444 Needlerush Pkwy., Mt. Pleasant).

The following companies offer kayak rentals and instruction on the Sea Islands around Charleston. The 1998 price for rentals of kayaks, safety equipment, and basic instruction was about $35 per day; $25 per half day. Tours, depending on their length, cost between $45 and $65.

**Bohicket Boat** (843-768-7294).

**Carolina Heritage Outfitters** (843-563-5051).

**Coastal Expeditions** (843-884-7684).

**Half-Moon Outfitters** (843-853-0990).

**Low Country Paddlesports** (843-863-1096).

**Whitewater Boat Co.** (843-406-0034).

## JET SKIING

Riding a jet ski offers the travel in shallow creeks and marshy inlets that sailing and kayaking afford, but at a much faster, and noisier, pace. Here are some places that rent jet skis. Prices in 1998 were from $50–$75 per hour, depending on whether you take a guided group tour or ride alone.

**Ashley Marina Jet Ski Rentals** (843-722-1996; Charleston).

**The City Marina** (843-853-4386; Charleston).

**Sun & Ski** (843-588-0033; Folly Beach).

**Tidal Wave Runners** (843-886-8456; Isle of Palms).

*Ocean-racing yachts streak across the broad harbors and inlets of Charleston.*

Wade Spees

## SAILING

For a sailor unfamiliar with Lowcountry coastal waters, the tides and currents can be strong and tricky to navigate. If you're interested in renting a sailboat, either for a day's excursion or for a trip along the Intracoastal Waterway, it's best to check out local conditions thoroughly, discussing your plans with the rental outfitter before you go.

Sailboats in a range of sizes are available for hire from the following:

**Argo Charters** (843-577-8804; 3 Lockwood Dr., Charleston, SC 29401).

**Bohicket Boat** (843-768-7294; Bohicket Marina Village, Seabrook Island, SC 29455).

**Wild Dunes Yacht Harbor** (843-886-5100; P.O. Box 527, Isle of Palms, SC 29451).

If you're towing your own boat, there are dozens of landings, most often simple ramps, where you can park your trailer and launch. Parking is free, but unmonitored. Listings or maps which show the locations of public boat landings in South Carolina are available from the state's *Marine Resources Division* (843-762-5000; P.O. Box 12559, Charleston, SC 29412) and the *Lowcountry Resort Islands and Tourism Commission* (800-528-6870; P.O. Box 615, Point South, SC 29945).

## BOWLING

**AMF Triangle Lanes** (843-766-0241; 1963 Savannah Hwy.).

**Ashley Lanes** (843-766-9061; 1568 Sam Rittenberg Blvd.).

## CAMPING

In the old days, a camping expedition usually involved sailing or rowing — or being sailed or rowed — in boats as heavily loaded as barges to the uninhabited barrier islands. Upon arrival there, the party would set up housekeeping at a "fish camp" for several days. These same spots would be revisited year after year, although they might consist of nothing more than driftwood chairs, a palmetto-log windbreak, and a fire pit. The tradition was rustic, the site well off the beaten track. Many Lowcountry residents still camp this way, though stories they bring home definitely outclass their accommodations!

Today's visitor can approximate this experience (but near running water, toilets, a campground store and gnat repellent) at *public campgrounds* at the following sites:

**Buck Hall, Francis Marion National Forest** (843-887-3257; Wambaw Ranger District, P.O. Box 106, McClellanville, SC 29458) 15 sites; hiking trails, boat ramp, fishing.

**James Island County Park** (843-795-9884; 871 Riverland Dr., Charleston, SC 29412) 125 sites, 10 cabins; paved bike trails, fishing and crabbing docks, playground, RV hookups.

Privately operated campgrounds in the area include:

**Lake Aire RV Park and Campground** (843-571-1271; S.C. 162, just off Hwy. 17) 100 sites including full hookups, primitive sites, and camper sites. Seven-acre fishing lake, swimming pool, paddle-boat and canoe rental, showers, laundry, recreation area, bike and foot trails.

**Oak Plantation Campground** (843-766-5936; Hwy. 17, 4 miles south of the intersection with S.C. 7 near the John's Island Road) Full hookups with 15-, 30-, and 50-amp. service; 100 tent sites, 150 camper sites, propane, laundry, groceries, bathrooms.

**Wood Brothers Campground** (843-844-2208; Hwy. 17, 37 miles south of Charleston) Wooded and open sites for RVs, campers, and tents; grocery, propane, showers, fishing pond.

## DIVING

If all those people who wear the wrist watches divers wear — thick black band, fluorescent numbers, rimmed with rings and buttons — ever actually suited up and went under, they'd clog the inshore waters of the Lowcountry; offshore, they might be taken for manatees.

Several outfitters provide rentals, guides, ocean-charters, and instruction in the sport. They include:

Aqua Ventures (843-884-1500).

Charleston Downunder (843-571-0860).

Charleston Scuba (843-763-3483).

Wet Shop (843-744-5641).

## FAMILY FUN

The Lowcountry's long summer nights, when dusk comes as late as nine o'clock, mean there's always extra time for that round of miniature golf or walk on the beach. By day, there are waterslides to offer cooling thrill rides. Here are some activities that adults and kids can enjoy together.

**Classic Golf** (843-881-3131; 1528 Ben Sawyer Blvd., Mt. Pleasant) Miniature golf landscaped and lit for night play.

**Frankie's Fun Park** (843-767-1399; 5000 Ashley Phospate Rd.) Two 18-hole mini golf courses, go-cart tracks, game rooms, batting cages, and bumper boats. Open daily, 10 a.m. to midnight. A great reward for kids who have been sightseeing all day.

**Palmetto Islands County Park** (843-884-0832; Long Point Rd., off Hwy. 17 N) Picnic areas and shelters, walking and biking trails, marsh boardwalk and fishing sites. Bicycles, canoes, and paddleboats are available for rent. **Splash Island** is a water fun park with slides, pools, and chutes.

**Sand Dollar Mini Golf** (843-884-0320; 1405 Ben Sawyer Blvd., Mt Pleasant) Open summer nights until 10 p.m.

## FISHING

There's *always* fishing in the Lowcountry, the time of year notwithstanding. Whether you choose to cast flies or live-bait from a pier, a flat-bottomed boat, a small powerboat, or a fancy charter headed for the Gulf Stream, you're bound to bring something home. The 1998 prices for charter boat rentals ranged from $185 for six passengers for a 5-hour excursion to about $60 per person with a guide in a smaller boat. Most charters accept credit cards. Call for reservations. Here are some suggestions for chartering in the Charleston area:

**Bohicket Boats** (843-768-7294; Bohicket Marina Village, Seabrook Island) Large selection of boats from 14 to 55 feet for inshore bass and trout fishing, jetty fishing, and offshore fishing for shark, mackerel, tuna, marlin. Full-and half-day trips.

*Like the early bird who gets the worm, the early riser catches the early charter and heads for Gulf Stream fishing grounds.*

Wade Spees

**Captain Ivan's Island Charters** (843-762-2020) Captain Ivan Schultz. Thirty-foot, wide beam boat with 21-passenger capacity, full- and half-day excursions to offshore reefs, trips to the Gulf Stream (12 hours).

**Carolina Clipper** (843-884-2992; Shem Creek, Mt. Pleasant) Captain Randolph Scott pilots a large boat with a snack bar and sundeck, and fully outfitted with gear and bait. Beginners welcome.

**Happyniss Sportfishing Charters** (843-884-3225; Mt. Pleasant) Maximum party of six aboard 42-foot Bertram. Full-day for marlin and tuna; half-day for sailfish, wahoo, king mackerel.

**Lowcountry Inshore Charters** (843-559-5040) Fly fishing and inshore light tackle for drum, jack crevalle, trout, and mackerel.

**Marsh Grass Charters** (843-766-1464; Charleston) Trolling and bottom fishing for 1–6 passengers; customized expeditions from 4 to 12 hours.

## FITNESS FACILITIES

Contemporary travelers may leave their troubles behind when they're on vacation, but few of them forget to pack their workout clothes. Though physical fitness for its own sake hasn't ranked as high on a list of Charleston's preferred pastimes as, say, hunting or being on the river, or talking about fishing or politics, or having a drink and meal with friends, nevertheless the city has accommodated itself to the national trend.

The idea of working out in an air-conditioned facility — when most of the year, even a short walk will produce beads of sweat — has its appeal. Fitness centers offer a range of machines and free weights; some of them offer day-rates for visitors. Your hotel concierge or bed-and-breakfast host may be able to steer you toward one, or recommend a personal trainer. Resorts generally have their own facilities. The 1998 fees for daily use ranged from $8–$35.

**The Firm** (843-723-3476; 77 Wentworth St.).

**Fitness Attitude Training** (843-769-5151; 1662 Savannah Hwy.).

**Lifequest Fitness** (843-849-1414; Mt. Pleasant or 843-571-2828; West Ashley).

**St. Andrew's Family Recreation Center** (843-763-3850; 1642 Sam Rittenberg Blvd.).

## GOLF

The first golf course in America was built in Charleston, and the founding of the nation's first golf club in 1786 followed immediately. Golf, it seems, is just another sublime activity, like building great houses or cultivating gardens, that Charleston's been doing for more than 200 years.

The best overview of golf-vacation possibilities is offered by any of the following reservation services. They provide information and will customize a golf package including course selections, tee times, lodging, and transportation.

**Charleston Golf, Inc.** (800-774-4444; ask for the *Golf Guide*).

**Charleston Golf Partners** (800-247-5786).

**Charleston SC Registry for Golf & Tourism** (800-952-7513).

If you're pursuing the links on your own, here are some general guidelines. Fees range according to the season, lower from Dec.–Feb., and in the heat of summer. Carts are required at peak playing times on many courses. For resort play, golf privileges are usually extended to non-resort guests: check with your concierge or call the resort directly. Club rentals and instruction are available at all courses. Greens fees/cart rentals reflect 1998 prices and do not include tax.

## PUBLIC AND SEMIPRIVATE COURSES

**Charleston Municipal Course** (843-795-6517; 2110 Maybank Hwy.) Par 72, 6,400 yards. Greens fees for non-residents: $12 if you walk, $22 with a cart; for seniors (62 and over) $10 if you walk, $20 with a cart. Twilight rates (after 3 p.m.) are $5. Pro: Jimmy Murray

**Charleston National** (843-884-7799; 1360 National Dr., Mt. Pleasant) Par 72. Five sets of tees spread over three small islands overlooking Hamlin Sound and the Intracoastal Waterway. Range: 5,045-yard forward course to 6,975-

yard champion course. Fees: $42 (weekdays) and $47 (weekends). Pro: David Jeffcoat.

**Coosaw Creek Country Club** (843-767-9000; 4210 Clubhouse Dr., North Charleston) Par 71. Range: 5,064-yard forward course to 6,593-yard champion course. Fees: $35–$45 (weekdays) and $39–$49 (weekends). Pro: Eric Lindfield.

**Crowfield Golf & Country Club** (843-764-4618; Goose Creek) Par 72. Range: 5,682-yard forward course to 7,003-yard champion course. Fees: $45–$65. Pro: Marty Mikesell.

**Dunes West** (843-856-9000; 3535 Wando Plantation Way, Mt. Pleasant) Par 72. Range: 5,278-yard forward course to 6,871-yard champion course. Fees: $32–$55 (weekdays) and $42–$75 (weekends). Pro: Keith Cain.

**Oak Point** (843-768-7431; Johns Island) Par 72. Range: 4,671-yard forward course to 6,759-yard championship course. Fees: $40–$60. Pro: Martin Shorter.

**Patriots Point Links** (843-881-0042; Mt. Pleasant) Par 72. Range: 5,562-yard forward course to 6,838-yard championship course. Fees: $32–$42. Pro: David Nelson.

**Shadowmoss Plantation Golf Club** (843-556-8251; 800-338-4971; Hwy. 61) Par 72. Range: 2,700-yard forward course to 6,700-yard championship course. Fees: $24–$29 (weekdays) and $25–$36 (weekends). Pro: Bob Wolfe.

**The Links at Stono Ferry** (843-763-1817; 5365 Forest Oaks Dr., Hollywood) Par 72. Range: 4,928-yard forward course to 6,616-yard championship course. Fees: $22–$36. Pro: Pam Weeks.

## *Courses at Charleston-area Resorts*

If you wish to plan your vacation around golf, you might save yourself travel time by staying in resorts or private residential communities where the game is the center of focus. Accommodations range from deluxe hotel rooms to villas and rental homes. These resorts also have complete recreational layouts which include swimming pools, tennis courts, and marinas. Here's a list of some well-known resort golf courses near Charleston.

**Kiawah Island** (843-768-2121 / 800-654-2924; 12 Beach Dr., Kiawah) Four championship courses have been carved out of gorgeous Sea Island landscape by the game's top designers: Pete Dye, Jack Nicklaus, Gary Player, and Tom Fazio. *The Ocean Course* (Par 72. Range: 5,327-yard forward course to 7,371 championship course) is probably the best known: the 1991 Ryder Cup was played here, and it was recently cited by *Golf Digest* as the toughest resort course in the country. *Osprey Point* (Par 72. Range: 5,122-yard forward course to 6,678-yard championship course) is consistently ranked in the country's top 75 courses. *Cougar Point* (Par 72. Range: 4,944-yard forward course to 6,861-yard championship course) and *Turtle Point* (Par 72. Range: 5,242-yard forward course to 6,925-yard championship course) make good use of Kiawah's unique geography — bracketed by the Atlantic and the River. Fees for the *Ocean Course* are $100–$125 (non-resort guests) and $81–$101 (resort guests). For all other courses, fees are $71–$106 (non-resort guests) and $56–$73 (resort guests).

**Seabrook Island** (843-768-1000; 800-845-2475;1002 Landfall Way, Seabrook Island). *Crooked Oaks* (Par 72. Range: 5,250-yard forward course to 6,832-yard championship course, designed by Robert Trent Jones, Sr.) and *Ocean Winds* (Par 72. Range: 5,524-yard forward course to 6,805-yard championship course, a Willard Byrd design) won the resort a silver medal commendation from *Golf* magazine. Players must either be members of the club or resort guests. Fees are $50–$80.

**Wild Dunes** (843-886-2164 / 800-845-8880; Isle of Palms) Tom Fazio designed both courses: *The Links* (Par 72. Range: 4,849-yard forward course to 6,722-yard championship course) offers oceanfront golf at its best, wind and water hazards notwithstanding. Fees: $70–$145. Pro: Tommy Young. *The Harbor* (Par 70. Range: 4,774-yard forward course to 6,446-yard championship course) features challenging holes that are, in some cases, an island apart. Pro: Steve Behr. Fees: $39–$69.

## HORSEBACK RIDING

*Recreational riding, dressage, and competitive polo keep equestrians busy.*

Wade Spees

The first racecourse in the Lowcountry was built near Charleston in 1735, and the South Carolina Jockey Club was founded there in 1758. It seems natural that equestrian showmanship should be a popular form of recreation.

If you want to take a lesson or trial ride during your visit, call one of the following stables to make advance arrangements, The prices in 1998 were $25 per hour for lessons; $15–$20 per person for trail rides.

*Seabrook Island Resort* (843-768-1000) features trails, an equestrian center and beach rides; *Stono River Riding and Boarding Stable* (843-559-0773) offers lessons in a stadium arena and trail rides; *Stono Ferry Stables* (843-763-0566) has hourly lessons in a ring; *Storybrook Farm* (843-571-2820) offers trail rides through adjacent cypress swamps and forests.

## HUNTING

In the Lowcountry you can hunt a wide variety of quarry including deer, wild turkey, dove, quail, feral hog, duck, fox, rabbit, woodcock, snipe, and clapper rail. What's more, you can do so during seasons which start as early as late summer (deer) and last through fall and winter until late spring (turkey). The Lowcountry has the longest deer season in the country and is considered the premiere spot on the East Coast to bag marsh hens.

There are six Game Management Areas in the Lowcountry; hunters at work within them are required to have a variety of licenses and permits, to abide by strict size and bag limits, obtain landowners' permission before hunting on private lands, and observe safe and ethical hunting practices in the field. For information, maps, and regulations concerning South Carolina hunting areas, contact the *Wildlife and Marine Resources Dept.* (843-734-3888; P.O. Box 167, Columbia, SC 29202). Outdoor recreation stores that specialize in hunting may also provide tips, information, and licenses.

Some of the most popular public hunting grounds in the Charleston area are located in the *Francis Marion National Forest* (843-825-3387; Berkeley County), *Webb Wildlife Center and Palachucola* (843-625-3569; Hampton and Jasper Counties), and *Bear Island* (843-844-2952; Colleton County).

If you prefer a more managed hunt, consider the guiding, cleaning, and transportation services of plantations that specialize in various kinds of game-hunting, according to the season. Some offer overnight accommodations. For information contact the *Lowcountry Tourism Commission* (800-528-6870; P.O. Box 615, Point South, SC 29945).

The *Southeastern Wildlife Exposition,* which takes place every February in Charleston, is the region's largest and best gathering of fishermen, hunters, outfitters, and artists who specialize in subjects of interest to sportsmen. Display sites scattered throughout the Charleston area feature Lowcountry and Western collectibles, crafts, decoys, antiques, and posters. A free shuttle bus service can take you to them. In addition, there are presentations and demonstrations. Admission is $10.50 per day. Write: *EXPO Information*, 211 Meeting St., Charleston, SC 29401; (843-723-1748; e-mail: sewe@aol.com).

## NATURE PRESERVES

M any small islands, swamps, or boggy necks nestled in the creeks and riverways of the Lowcountry offer natural camouflage and a near-wild habitat to the wildlife that live or migrate there. Some are more developed than others — with boardwalks or marked trails — but none require strenuous activity or advanced knowledge for enjoyment. If you are interested in the ecology of the Lowcountry, the life-cycle of the marsh, the effects of tidal flow on vegetation, and the interdependence of plant and animal life, then these sites will give you a feel for the rhythms of the Lowcountry beneath the surface.

**ACE Basin** (Access off Hwy. 17 at Green Pond, S.C. 26, Bennett's Point, Bear Island) A consortium of private individuals and state and federal groups have joined together to preserve some 350,000 acres of incredibly diverse habitat, including several islands, at the center of the Lowcountry. It is one of the largest undeveloped estuarine sanctuaries left on the East Coast. ACE takes its name from the area it embraces: the lands and waters amidst the Ashepoo, Combahee and Edisto Rivers on both sides of St. Helena Sound, a fishery so rich and pristine it accounts for nearly 10 percent of the state's shellfish harvest. Seventeen endangered species make their home here. Bring binoculars and cameras.

**Audubon Swamp Garden** (843-571-1266 / 800-367-3517; Hwy. 61 at Magnolia Plantation) Sixty acres of blackwater cypress and tupelo swamp, with trails through virgin pine forests, wild flowers, and exotic plants, this is a place that impressed John J. Audubon 150 years ago. Admission $4 (adults); $3 (teens); $2 (children 6–12).

**Cypress Gardens** (843-553-0515; Goose Creek. I-26 West to Exit 208, then to Hwy. 52 north) Take a guided tour or paddle a flat-bottom boat yourself through an old rice plantation reserve, now a protected natural swamp garden. A succession of blooms, from the earliest camellia and narcissus to trumpet vine and azalea, brightens the shadowy cypress forest. Open 9–5 daily. Adults $5, children $2, under 6 free.

**Francis Biedler Forest in Four Holes Swamp** (843-462-2150; Harleyville. From I-95 take I-26 east to Exit 177, then south on S.C. 453 to U.S. 178. Follow signs east on 178. From Charleston, take I-26 west to Exit 187, then south on S.C. 27.) The 5,415 acre forest, managed by the National Audubon Society, contains the largest remaining virgin stand of bald cypress and tupelo gum

*Walking in the evening at Magnolia Plantation.*

Wade Spees

trees in the world. There's a self-guided boardwalk and Visitor Center, but the point here is to walk quietly and observe well, to absorb what you can on your own without the experience being "packaged" in any way. Open 9–5 daily except Mondays. Adults $3.75, children $1.75, under 6 free.

## POLO

Spectators can pack a tailgate picnic and enjoy Sunday afternoon polo games in September and October, April and May at *Stono Ferry* (843-766-6208) located south of Charleston. Take Hwy. 17 to S.C. 162, Hollywood.

## TENNIS

Like golf, tennis is a popular Lowcountry sport around which an entire vacation could be designed. There are courts in city parks, tennis centers, and county recreation areas. Your hotel concierge or bed and breakfast host should be able to direct you to ones close by, or call the town halls for the location of their recreation centers.

**Charleston Tennis Center** (843-724-7402; Farmfield Rd., west of Charleston on Hwy. 17) has 15 outdoor hard courts, lit for night play. $2.50 per hour per person. Visitors should call ahead to check availability, or may reserve by paying in advance.

Some Lowcountry resorts also offer playing-time for non-resort guests. Fees vary depending on season and time of day. Reservations are required. Inquire about tennis packages.

**Kiawah Island** (843-768-2121).
**Shadowmoss Plantation** (843-571-2914).
**Wild Dunes** (843-886-2113; Isle of Palms).

## WINDSURFING

Although the currents and tides make for tricky windsurfing conditions, the Lowcountry's warm water temperature and wide open spaces have attracted windsurfers for years. It is very important to check the local forecasts and tides before you go (843-744-3207 is the number for Charleston weather) and to surf in well-known areas. Even experienced windsurfers have found themselves thrust well beyond the confines of, say, Charleston Harbor by the outgoing tide, only to find they have to wait until it turns to paddle or sail in.

Many resorts have windsurfers to rent ,or provide instruction first on land, then in sheltered creeks or on a quiet stretch of beach. For more information, inquire at sporting goods shops or call some of the following rental/instruction agencies.

**Barrier Island Surf Shop** (843-588-6666, Folly Beach).
**Folly Windsurfing** (843-795-8872; Folly Beach).
**McKevlin's Surf Shop** (843-886-8912, Isle of Palms; 843-588-2247, Folly Beach).
**Timeout** (843-577-5979; downtown Charleston).

# SHOPPING

The time has long passed since Charleston's ports operated on a small scale; small enough for residents to have the incidental pleasures of observing ships at the wharf and wondering what lay in their hold. Yet such pastimes of commercial life were once commonplace. Life was measured by the anticipation of an import — teas or seeds, books, furniture, food, or mail — and the reciprocal, satisfactory delivery of an export. If the export represented the summing up of what plantation culture and slavery had been designed to produce, the import confirmed Charleston's view of itself as a tasteful, cultivated, wealthy society. It was as if the sight of bustling, wharf-side activity enhanced, gave value to, the rather ordinary impulse to consume.

Today, the thrill is not gone, it's just been moved. The fun in shopping still emerges from its setting. Here it happens in smallish places: in glossy boutiques, in shops in old houses, in commercial buildings on ballast-stone alleys, under market sheds, or out in the open air of a busy corner.

Some of these places are run by partnerships of family members, or have

*HOME in Charleston is a store that symbolizes the pride of a city that values domestic beauty, utility, and tradition.*

Wade Spees

been passed on — tin ceilings and all — to their present owners. Others have taken root in jam-packed shopping areas like the *Market Area* where the old, open-air sheds claim the center of the street, which is itself bisected at several points by lateral shopping streets. Take a nice after-dinner walk here, or have coffee and dessert at a sidewalk cafe and watch the Citadel cadets with their dates, or the tourists, pass in drifts. The range of what you can buy is enormous, from a hand puppet to a turnip.

## ANTEBELLUM ARTIFACTS

**Charleston Shoreline** (843-723-6213; 40 N. Market St.) Civil War prints, engravings, stamps, artifacts, and documents.

**D & D** (843-853-5266; 190 King St.) Old books about the South and Charleston; artifacts of marine life.

## ANTIQUES

The period of poverty that engulfed the Lowcountry after the Civil War called for living by austere means and resourcefulness. It was not a time when renovating and redecorating was considered remotely possible.

Some residents count this as a blessing: a lot of old houses, and all they contained, were spared the wrecker's ball. In the 1920s, they caught the eye of northern decorators and curators, who either imitated their look or purchased them, literally, lock, stock, barrel, and window sash. Later, when the families who had lived in the old houses produced a generation with the means to redecorate them, the urge to adorn them in the old style prevailed. Today, antiques stores throughout the Lowcountry retail this classic look, both in original pieces and in excellent reproductions.

While taste, or a good eye, is hard to define, it seems clear that the very experience of living in Charleston has produced antiques dealers who have absorbed its lessons of enduring beauty. They seem to know what fits — whether it's a pair of simple sterling candlesticks or a stunning chest-on-chest.

A short list of some of the more distinctive antiques shops follows. If you are poking around for something in particular, or a type of thing, ask for it. It's a small world, and dealers should be able to direct you elsewhere.

**A'Riga IV Antiques** (843-577-3075; 204 King St.) An impressive collection of old scientific instruments and medical kits, some of which can be oddly beautiful as art objects, as well as apothecary jars and ceramic containers that were put to domestic use years ago.

**George C. Birlant & Co.** (843-722-3842; 191 King St.) In business for nearly 70 years, selling brass, silver, crystal, and small and large English antiques, which they import directly. Big old-fashioned picture windows open onto the street; inside there's lots of room to walk around. Reproductions of Charleston's own cypress-and-iron "Battery Bench" available.

**Century House Antiques** (843-722-6248; 85 Church St.) There's a fineness about this shop which may have to do with the nature of its stock — English and Chinese export porcelain — or the feeling you get from being in the presence of an eye that's appreciated beauty for a long time. Botanicals, bird prints, and old books, too.

**Estate Antiques** (843-723-2362; 155 King St.) A superb collection of American antiques, especially Southern and Charleston pieces, and accessories. Jim and Harriet Pratt know their merchandise from the inside out and they willingly share their knowledge with even the most committed browsers. The pieces here have good bones. The best antique store in Charleston.

**Grey Goose Antiques Malls** (843-763-9131; 1011 St. Andrews Blvd.; 1119 Johnnie Dodds Blvd., Mt. Pleasant; 843-856-9525) Many rooms filled with antiques, from lap desks and pie birds to Southwestern jewelry and Depression-glass.

**Historic Charleston Reproductions** (843-723-8292; 105 Broad St.) Adaptations and reproductions of 18th- and 19th-century furniture, lamps, fabric, brass, wallcoverings, and accessories that once graced Charleston homes. High-quality workmanship by companies like Baker Furniture, Scalamandre, and Mottahedeh.

**Period Antiques** (843-723-2724; 194 King St.) Several different stylistic rhythms carry on here: there are 20th-century decorative art and furniture, country-style pine pieces, mirrors, antiques of one sort or another, and funky things that could brighten a corner.

**Piazza** (843-853-4555; 56 Queen St.) Wonderful French needlepoint pillows and small European antiques.

**Ridler Page Rare Maps** (843-723-1734; 205 King St.) Antique maps in a variety of sizes, some as old as the 16th century, many hand-colored.

**Shalimar Antiques** (843-766-1529; 2418 Savannah Hwy.) A totally unprepossessing place from the outside — it looks like an old motel and probably was — but inside, the collection of grandfather clocks, pine tables and beds, primitives, and trunks is lovely indeed.

## BOOKS

The personal style of book selling, in which a store's proprietor knows the taste of his customers and alerts them to new volumes, is prominent in Charleston, where readers may live at some distance from the city and depend on a bookseller's recommendations and mailing services. The advantage for the visitor is that clerks really know their stock, can suggest local favorites, and will find out-of-print volumes.

There are also several shops for used books which, if a person could track them the way the wildlife experts track fish, could be seen migrating from one home library to another. The national chains, for their part, showcase titles relating to local topics in history, gardening, culture, and photography.

**Atlantic Books** (843-723-4751; 310 King St. and 191 E. Bay St.; 843-723-7654.) Thousands of used books on many subjects. Very strong in local history and memoir, military titles, fiction, Civil War, Southern authors.

**Audubon Shop and Gallery** (843-723-6171; 311 King St.) Field guides galore.

**Book Exchange** (843-556-5051; 1219 Savannah Hwy.) New and used books and collectible comics.

**Boomers' Books** (843-722-2666; 420 King St.) Broad selection in fiction, children's, antiques, and architecture.

**Cady & Daughter Books** (843-722-6951; 40 N. Market St.) Big selection of used books and remainders.

**Chapter Two** (843-722-4238 / 800-722-4238; 249 Meeting St. at Wentworth.) The best in Charleston, consistently rated among the best in the region. Superb history and art sections, fine magazines. Open late for browsers on Thursdays and Fridays. Frequent book-signings held here.

**Charleston Rare Book Co.** (843-723-3330; 66 Church St.) Specializing in Charleston and Lowcountry books, including a good nautical section.

**Doubleday Book Shops** (843-723-6186; 126 Market St. at Charleston Place) Good children's section, best-sellers of the Lowcountry (Pat Conroy, Eugenia

*You could easily spend a quiet hour browsing at Charleston's Chapter Two — and you're more than welcome to do so.*

Wade Spees

Price, Alexandra Ripley, Jo Humphries) as well as a nice collection of photography books with a regional focus.

**Historic Charleston Foundation Museum Shop and Bookstore** (843-724-8484; 108 Meeting St.) If you want to know more about regional history and the decorative arts, preservation efforts, architecture and related topics, stop in here. Also many volumes about historic properties here and elsewhere, as well as an excellent children's section.

**Hoppin' John's** (843-577-6404; 30 Pinckney St.) A two-room shop that is nothing more or less than an institution. John Martin Taylor, author of two cookbooks, food historian and raconteur, has assembled an impressive collection of cookbooks — and he's probably read every one.

**Noble Dragon** (843-577-9334; 106 Church St.) Old, new, and rare books amidst a little cafe with excellent cookies, beer and wine, and light snacks. A great late-afternoon stop.

**Pauline Books & Media** (843-577-0175; 243 King St.) A religious bookstore with Bibles and a nice selection for younger readers.

**Petterson Antiques** (843-723-5714; 201 King St.) If the old books and magazines that sit on carts outside the store don't attract your eye, duck in and cast your gaze to the shelves and cases within. It may take time to find a treasure, but after all, you can never get enough of the atmosphere, which is free.

**Preservation Society of Charleston** (843-723-4381; 147 King St.) The headquarters of the Preservation Society has an unhurried, old-world feeling and many books on Charleston history, art, architecture, and culture.

**Waldenbooks** (843-797-3558; Northwoods Mall) Best-sellers, good history and military section.


## CLOTHING

In Charleston, people still wear hats. Not just baseball caps or fedoras — hats with attitude and purposeful brims — either, but straw hats, garden-party hats, fishing caps, and velvet berets. They also dress their children, boys and girls, in smockery and suits. Yet among a population that tends to sartorial conservatism, there is usually a fillip of embellishment to be found, accompanied by the natural confidence to pull it off.

Women will be especially fortunate to be shopping for clothes here, as there are several comfortable boutiques that offer unusual suits and separates in linen, silk, and cotton blends, in a range of styles to suit most ages.

The following suggestions do not list clothing stores that are part of a national chain, although those to be found in Charleston include: Polo, Laura Ashley, Banana Republic, Gap, Express, The Limited, Saks Fifth Avenue, and Talbot's.

**A.J. Davis & Co.** (843-577-3088; 296 King St.) Men's clothes, plain and cheerfully sporty, and accessories.

**Berlin's** (843-722-1665; 114 King St.) Men's and women's clothes in traditional styles and top quality brands. Since 1883.

**Bits of Lace** (843-577-0999; 212 King St.) Fine lingerie and other little fancy things for women.

**Bob Ellis Shoes** (843-722-2605; 332 King St.) Vast selection of fine footwear for men and women and a sales staff that keeps bringing out the boxes.

**Christian Michi** (843-723-0575; 220 King St.) For women, high-fashion and sporty lines from top European and American designers. It's as if a small section of a hip New York department store left the city for life in the provinces.

**Cousins** (843-723-2643; 150 King St.) Simple, elegant, understated clothes with classic lines, for women. There's a quiet, relaxed atmosphere of real attention to your own style here.

**Eighty-Two Church** (843-723-7511; 82 Church St.) If this store were anywhere but in the "South of Broad" district, it would probably be a museum by now. A lovely selection of hand-smocked dresses for girls to size 14, bonnets, clothes for newborns, christening outfits, sweaters, cotton rompers, and seersucker playsuits. Boy's clothing to size 6. Very nice baby gifts, too.

**Ellington** (843-722-7999; 193 King St.) If you're returning to office life after a

*A new generation ready to be outfitted at Eighty-Two Church Street.*

Wade Spees

break and need something unusual and spiffy, or if you don't dress up much but like to wear a finely tailored piece when you do, look here for clothes with simple lines and solid construction.

**Granny's Goodies** (843-577-6200; 301 King St. ) Antique and vintage clothes for men, women, and children: poodle skirts, Hawaiian shirts, gloves and gauze, fur-trimmed opera capes, boas. Great selection and guaranteed laughs.

**M. Dumas & Sons** (843-723-8603; 294 King St.) Even the wallpaper here is riding to hounds. The old original source for what has become an "American Country" look.

**RTW** (843-577-9748; 186 King St.) A boutique for women who delight in gorgeous fabrics, sweaters that tumble with color, one-of-a-kind shirts, hats, shoes, and accessories, and who like to dress with a sense of fun and beauty. A rare find in any city.

**Three Nineteen King** (843-577-2699; 319 King St.) Chic fashions for men and women with attitude.

**Urban Cotton** (843-937-8500; 287 King St.) The best look in basic cotton: knits, tee-shirts, sarongs, stylish cardigans, and tunics.

**Utopia** (843-853-9510; 27 Broad St.) A funky store of up-to-the-minute downtown, MTV fashion, paintings, jewelry, accessories, and shoes.

## CRAFTS

The Lowcountry's *sea grass baskets* are a regional specialty, and if you're interested in them, you won't have far to look. The basket weavers are out every day along *Broad and Meeting Streets,* and in the *Market Area.* Prices vary for items as small as keepsake decorations or as large as fanner baskets and hampers. You're welcome to watch the process, which incorporates palmetto strips and pine straw with the pale grass. Other weavers sell their work at stands located north of Charleston on *Highway 17.*

**American Originals** (843-853-5034; 153 East Bay St.) Crafts by local and national artists: pictures, baskets, rugs, pottery.

**Beadstreet** (843-577-7192; 72-A Wentworth St.) Beads and supplies for stringing, gluing, and fastening, as well as books on jewelry styles and technique.

**Charleston Crafts** (843-723-2938; 38 Queen St.) Crafts and exhibits by members of this local co-op, who are considered superior in their fields, be they weavers, soapmakers, or photographers.

**East Bay Gallery** (843-723-5567; 264 King St.) Ironwork tables, pottery lamps, wooden inlaid boxes, colorful blown stemware.

**Laura's Closet** (843-849-9602; 280 W. Coleman Blvd., Mt. Pleasant) A treasure trove for people who like to sew, embroider, and smock. There are heirloom patterns, fabrics, accessories, books, and needlework materials.

## FARMS AND FARMERS' MARKETS

Wade Spees

*Fields of the Lowcountry have produced indigo, rice, cotton, and now tea.*

The Lowcountry grwing season lasts from February to the first frost in November, with many crops being planted more than once. A visit to the outdoor market held in **Marion Square** on Saturday mornings between April and November may yield anything from herbs to watermelon. If you're interested in getting out into the fields yourself, you may do so at any number of roadside farm stands scattered across the Sea Islands. Here you pick your own tomatoes, peppers, melons, beans, squash, blueberries, and strawberries and pay by the basket or the pound. Look for notices in the newspaper announcing the opening of fields or call the local Chamber of Commerce for information.

Two other farms are worth a stop if you're exploring. *The Charleston Tea Plantation* (843-559-0383 / 800-443-5987) where American Classic Tea is grown, is unique in the nation. Tours lasting 30 minutes are usually scheduled the first Saturday of the month, May through October, starting at 10 a.m. There are also weekday tours, by appointment, for groups of 20–45 people. The tours last one hour and cost $5.00. The last tour of the day is at 1:30 p.m. and they are cancelled in case of rain. It's located on Wadmalaw Island about 20 miles south of Charleston. Take Hwy. 17 to SC 171. Turn east (toward Folly Beach) and soon after turn south on SC 700 (Maybank Highway). The plantation is located at nearly the end of this road. *Rosebank Farms* (843-768-9139) is on John's Island, shortly before the entrances to Kiawah and Seabrook. There are many varieties of premium vegetables and herbs for sale, glorious bouquets of fresh-cut flowers, dried wreaths, bedding plants, and holiday garlands.

## GALLERIES

Art galleries are proliferating in many sectors of the city, especially in the *French Quarter* (an area roughly four blocks square, bounded by E. Bay St., Broad St., Meeting St., and Cumberland St.), and on lower Broad St. You can tour the Charleston gallery scene on line, too: *http://www.discovernet.com/charleston/gallery/*.

**Art Thomas Gallery** (843-577-0534; 2 Queen St.) Contemporary art that is strong, dramatic, and complex, from artists such as Eva Carter, Phillip Garrett, Tom Durham, and William Halsey.

**Birds I View Gallery** (843-723-1276; 119-A Church St.) Realistic paintings and prints — her birds and rabbits are drawn from those she's cared for — by longtime Charleston artist Anne Worsham Richardson.

**Carolina Prints** (843-723-2266; 188 King St.) Antique prints by masters such as Audubon, Catesby, and Schwert, pre-1945 American art, and contemporary realistic art by local artists, including the proprietors. From time to time, there are beautiful examples of the works of Charleston artists from the earlier part of the century, such as Alice Ravenel Huger Smith, Anna Heyward Taylor, and Alfred Hutty.

**Coleman Fine Art** (843-853-7000; 45 Hasell St.) Members of the gallery include a number of superior artists working in a realistic style in oils and watercolors. Smith Coleman, III, who owns the gallery, also restores damaged works of art. There's a lot of accomplishment inside these four walls.

**Fraser and Co. Fine Arts** (843-577-6039; 17 B Broad St.) Landscapes, cityscapes, maritime watercolors, prints, oil paintings, and sculptures of the Lowcountry and the Eastern seaboard by West Fraser and others. Very fine work.

**Gallery Chuma** (843-722-8224; 43 John St.) A large, handsome gallery dedicated to work by African-Americans, including original work by regional artists Joe Pinckney, Jonathan Green, and Leo Twiggs.

**Gordon Wheeler Gallery** (843-722-2546; 180 E. Bay St.) The realistic paintings of the artist, mostly watercolor, many in print editions, of the Lowcountry, including vistas and sporting scenes.

**Lowcountry Artists, Ltd.** (843-577-9295; 148 E. Bay St.) A small, intimate gallery showing the work of nine distinctive artists. The woodcuts and pencil drawings are especially noteworthy.

**Margaret Petterson Gallery** (843-722-8094; 125 Church St.) At a time when cityscapes and bucolic scenes of Charleston seem to be everywhere, those by the gallery's owner seem fresh and interesting, especially the closeups. Sculpture and pottery sometimes on view.

**Marty Whaley Adams Gallery** (843-853-8512; 120 Meeting St.) The work of a prolific artist who works in many media, including watercolor, oil, monotype, wood, iron, and pottery. The results are most often still lifes and Lowcountry landscapes rendered in vivid color.

**Nina Liu and Friends** (843-722-2724; 24 State St.) Wonderful contemporary art in media such as fabric, collage, ceramic, paper, and glass, that can be startling, magical, and strong. The owner is herself an artist with a fine eye.

**Unity Gallery** (843-853-7263; 149 E. Bay St.) A new gallery located in the French Quarter showing boldly drawn and colored representational work.

**Virginia Bolton and Friends** (843-577-9351; 125 Meeting St.) Classic scenes of Charleston, its houses and people, including miniatures reproduced from original watercolors which make nice keepsakes.

**Waterfront Gallery** (843-722-1155; 167 E. Bay St.) A collection of artists who generally take the Lowcountry as their theme and express it in diverse ways. The gallery provides a helpful overview of regional work.

**Wells Gallery** (843-853-3233; 103 Broad St.) Contemporary art of nationally recognized artists such as Susan Mayfield West, John Carroll Doyle, Betty Anglin Smith, and Rhett Thurman.

**William McCullough Studio** (843-577-4458; Rutledge Ave.) The artist's studio, open by appointment, features work in oil and pastel that captures the special light and texture of the Lowcountry.

## GIFTS

**Birds & Ivy** (843-853-8534; 235 King St.) Accessories for your garden and even the coffee beans to brew while you're sitting in it.

**Cabbage Row Shoppe** (843-722-1528; 110 Church St.) Original, hand-painted, needlepoint canvases and needlework accessories, as well as little treasures for the bureau and greeting cards.

**Indigo** (843-577-5563; 189 E. Bay St.) A changing mixture of English pine furniture, wrought iron tables and benches, handsome leather luggage that has seen the world, folk art, and pottery.

**Kites Fly' N Hi** (843-577-3529; 40 North Market) These kites, wind socks, and flags look good standing still; how fine they'd be in a breeze back home.

**Native Son** (843-723-3008; 308 1/2 King St.) Folk art, painted furniture, quilts, and jewelry.

**Porgy & Bess** (843-723-1887; 89-91 Church St.) What's here in the way of clothing and accessories is likely to be bright in color and long on puckishness, as in paper goods that read "This napkin has no cholesterol."

**The Smoking Lamp** (843-577-7339; 197 East Bay St.) Everything for the smoker, that most maligned modern species.

## GOURMET AND HEALTH FOOD STORES

**Aloha Natural Foods** (843-849-5521; 628 Coleman Blvd., Mt. Pleasant) Organic produce and juice bar, books, herbs, face and body products.

**Books, Herbs & Spices** (843-722-9024; 480 E. Bay St.) The store is filled with herbs, roots, extracts, cooking spices, and vitamins, and lots of books that explain homeopathy and care of the body.

**Carolina Wine and Cheese** (843-577-6144; 54 1/2 Wentworth St.) Fresh German bread, excellent deli meats, coffees and teas, gourmet items, and all the makings for home-brewed beer.

**Hoppin' John's** (843-577-6404; 30 Pinckney St.) A wonderful culinary bookstore that also sells fresh stone-ground grits and food-related items such as cards and kitchen accessories. If you're interested in Lowcountry cooking, this store is a must.

**Raspberry's** (843-556-0076; 1331 Ashley River Rd.) Natural, unprocessed foods including grains, herbs, bulk flour, and organic produce. Vitamins and body care items, too.

**Tinder Box Internationale** (843-853-3720; 177 Meeting St.) The largest selection of cigars for sale in the city, including vintage cigars and hand-rolled specimens long enough for Winston Churchill. Smoking on premises encouraged.

## HOME FURNISHINGS/KITCHENWARE

**Blink** (843-577-5688; 62 B Queen St.) The owner, and the gifted eye behind the wonderful ceramic, glass, metal, and fabric objects in this tiny shop, is Mary Leonard. Nothing in Charleston compares — perhaps nothing south of SoHo.

*Gardening may be the latest national trend, but they've been doing it in Charleston for two centuries.*

Wade Spees

**Charleston Gardens** (843-723-0252; 61 Queen St.) Furnishings and accessories (botanical prints, old posters, lamps, and pots) for the gardener at heart, as well as serious gardening tools and live topiaries. In a creatively renovated space, with a back garden courtyard.

**fred** (843-723-5699; 237 King St.) Clean, spare design in black and white and stainless steel: kitchen basics, cutlery, towels and racks, mechanical wonders. A local favorite.

**Home** (843-723-9063; 268 King St.) Cookbooks, gifts, ceramics, table settings that bring Provence or Tuscany to your sunny rooms.

**Le Creuset** (843-723-4191; 242 King St.) Famous French enameled cookware at factory prices. (The factory, and another store, is located off I-95 at Yemassee if you're heading south.)

**Metropolitan Deluxe** (843-722-0436; 164 Market St.) Located in what looks like an old warehouse, featuring several large rooms decorated and piled high with household goods that range from the opulent (velvet upholstery, leather boxes, brass lamps) to the funky (wire baskets, painted benches, canvas chairs.) The old mercantile store has been updated.

**Studio Marc Howard** (843-722-2762; 314 King St.) Lush, multi-colored leather pillows, museum-store desk accessories, modern clocks, high-tech floor lamps.

## SPORTING GOODS AND CLOTHING

**Bicycle Shoppe** (843-722-8168; 280 Meeting St.) Rent or buy bikes here, or choose from cases full of bike hardware and gadgets.

**Half-Moon Outfitters** (843-853-0990; 320 King St.) The most durable and fashionable outdoor wear (like Patagonia) is here, plus coats, tents, packs, camping supplies, and the best advice on local outdoor adventuring to be found in the city.

**Outdoor Outfitters** (843-763-9115; 1662 Savannah Hwy.) A one-stop shop if you're going to be in the woods, the marsh, or on the water.

**Palmetto Cyclery** (843-571-1211; 1310 Savannah Hwy.) Bikes and gear galore — and an unusual art gallery within the shop.

*High-end outdoor stores — filled with wet suits and sandals, kayaks and backpacks, maps and good advice — set the youthful tone on Upper King Street.*

Wade Spees

# CHAPTER FOUR
# *An Old City, A Modern City*
## SAVANNAH

It's no secret that the preservation of the great places of the Low-country, including the city of Savannah, came about less as a result of enlightened social policy than as the backhanded result of post-Civil War impoverishment. Indeed, the many years of slow growth and stalled expectations treated Savannah as they did Charleston, and to this day, the cities share similar assets as a result: vibrant, intact, downtown historic districts; a heritage that reflects the contributions of wealthy

Wade Spees

*The Waving Girl statue on River Street, expressing the sadness of a farewell, is a memorial to the lives of lighthouse keepers and the safe passage their watchfulness provided for generations of sailors.*

planters and merchants, talented local artisans who had been former slaves or European immigrants; and a culture enriched by unique musical, religious, culinary, and artistic contributions.

Yet in several subtle ways, Savannah today is a far more complex and interesting *modern* city than Charleston is. For whatever historic reasons, and they run deep, it seems to have achieved an unusual sense of detachment. For every bold statement claimed about its history or beauty, there will be lurking on the lips of someone nearby a counter-claim, a wee sarcasm. (Once upon a time during the cotton boom, Savannah madly envied New York City for its commercial muscle; 160 years later the two cities share a liking for gesture and attitude.)

This trait was evident even during the Civil War. Legend has it that General W. T. Sherman spared Savannah because the city was beautiful, the women were gracious, and the parties were just what he needed at the end of his blazing "March To the Sea" campaign. He took up residence, was indeed feted, and, in a remarkable telegraph of 1864, offered the unmolested city to President Lincoln as a Christmas gift.

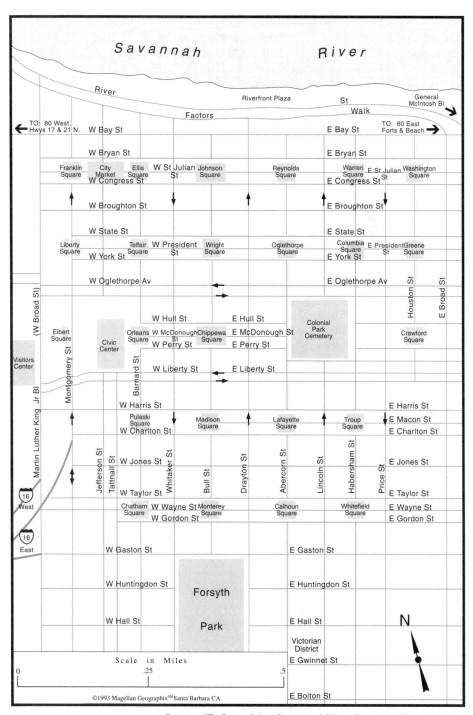

Courtesy of The Savannah Area Convention & Visitors Bureau (used by permission)

**SAVANNAH**

Well, Savannah is still beautiful, and they're still partying. (This quality, and the world it describes, is revealed with great skill in the best book on Savannah, John Berendt's 1994 work, *Midnight in the Garden of Good and Evil*.) The blend of reverence and hilarity, of high-mindedness and getting by, gives the city its character. In fact, as time passes, it becomes more palpable. When the local minor league baseball team renamed itself the Sand Gnats (the top choice in a city-wide poll), it chose for its slogan *"Bite Me."* The city literally shuts down every St. Patrick's Day to accommodate 24 hours of revelry. Clearly, this is not Charleston, a city thought by some Southerners as being "wrapped too tight." Savannah doesn't mind having been thought of as too sleepy or too indifferent to capitalize on its own potential.

By the time that national economic and social development did recommend change — after World War II, after a manufacturing and military base under-girded the economy, after federally mandated integration — Savannah residents with the means and interest to do so were faced with reconciling their historic cultural identity, on which they relied so deeply, with a post-war world which placed increasing value on money, mobility, and a celebration of things modern and new. The time had come to set the ongoing physical and intellectual activities associated with historic preservation, neighborhood renovation, and tourist attraction on a larger and more public stage. This they did, and in the process became what might be called curators of their own collection, a collection, it must be said, whose very display case — the old city — is a work of art.

Originally laid out in an orderly, compact grid, downtown Savannah retains this geography today. It is defined by 22 handsome squares that function as vest-pocket parks, are embowered and rimmed with native flowering species, and are linked by narrow cross streets or broad parkways divided by columns of trees. It is the nation's largest registered Urban Historic District, containing some 1,200 buildings of architectural and historic significance. These include blocks of magnificent townhouses, many 19th-century places of worship, and several examples of Regency architecture popularized in this country by an Englishman, William Jay.

Some sections deserve particular note. One is the old City Market area, which has been transformed into a largely pedestrian streetscape, with shops, galleries, restaurants, and clubs. Another is the waterfront, site of the old Cotton Exchange, where the brick warehouses and cotton factor's offices are filled with commercial and tourist-related attractions. The Victorian District, the latest section of Savannah to be renovated, features large wooden houses faced with decorative moldings, fretwork, and porches, and many gingerbreaded-bungalows.

The restoration and adaptive re-use of private and institutional buildings throughout the city (especially by the dynamic Savannah College of Art and Design) continues in very imaginative ways. In each of these areas, visitors are given the privilege to feel as residents: nothing is frozen in amber. There is still motion in and around the most awe-producing architectural icons: people going to work, to school, home to lunch, to the market, just hanging out, or visiting.

The ways in which Savannah chose to survive have served it well. It has withstood General Sherman and Forrest Gump. Relishing its contradictions as it does, it faces the millennium with an extraordinary cultural and historic landscape, and a population with the sass and ginger pop to really enjoy it.

# LODGING

Savannah and its Sea Island neighbor, Tybee Island, offer a pleasing range of accommodations, from upscale inns to downright funky beach villas. Tybee is closer to Savannah than Charleston's beach areas are to that city, and unlike Savannah's other nearby resort islands, it is not private.

Like Charleston, Savannah had its tradition of providing guest accommodations in city mansions whose owners had rooms to spare. As more visitors came to the area, "tourist homes" and "guest houses" sprang up to serve the mainly Northern clientele who flocked in springtime to see Savannah's gardens and experience its faded charm.

The only thing you'll find faded in Savannah today is a shirt that's been left out in the sun too long. As the old houses have been renovated and the cityscapes renewed, dozens of splendid inns have emerged, which are listed below.

The caveats invoked in earlier chapters hold true here: reservations are highly recommended, especially in the "high season" of spring, when a two-night's minimum stay is the usual practice; cancellation policies and room deposits are standard; rules exist regarding smoking on the premises and provisions for guests under age 10; access for handicapped persons can be problematic. For a refresher on these and other topics concerning lodgings, refer to the *Introduction* and don't hesitate to ask your innkeeper when inquiring about reservations.

The same range of rates applies in Savannah as in other Lowcountry places. They are:

| | |
|---|---|
| Inexpensive | Up to $50 |
| Moderate | $50 to $110 |
| Expensive | $110 to $180 |
| Very Expensive | $180 and up |

These rates do not include room taxes or special service charges that might apply during your stay.

## *Credit Cards*

AE — American Express
CB — Carte Blanche
D — Discover Card

DC — Diner's Card
MC — MasterCard
V — Visa

## HOTELS AND LARGER INNS

**DE SOTO HILTON**
912-232-9000 / 800-426-8483.
15 E. Liberty St., Savannah,
GA 31412.
Price: Expensive.
Credit Cards: AE, DC, MC,
V.
Handicap Access: Yes.

This is a wonderful location in the heart of the Historic District, a short walk to the riverfront. Some of the 245 rooms have private balconies, many are non-smoking, many have great views of Savannah's splendid squares. Pool and health club.

*A glossy new hotel shines in the midst of old Savannah.*

Wade Spees

**HYATT REGENCY
SAVANNAH**
912-238-1234 / 800-233-1234.
2 W. Bay St., Savannah, GA
31412.
Price: Expensive to Very
Expensive.
Credit Cards: AE, DC, MC,
V.
Handicap Access: Yes.

This big, fancy hotel (346 rooms), with the trademark Hyatt atrium lobby, towers over the riverfront with an unparalleled view of the ship and tugboat traffic. It is thoroughly modern, but not a tower of concrete and glass. There's an indoor pool and shopping arcade, and you're steps away from all the nightlife and daytime shopping on River Street, the main avenue of restored warehouses and commercial marine buildings.

**THE MULBERRY**
(A Holiday Inn property).

Right across the street from the commercial riverfront, this 122-room inn blends the close

912-238-1200 /
   800-465-4329.
601 East Bay St., Savannah,
   GA 31401.
Price: Expensive.
Credit Cards: AE, MC, V.
Handicap Access: Yes.

**SAVANNAH MARRIOTT
   RIVERFRONT**
912-233-7722.
100 General McIntosh Blvd.,
   Savannah, GA 31401.
Price: Expensive.
Credit Cards: AE, D, DC,
   MC, V.
Handicap Access: Yes.

**LUXURY INNS**

attention found in smaller inns with the services of a hotel. Informal piano concerts set the tone for afternoon tea, and complimentary hors d'oeuvres are served. Before you venture out to dinner, you can relax in the heated, rooftop Jacuzzi. There's an outdoor pool, too.

This waterfront hotel served as the 1996 Olympic housing village for all yachting athletes. It's luxurious, with large lounges and a soaring atrium, an outdoor pool, and exercise facilities. Not intimate, but new and on a great site.

*Teatime in the parlor at The Ballastone Inn renews the Southern custom of visiting.*

Wade Spees

**BALLASTONE INN**
Innkeeper: Jean Hagens.
912-236-1484 /
   800-822-4553.
Fax: 912-236-4626.
14 E. Oglethorpe Ave.,
   Savannah, GA 31401.
Price: Expensive to Very
   Expensive.
Credit Cards: AE, MC, V.
Handicap Access: Limited.

At Christmas, the Ballastone Inn looks like a scene out of Dickens — holly, magnolia leaves, native mistletoe, and garlands of smilax carry its grand front parlor back in time to the townhouse's mid-19th century beginnings, when English style held such sway in the city. The English influence is still felt here today, expressed in antiques, chintzes, moiré wallpapers, porcelain, and afternoon tea. There are 18 rooms, including three deluxe suites — many of them with Jacuzzis and fireplaces. A handsome full-service bar on the first floor is a wonderful amenity, as are the plush robes provided for guests. Full hot Southern breakfast is included. Cancellation of a reservation must take place ten days before scheduled arrival or you will be charged the total cost of the stay.

**EAST BAY INN**
Innkeeper: Glen Anderson.
912-238-1225 / 800-500-1225.
225 East Bay St., Savannah, GA 31401.
Price: Expensive.
Credit Cards: AE, D, DC, MC, V.
Handicap Access: No.

This inn — a modestly appointed establishment — is at a great location, across the street from the busy retail and nightlife hub of River Street. There are 28 guest rooms in this circa-1853 cotton warehouse, each furnished with queen-sized, four-poster beds, reproduction antiques, and coffee-makers. Continental breakfast is included and children under 12 stay free.

**ELIZA THOMPSON HOUSE**
Innkeepers: Carol and Steve Day.
912-236-3620 / 800-348-9378.
5 W. Jones St., Savannah, GA 31401.
Price: Expensive to Very Expensive.
Credit Cards: AE, MC, V.
Handicap Access: Limited.

If you're interested in antiquing, you'll find the conversations here, as well as the accommodations, to your liking. The 25-room inn gives off a sense of family warmth amidst beautiful old objects. This was one of Savannah's first luxury bed-and-breakfast inns, and for years it was the benchmark by which others were measured: its Federal style, its spacious courtyard and fountain, its wonderful location (on a brick-paved street embowered by oaks and lined with iron-balconied townhouses) all fulfill the expectations of visitors who come in search of the cities of the "Old South."

**FORSYTH PARK INN**
Innkeepers: Hal and Virginia Sullivan.
912-233-6800.
102 W. Hall St., Savannah, GA 31401.
Price: Expensive to Very Expensive.
Credit Cards: AE, D, MC, V.

This is a modest, quiet inn with 10 rooms, including a courtyard cottage that can accommodate up to four, but might best be used for a romantic weekend getaway for a busy couple. The main house is a Victorian-era mansion, furnished in the same style with reproductions and four-poster beds. The baby grand piano in the entrance hall seems right in scale with the tall ceilings and long windows. Continental breakfast is included. During special seasonal events, such as the St. Patrick's Day celebration and the annual tours of homes, a minimum stay may be required.

**THE GASTONIAN**
Innkeeper: Anne Landers.
912-232-2869 / 800-322-6603.

This grand residence of 1868 has lost little of its imposing feel. Period-appropriate decor and muted colors take a visitor back to the post–Civil

Wade Spees

*Modern luxuries like spacious Jacuzzi tubs are nestled within historic beauty at Savannah's inns: here, The Gastonian.*

220 E. Gaston, Savannah, GA 31401.
Price: Expensive to Very Expensive.
Credit Cards: AE, D, MC, V.
Handicap Access: 4 rooms.

War era when "the Old South" was becoming "the New South." Each of the 17 guest rooms has a gas fireplace. All are non-smoking rooms; many have four-poster beds and some have Jacuzzi tubs. There's a sun deck with a hot tub, too. Local people often reserve months in advance for special occasions. The Carriage House suite, with its own balcony and kitchen, is a favorite for honeymooners. Full Southern breakfast.

**THE KEHOE HOUSE**
Innkeeper: Melissa Exley.
912-232-1020 / 800-820-1020.
123 Habersham St.,
  Savannah, GA 31401.
Price: Expensive to Very Expensive.
Credit Cards: All major.
Handicap Access: Elevator from street level.

A meticulously-restored Victorian mansion is the site of The Kehoe House, one of Savannah's newest and most luxurious inns. There are one dozen guest rooms (many with private balconies) and several grand public rooms adorned with huge urns of fresh flowers in the main building, and three additional rooms in the townhouse across the courtyard. Everything here is scaled to appropriate *fin-de-siècle* oversize: the ceiling moldings, the valances, the draperies, the armoires, the library tables, even the banisters and paneling. Not a corner's been cut in refurbishing, nor is there any stinting in guest services: a concierge is on duty 24 hours; there's off-street parking; a full breakfast is served in the double parlor; and a complimentary cocktail hour rounds out the day.

**MAGNOLIA PLACE INN**
Innkeepers: Rob Sales,
  Jane Sales, and
  Kathy Medlock.

This late-19th century inn of 13 rooms faces Forsyth Park, next door to the Georgia Historical Society. It has one of the nicest looking

912-236-7674 / 800-238-7674.
503 Whitaker St., Savannah,
GA 31401.
Price: Expensive to Very
Expensive.
Credit Cards: AE, MC, V.

interiors of all the Savannah inns, partly because a good eye selected the fabrics, rugs, and furniture, and partly because the rooms themselves have retained, even through renovation, the sense of scale and period detailing that originally distinguished them. Some people praise the inn because it is so luxurious (seven rooms have their own Jacuzzi or soak tub in the bathroom and most have gas fireplaces). But we liked it because it provides a total sense of privacy. It's comfortable without being folksy, sophisticated without being stiff. There's a lot of repeat business and word-of-mouth referral. Continental breakfast is included; children 12 and older are welcome, pets are not. Reserve with a credit card, cancel within 72 hours. Ask to see the butterfly collection.

**PLANTERS INN**
Manager: Deborah Wade.
912-232-5678.
29 Abercorn St., Savannah,
GA 31401.
Price: Expensive to Very
Expensive.
Credit Cards: AE, DC, MC,
V.
Handicap Access: Yes.

This was the old John Wesley Hotel near the Pink House restaurant, and if you remember those landmarks, you know Savannah from the old days. Even though it's been updated and refurbished, the framework of the old hotel and its old-fashioned touches — beautiful heavy moldings and an expansive, cheerful lobby with lots of comfortable seating areas — give it a substantial feeling. There are 56 rooms, most of them outfitted with queen-sized beds, and several larger suites which have two private baths apiece. Non-smoking rooms are available.

**PRESIDENT'S
QUARTERS**
Owner: Stacy Stephens.
912-233-1600 / 800-233-1776.
Fax: 912-238-0849.
225 E. President St.,
Savannah, GA 31401.
Price: Moderate to
Expensive.
Credit Cards: AE, D, DC,
MC, V.
Handicap Access: Yes.

The theme here is United States Presidents — yes, there's a "Richard Nixon Room" for guests — and authentic memorabilia are everywhere. There are 16 rooms in all, 4 double, 8 king, 4 queen, and you will find fruit and wine in them when you arrive. Breakfast features several kinds of homemade bread and it can be enjoyed in the courtyard patio. Extensive video library. First night's tariff is required with reservation; 72-hour cancellation notice for refund. Four "smoking" rooms available. Children are okay, under 12 free, and cribs are available.

## BED AND BREAKFAST ACCOMMODATIONS IN HOMES

Savannah has listing services for accommodations in private homes in the Historic District. Just let them know what you have in mind, and they'll be able to find appropriate lodgings. Credit cards are accepted for some — but not all — lodgings; deposits required, usually seven working days in advance, with penalties or charges for cancellation. Handicap access is available; some hosts allow pets. Rates are Moderate to Expensive.

**R.S.V.P. Savannah** (800-729-7787) Thirty listings in historic inns and homes.

**Savannah Historic Inns and Guest Houses** (912-233-7666 / 800-262-4667; 11 Silver Leaf Ct., Savannah, GA 31406) Accommodations in a dozen or so homes and small inns.


## RESORTS AND RENTALS — TYBEE ISLAND

Savannah's main beach is *Tybee Island,* a place of character (and characters) and informality, with shops, bars, and a down-home feeling. You may find yourself in the midst of what seems like one huge beach party. Condo complexes and inexpensive motels are the order of the day. Be prepared to have fun — concentrate on your tan.

**BEST WESTERN DUNES INN**
912-786-4591 /800-528-1234.
1409 Butler Ave., Tybee Island, GA 31328.
Price: Moderate.
Credit Cards: AE, D, DC, MC, V.
Handicap Access: Yes.

Tybee's newest motel in a slightly revised version of the chain motel. Some of the 32 rooms have kitchenettes, some king-sized beds and Jacuzzis. It's simple and clean, and close to the beach. It also has a swimming pool.

**HUNTER HOUSE BED AND BREAKFAST**
Innkeeper: John Hunter.
912-786-7515.
1701 Butler Ave., Tybee Island, GA 31328.
Price: Moderate.
Credit Cards: AE, MC, V.

Four rooms in a circa 1910 house at the beach — sounds like an old-fashioned vacation. It's one block away from the water, just 20 minutes from downtown Savannah. Each room has queen-sized beds and a private bath. There's a good restaurant (not really suitable for young children) and an informal lounge, too.

**SAVANNAH BEACH & RACQUET CLUB**
912-786-6284 / 800-864-7985.
1217 Bay St., Tybee Island, GA. 31328.
Price: Moderate to Expensive.
Credit Cards: MC, V.

Modest condo lodgings with pool, tennis, and beach access, available by the night, week, or month.

**TYBRISA BEACH
  RESORT**
912-786-4080 /
  800-868-4080.
One 15th St., Tybee Island,
  GA 31328.
Price: Moderate to
  Expensive.
Credit Cards: AE, MC, V.
Handicap access: Yes.

Condos and villas rent by the night, week, or month here. There are 48 in all, and they're very comfortable and basic. There are tennis courts and a pool on the premises.

## RENTAL AGENTS AT TYBEE ISLAND

**Tybee Beach Rentals** (912-786-8805 / 800-755-8562; 211 Butler Ave., Tybee Island, GA 31328) Weekly and monthly rentals of properties at Lighthouse Point, Savannah Beach and Racquet Club, and private homes, including townhouses and villas.

**Tybee Island Rentals** (912-786-4034 / 800-476-0807; 203 First St., Tybee Island, GA 31328) Some 120 properties are available for rent by the week or month, with a two-night minimum stay.

# DINING

> "Nothing helps scenery like ham and eggs."
> — Mark Twain

By the end of the American Revolution, visitors to Savannah were impressed with the abundance and variety of its foods, the sophisticated way they were prepared, and the splendid manner in which meals arrived at the table. The habit of lavish, at-home dining had established itself as a mark of high status in a society committed to living well. Given the region's plentiful supply of game and fish, its gentlemen of leisure who enjoyed the chase, and its slaves to tend gardens and kitchens, it was an easy habit to support.

The art and pleasure of dining stayed home-based for many years after that, well into this century. There were few places to dine out and few reasons to do so. The culture centered around home, family, the connections of friends and neighbors, and a convivially shared history. You could conduct your business in a restaurant but not your social life.

Savannah's many restaurants show how that has changed. Today, the city is filled with plain and fancy places to eat. The local population, including hundreds of students, are eager to dine out, and have the means to do so; visitors arrive with high culinary expectations. While there may be fewer no-frills places than in the past (Smitty's, a place with five booths, ten stools, get-the-job-done waitresses, and, as the menu pointed out "no chandeliers, no carpet" has shut its doors) there are plenty of informal cafes, taverns, and beachside bistros to take their place.

The hours and prices of restaurants listed below have been checked as close to the date of publication as possible, but a call ahead to confirm is always wise. The general price range we list is meant to reflect the cost of a single meal, usually dinner, featuring an appetizer, entree, dessert, and coffee. Cocktails, beer and wine, gratuity, and tax are not included in the estimated price.

### *Dining Price Code*

| | |
|---|---|
| Inexpensive | Up to $10 |
| Moderate | $10 to $20 |
| Expensive | $20 to $30 |
| Very Expensive | $30 or more |

### *Credit Cards*

| | |
|---|---|
| AE — American Express | DC — Diner's Club |
| CB — Carte Blanche | MC — MasterCard |
| D — Discover Card | V — Visa |

Delicatessens, sweet shops, and bakeries are listed below larger restaurants; gourmet and health-food stores are listed under **Gourmet Food** in the **Shopping** section of this chapter.

*Savannah is a small city full of confidence and easy sophistication, and so is the Bistro.*

Wade Spees

**BISTRO SAVANNAH**
912-233-6266.
309 W. Congress St.
Open daily.
Price: Moderate to
   Expensive.
Cuisine: American,
   Southern.
Serving: D.
Credit Cards: AE, MC, V.
Reservations
   recommended.
Handicapped Access.
Special Features: All food
   available to go.

The Bistro has steadily drawn a mix of residents and visitors staying at the downtown B&Bs. Repeat customers come for the homemade soups and desserts, the house smoked pork, greens, and hot pepper cornbread, and the casual, upbeat atmosphere. The menu is full of fresh market specials featuring organic produce. The "small plates" feature warm salads, and roasted garlic, squeezed on goat cheese with Vidalia onion relish. Extensive wine list, specializing in California vineyards.

**CITY MARKET CAFE**
912-236-7133.
224 West St. Julian St.
Open daily.
Price: Moderate.
Cuisine: American.
Serving: L., D.
Credit Cards: AE, CB, D,
   MC, V.
Special Features: Kids'
   menu.

This popular and unpretentious restaurant covers a lot of bases well. The menu includes pasta, sandwiches, rotisserie chicken and ribs, ice-cream sundaes and fountain concoctions, desserts from the Silver Palate cookbook, Cokes in the bottle and 16 brands of beer. The place itself seems full of fizz: brick walls, a black tin ceiling, starched tablecloths, and indoor and outdoor dining. The staff is unfazed by children and won't even blink if you order a hefty grilled sandwich for dinner while your companion has beef tenderloin and fine wine.

**CLARY'S CAFE**
912-233-0402.
404 Abercorn St. at Jones St.
Open daily.
Price: Inexpensive.
Cuisine: American.
Serving: B, L, D,
Credit Cards: AE, MC, V.
Wheelchair accessible
   seating.

A bacon-and-egg sandwich on wheat and coffee is a typical order at Clary's, a downtown eatery where your cup stays refilled and the food is simple and good. At lunch, the Greek salad is big enough to share, or if you're hungry you might try the chicken pot pie which includes salad and a roll. Top it off with a root beer float. Clary's is a featured venue in John Berendt's terrific book about contemporary Savannah, *Midnight in the Garden of Good and Evil*.

**CRYSTAL BEER PARLOR**
912-232-1153.
301 W. Jones St.
Closed Sunday.
Price: Inexpensive.
Cuisine: American.
Serving: L, D.
Credit Cards: AE, D, MC, V.

Located at the end of one of Savannah's prettiest residential streets, the Crystal is a bar with leather banquettes and frosted mugs that has been serving for some 65 years. It's not undiscovered — it's been written up time and again — but fame has not altered its unprepossessing style and probably never will. It would be like urging a sleepy dog lying in the sun to move on. The fried oyster or shrimp salad sandwiches are among the best around; the crab stew is thick and filling. Fine for youngsters, too.

Wade Spees

*Meals prepared by Elizabeth Terry at her namesake restaurant have been singled out for praise in the South, and the country.*

**ELIZABETH ON 37TH**
912-236-5547.
105 E. 37th St.
Closed Sun.
Price: Expensive to Very Expensive.
Cuisine: American; gourmet Southern.
Serving: D.
Credit Cards: AE, MC. V.
Reservations recommended.

Dinner is served in four beautifully decorated dining rooms with lovely table settings and formally attentive service. Nationally-acclaimed chef and cookbook author Elizabeth Terry has created a menu using superior seasonal products and signature flavorings that have earned the Terry's restaurant a place on many critics' best-in-the-country lists. Some favorites include grouper and smoked salmon cake, venison medallions, or seafood soups. Southern standards such as corn relish, fried grits, shrimp, or red rice take on a new image here—and "low fat" is not in the picture. Michael Terry is the wine steward, and his cellar is remarkable.

**45 SOUTH**
912-233-1881.
20 E. Broad St.
Closed Sun.
Price: Very Expensive.
Cuisine: Continental; gourmet Southern.
Serving: D.
Credit Cards: AE, MC, V.

A softly lit place, lots of dark green in the decorating, almost like a row house, with elegant tables situated in three sections and a small bar. The service is here in abundance — a waiter to refill your water glasses; another to grind the pepper. Soft breadsticks give way to well-dressed food, especially the crab cake appetizer with roasted red pepper remoulade, or scallops of veal with garlic potatoes and spicy mustard.

**GARIBALDI'S**
912-232-7118.
315 W. Congress St.
Open daily.
Price: Moderate to
    Expensive.
Cuisine: Italian.
Serving: D.
Credit Cards: AE, MC, V.
Handicapped Access.
Reservations
    recommended.
Special Features: Take-out
    available.

Two things should draw your attention as you enter this very busy place: the blackboard with its daily specials, and the crowd, likely to include a sampling of civic leaders, politicians, writers, and artists. Even if you have to wait for a table — or for your meal if it's really crowded — the people-watching will be fun. The pasta dishes come as simple as fettucine Alfredo, to which you can add a spinach salad. But if you're more adventurous, start with eggplant and chevre and move on to veal, cooked five ways. Or just come for dessert and coffee and after-dinner drinks.

**JEAN LOUISE**
912-234-3211.
321 Jefferson St.
Open daily.
Price: Very Expensive.
Cuisine: American;
    gourmet Southern.
Serving: D.
Credit Cards: AE, D, MC, V.

This small restaurant of ten tables arranged on an enclosed "shotgun-style" piazza is one that requires its patrons to take a leap of faith. There's not really a menu (you *can* order a few things a la carte); instead, there's a "chef's table" approach, which means Jean Jawback is preparing several dishes he's confident will appeal. Well, they do. They include appetizers like mussels or salmon mousse with caviar, entrees like pork and stuffed flounder, and dreamy desserts. There's a sorbet and champagne course to cleanse your palate; salad; old-fashioned country biscuits; and a coffee service that might as well be its own course. The mystery surrounding the night's meal (there is one seating) may sound a little precious, but the atmosphere and service are not stuffy at all. It's a spirited, intimate place for a very special, expensive meal.

**MRS. WILKES'**
    **BOARDING HOUSE**
912-232-5997.
107 W. Jones St.
Open Mon.–Fri.
Price: Inexpensive.
Cuisine: Southern.
Serving: B, L.
Credit Cards: None.
Handicapped Access.
Special Features: Take-out
    available.

This is truly homemade cooking served as it would be at home: the diners seated around large tables, with heaping platters of fried chicken, baskets of biscuits, and bowls of slaw, vegetables, red rice, and black-eyed peas or green beans placed before them. You take the dishes to the kitchen when you're done. It's located in the basement of an old, red-brick house, but you'll recognize it best by the line forming at mealtime.

**RIVER HOUSE**
912-234-1900.
125 W. River St.

Eat in a converted cotton warehouse overlooking River St. and the boat traffic, too. Fresh fish is the speciality; service is very efficient even if there

Open daily.
Price: Moderate to
Expensive.
Cuisine: American;
Seafood.
Serving: L, D.
Credit Cards: AE, MC, V.
Reservations
recommended.
Handicapped Access.

are crowds, which there may be: it's in a great location, just down the street from the Hyatt, and is a favorite of visitors. Try some take-out from the Pecan Pie and Cookies Co. located on the premises to satisfy a late-night craving.

**SAPPHIRE GRILL**
912-443-9962.
110 W. Congress St.
Open daily.
Price: Expensive.
Cuisine: American.
Serving: D.
Credit Cards: AE, MC, V.

A sharp, stylish restaurant for a first-rate dinner in the City Market area. It's sleek — bare hardwood floors, wooden blinds, white tablecloths, and lots of brushed metal. The bar, along one side, can get crowded and create a lot of traffic, and the restaurant tends to be noisy. Nonetheless, it's a special place. There's always an excellent beef choice and many fish entrees, but special attractions are the baby greens, wads of seasoned polenta, or fried tomatoes.

**SAVANNAH RIVER
QUEEN DINNER
CRUISE**
912-232-6404 / 800-786-6404.
9 E. River St.
Hours: Fri., Sat., Sun at 7
p.m.
Price: Expensive to Very
Expensive.
Cuisine: American.
Serving: D.
Credit Cards: AE, MC, V.
Handicapped Access.

E njoy a complete meal of fish or prime rib, salad, vegetables, and dessert while your cruise boat plies the Savannah River, upstream and down. There's live entertainment and a dance floor; the band even plays requests. Tickets for the two-hour cruise are $32.95 for adults and $21.95 for children, including tax. Tip and bar beverages are extra. Fully prepaid reservations are required, and there are no refunds. A change of date will be honored given 48 hours' notice. Call ahead to confirm schedule; fewer trips in colder months.

**THE PINK HOUSE
RESTAURANT**
912-232-4286.
23 Abercorn St.
Open daily.
Price: Expensive.
Cuisine: Southern.
Serving: D.
Credit Cards: All major.

T he restaurant is located in an elegant 18th-century mansion which has been designated a National Landmark: it was the site of the first reading in Savannah of the Declaration of Independence. Yet a lot of life resides in this antique, exposed-beam, setting: there's a quiet dining room upstairs, and a more lively one downstairs, where two fireplaces (roaring in winter), live piano music, a welcoming bar, and a full dinner menu attract the regulars. This is one of the most popular places downtown to have a cocktail or relax after dinner — that is, if the diners release their tables. The seafood

*The Pink House Restaurant has been one center of Savannah hospitality since the early years of the colony.*

Wade Spees

and the ham are recommended — but then, so are the architectural details, designed by Thomas Jefferson.

*Suits, strollers, and students mix congenially at Vinnie Van GoGo's pizza place in the City Market.*

Wade Spees

**VINNIE VAN GOGO'S**
912-233-6394.
317 W. Bryant St.
Open daily.
Price: Inexpensive.
Cuisine: Pizza, Italian
   specialities.
Serving: L (Sat., Sun); D
   (from 4 p.m.)
Credit Cards: None
Special Features: Delivery
   by bicycle courier to
   downtown area.

Calzones and thin-crust pizza by the slice or pie (14" or 18") made from dough prepared on the premises during the day and rolled and tossed while you watch from the counter. These cooks are having fun. Nineteen toppings including Italian sausage made in Chicago (by an Italian we're told) and shipped south. Large selection of imported beers and a concoction called spodeeodee (cheap red wine, 7-Up, splash of orange soda), which sells by the glass or pitcher as fast as they can mix it up. A perfect example of the new life that has ingrained itself into the old city.

**WINDOWS**
912-238-1234.
2 W. Bay St.
Open daily.
Price: Moderate to Very
  Expensive.
Cuisine: Continental.
Serving: B, L, D.
Credit Cards: AE, D, MC,
  V.
Handicapped Access.

Though it's located in the Hyatt, and has a brisk "hotel" feel, it seems more like an upscale urban restaurant. Sunday brunch is the best around — a full buffet where your eyes are guaranteed to be bigger than your appetite. Wonderful views and a staff that lets you take the time to enjoy your meal and linger over coffee.

## Savannah Area

Wade Spees

*The Crab Shack represents the best of the beach, with dining on the deck, a handmade Tiki Bar, and the trademark "Tybee Chandeliers," made of crab baskets.*

**CRAB SHACK AT
  CHIMNEY CREEK**
912-786-9857.
40 Estill Hammock Rd.,
  Tybee Island (second
  right past Lazaretto
  Creek Bridge).
Open daily.
Price: Moderate.
Cuisine: Seafood.
Serving: L, D.
Credit Cards: MC, V.

You won't find a more informal place outside your own kitchen: wooden tables inside and out, beer in the bottle, diners in bathing suits and sandy feet welcome. The food is strictly off-the-boat: raw bar selections, delicious, fat crab served in cakes or blended with spices and cheese, and Lowcountry boil, a platter including shrimp, corn, potatoes, and sausage. Located at a bend on the creek, the view is the Lowcountry at its best, whether you take it in from the homemade Tiki Bar, or on the deck, where "Crab Shack chandeliers" (made from old baskets) light up the night.

**PALMER'S SEAFOOD
   HOUSE**
912-897-2611.
Wilmington Island.
Open daily.
Price: Inexpensive to
   Moderate.
Cuisine: Seafood.
Serving: L (Tues.–Sun.), D.
Credit Cards: AE, D, MC,
   V.
Special Features: Dock
   space available for
   diners.

The top choices are broiled and fried seafood (done very well here), served in a casual setting overlooking a stupendous section of Turner's Creek. There are newspapers on the table, it's true, but the feeling is more upscale.

**NORTH BEACH GRILL**
912-786-9003.
At Fort Screven, Tybee
   Island.
Closed Tues.
Price: Inexpensive to
   Moderate.
Cuisine: Southern;
   Caribbean.
Serving: L, D.
Credit Cards: AE, MC, V.

Take an old beachside snack bar (where you could have rented surf boards and umbrellas as well as order a hot dog), screen it in, add island spices and African beer, and you're getting close to describing this place. It's very small, informal, and nonchalant, serving jerk chicken, salmon, and pork (sandwiches or plates), Cuban pot roast, crab with asparagus, and plantains. Success hasn't spoiled it one iota — but hurry up, places this unique sometimes find it hard to stay true, even in funky Tybee.

**THE OAR HOUSE**
912-786-5055.
1311 Butler Ave., Tybee
   Island.
Open daily.
Price: Moderate.
Cuisine: American.
Serving: L, D.
Credit Cards: AE, D, DC,
   MC, V.
Special Features: Kids'
   menu; smoking and
   non-smoking dining
   areas.

This is a friendly, local tavern on the beach, where you can sit at the bar on a Friday night and have the rib-eye dinner special or bring the family and feel comfortable. Nautical memorabilia decorate the walls — one wall is dedicated to pictures of the Tybee Lighthouse, whose upkeep the restaurant supports through sales of its private-label house wine.

**THE BREAKFAST CLUB**
912-786-5984.
1500 Butler Ave., Tybee
   Beach.
Open daily.
Price: Inexpensive.

Get a real feel of the kicked-back life of Tybee Beach at The Breakfast Club, where you can eat ham and eggs as early as 6 a.m. You might run into the shrimpers coming in or the early anglers just setting out. If you want to get a jump on the

Wade Spees

*On a clear day, you can see forever, or at least over Savannah, from the Tybee Island Lighthouse.*

Cuisine: Southern.
Serving: B, L.
Credit Cards: MC, V.

day, or take a quiet walk on a deserted morning beach, this is a great place to start.

## FOOD PURVEYORS

On Saturdays from 8 a.m. to 2 p.m., the City Market becomes an open-air Farmers' Market, with selections from the garden, the field, the sea, and the oven. There are good bargains: bread from the Metropole and inexpensive shrimp among them. Great treats are also available at the following locations:

### BAKERIES/COFFEEHOUSES

**Ex Libris** (912-238-2427; 228 Martin Luther King, Jr. Blvd.) Three floors of books, art supplies, and overstuffed sofas to sit on and sip your coffee after you browse.

**Express Cafe and Bakery** (912-233-4683; 39 Barnard St.) An upscale Art Deco-style bakery created in the shell of a downtown storefront. The breads and desserts are homemade, and the bagels taste like they're from Brooklyn. Fresh garden produce makes for excellent sandwiches and soups, too.

**Gallery Espresso** (912-233-5348; 6 E. Liberty St.) Coffees, baked goodies, local art, and poetry readings.

**Gryphon Tea Room** (912-238-2481; Madison Sq.) A real Edwardian-style cafe, with tile floors, stained glass, and potted palms.

**Il Pasticcio** (912-231-8888; 2 E. Broughton St.) A gourmet bakery and market, with Italian specialty cookies, cakes, and filled pastries.

## CANDY AND ICE CREAM

**Byrd Cookie Co.** (912-355-1716; 6700 Waters Ave.) A local institution since 1924. Delicious cookies and gourmet desserts made on site. Tours available.

**Rainbow Row Ice Cream and Espresso Bar** (912-692-0550; 5500 Abercorn St.) If you come with kids, get yourself an exotic coffee concoction, and just beg licks off their cones.

**Seaweed's Soda Shop** (912-786-5360; 1405 Butler Ave., Tybee Island) Here you'll find sno-cones in dozens of flavor combinations. The real, shaved-ice-and-syrup thing.

## DELIS AND FAST FOOD

**Brighter Day** (912-236-4703; 1102 Bull St.) A health-food store featuring a full line of natural foods and health-care products as well as excellent sandwiches to go, breads, and organic produce.

**Eli's Bakery** (912-355-3287; 4430 Habersham St.) Sandwiches to eat in or take out. Imported Greek products, fancy cheeses, and whole-grained breads. Locals' favorite.

**Fannies on the Beach** (912-786-6109; 1613 Strand, Tybee Island) You're on the beach and you're hungry: get a burger and fries or fried chicken and onion rings here.

**606 East** (912-233-2887; 319 W. Congress St.) Creative sandwiches like "muffaletta" (grilled ham, marinated olive salad and melted mozzarella) served on grilled Greek pita bread and veggie "wraps" of broccoli, zucchini, mushrooms, yellow squash, and tomatoes. There's a game room to entertain the kids, but the whole place is slightly funhouse.

*Restaurants in Savannah take advantage of the mild, sunny climate and wide streets with big windows and airy rooms.*

Wade Spees

# CULTURE

## ARCHITECTURE

Appreciating architecture in Savannah is a little like being a parent: you can read about it, you can hear it described fully and well, you can understand why people do it, and you can give it a rational and historic context. But you haven't begun to feel its power until you face it for yourself, four-square, on a lazy walk in the city.

There is no reason, when you are here, to arrive and hit the ground running. Whether or not you visit every historic house and church, or mentally catalogue its interior detailing, is not that important. You can buy an exquisite book for that (see the *Information* Chapter for suggestions, or visit a bookstore listed under **Shopping**). What's special about this region is that you can experience architecture in drifts, in vistas, as a harmonious whole that came into being as a response to the natural conditions of climate and the studied ones of prevailing fashions.

Further, the very settings of these built gems bear appreciation for their scale and for the surviving scale of the environment around them. This you can experience only by being there.

Savannah's architectural inventory includes Federal-period mansions and townhouses; buildings designed by William Jay, the Regency-period architect who delighted in fancy scrollwork and a free-hand imposition of Greek motifs; grand antebellum homes; and a whole district of Victorian homes (made of both wood and masonry). Whatever their specific style, the older buildings downtown seem to share a formal and restrained design, often colored from a muted palette of greys, greens, and tans, and echoing the geometry of Savannah's squares.

A good place to start is the *Savannah Visitors Center* (303 Martin Luther King, Jr. Blvd.) where you can join a tour or get a good overview of the city's history.

When you're out and about, you will find that local people appreciate your interest and are happy to chat. But since all but a few of the historic homes are privately owned, it is helpful to remember that while photographing is fine, entering gardens or taking you car up the driveway is not. For such closer looks, visit the area's many house museums where well-briefed and accommodating docents can answer your questions. In addition, there are annual tours of private homes and gardens, sponsored by local preservation organizations or churches. They usually take place in March and October, last all day, and range in price from $15 to $40.

## DANCE

**Ballet South** (912-239-9873; 2158 E. Victory Dr.).
**Company and Clark Modern Dancers** (912-231-0405; 11 W. Bay St.).

## FILM

**Abercorn Cinema** (912-925-2383; 12056 Abercorn Expy.).
**Carmike Cinemas** (912-353-8683; 511 Stephenson Ave.).
**Eisenhower Cinemas** (912-352-3533; 1100 Eisenhower Dr.).
**Tara Cinemas** (912-925-2135; 12319 Largo Dr.).
**Victory Square Cinemas** (912-355-0110; 3001 Skidaway Rd.).

## GALLERIES

The world of galleries and museums has been enhanced by the presence of the Savannah College of Art and Design. Frequently changing exhibitions of work are on display in college buildings throughout the city, and a glance at *The Georgia Guardian* will turn up undiscovered or short-run shows. Here are some places to look at art — it may or may not be for sale.

**Beach Institute** (912-234-8000; 502 E. Harris St.) Established in 1865 by the American Missionary Association to educate the newly-freed slaves of Savannah, the Beach continues to be an African American cultural center which features exhibits of arts and crafts. Of special interest is the collection

*Telfair Academy, Savannah's art museum for more than 100 years, has educated generations of viewers with classic and contemporary art.*

Wade Spees

of hand-carved wooden sculptures, including likenesses of Presidents, by acclaimed folk artist and Savannah barber Ulysses Davis. Open Tues.–Sun. 12–5. Admission for adults is $1.50; children $0.75.

**Exhibit A Gallery** (912-238-2480; 342 Bull St.) The gallery of the Savannah College of Art and Design, featuring work by students, faculty and occasional guests. Open Mon.–Fri. 9–5:30; Sat. 10–4.

**Telfair Museum of Arts** (912-232-1177; 121 Barnard St.) Savannah's main art gallery, housed in a Regency-style mansion, with a permanent collection of American and European Impressionist paintings, and frequent exhibits of modern art. Open Tues.–Sat. 10–5; Sun. 1–5, Mon. 12–5. Adults $6; seniors and AAA members $5; students $2; children (6–12) $2.

## HISTORIC HOMES, GARDENS & RELIGIOUS SITES

One of the most distinguishing qualities of longtime Lowcountry residents is that they are, to slightly alter the words of the Rolling Stones, "practiced in the art of perception"; that is, they know how to see and how to honor, over the generations, what they see. In Savannah, this means that historic sites — be they mansions, gardens, forts, or houses of worship — are cared for in a personal way. A site is valued not just because it is important and beautiful (though they all are), but because it has given meaning to the community. Structures that could be classified as monuments are familiar touchstones. Such an attitude puts flesh on the bones of historic preservation rhetoric — makes it real.

And it's not just buildings that are treated well: Savannah's squares and cemeteries are testimonials to public beauty. Observing the years of care that have been lavished on Savannah's historic places — from efficient, Federal-style frame dwellings to vast Romantic Revival warehouses — is one pleasure that will come naturally to every observant visitor.

**ANDREW LOW HOUSE**
912-233-1828.
329 Abercorn St.
Mon.–Wed., Fri.–Sat.
  10:30–4:00; Sun. 12–4;
  closed Thurs.
Admission: Adults $6;
  students $3; children $2.

A city house in the high style, although adapted to the rigors of Savannah's summer heat by means of jalousied rear porches. By 1848, when it was built, Savannah was in its prime: this is how the wealthy cotton merchants lived. It was from this house that Juliette Gordon Low founded the Girl Scouts and where she died in 1927.

**FIRST AFRICAN**
  **BAPTIST CHURCH**
912-233-6597.
23 Montgomery St.
Open daily, 9:30–4:30
  (advisable to call first).

The oldest church for black worshippers in North America, and the birthplace of the Civil Rights Movement in Savannah. Within the church (circa 1859) is a small museum and archive.

---

### The Gift

To His Excellency President Lincoln, Washington, D.C.: I beg to present you as a Christmas-gift the city of Savannah, with one hundred and fifty heavy guns and plenty of ammunition, also about twenty-five thousand bales of cotton.

— W.T. Sherman, Major-General. From Savannah, Dec. 22, 1864.

---

**GREEN-MELDRIM HOUSE**
912-233-3845.
1 W. Macon St., Madison Square.
Tues. and Thurs.–Sat. 10–4.
Admission: Adults $4; students $2.

Used as headquarters by General W.T. Sherman during his 1864 Christmas occupation of Savannah, this Gothic Revival mansion was considered the city's most expensive house when it was built in 1850. The exterior ironwork and porches are probably the best example of the style in the city.

**HAMILTON-TURNER INN**
912-233-1833; 888-448-8849.
330 Abercorn St., at Lafayette Sq.

Just at press time we learned that this former house museum has been turned into an inn. It will be reviewed as such in future editions of this book; in the meantime, you can visit the inn's website — www.hamilton-turnerinn.com — for pertinent lodging details.

**HISTORIC RAILROAD SHOPS**
912-651-6823.
601 W. Harris St.
Mon.–Sat. 10–4, Sun. 1–6.
Admission: Adults $2.50, students $2.

This National Historic Landmark is a collection of 13 structures first built in 1850 as used as a railroad manufacturing and repair facility. Today you can see the roundhouse and turntable, a 125-foot brick smokestack, antique steam engines, diesel locomotives, and rolling stock.

**ISAIAH DAVENPORT HOUSE**
912-236-8097.
324 E. State St.
Mon.–Sun. 10–4.
Admission: Adults $5; children (6–18), $3.

The proposed demolition of this landmark (built in 1820 by a master-builder from Rhode Island for his family) to salvage the brick and make way for a parking lot galvanized Savannah preservationists. That was 1954, and the effort marked the birth of the Historic Savannah Foundation. Today it's a museum adorned with furnishings and decorative arts of the Federal Period. There's a lovely garden out back and a fine museum shop.

**JULIETTE GORDON LOW GIRL SCOUT CENTER**
912-233-4501.

A Regency townhouse decorated in postbellum period style, this building commemorates the childhood of the founder of the Girl Scouts, who

142 Bull St.
Daily (except Wed.)10–4;
 Sun. 12:30–4:30.
Admission: Adults $5;
 children $4.

was born here in 1860. Gift shop with special things for Scouts.

**KING-TISDELL
 COTTAGE**
912-234-8000.
514 E. Huntingdon St.
Tues.–Fri. 12–4:30;
Sat.–Sun. 1–4.
Admission: Adults $1.50;
 children $0.75.

This charming, original Victorian cottage (circa 1896) houses a museum of the black history and culture of Savannah and the Sea Islands. Three walking or driving tours, highlighting events and significant sites that pertain to black history, can be arranged in advance.

**LAUREL GROVE —
 SOUTH CEMETERY**
912-651-6772.
802 W. Anderson St.
Open daily. Tours by
 appointment.

The South Cemetery of Laurel Grove (located at the west end of 37th St.) was dedicated in 1852 for the burial of "free persons of color" and slaves. Many of the city's most famous African-Americans are buried here.

**MICKVE ISRAEL
 TEMPLE**
912-233-1547.
20 E. Gordon.
Open Mon.–Fri. 10–12 and
 2–4.

The Gothic-style synagogue was built in the 1870s, more than 100 years after the congregation was established. The museum and library house the oldest Torah in America, as well as letters, books, and historical documents.

**OWENS-THOMAS
 HOUSE**
912-233-9743.
124 Abercorn St.

Designed in 1816 by Englishman William Jay and considered the best example of his Regency style for an urban villa, this house con-

*The Owens-Thomas House is a magnificent example of Regency architecture, a house museum that defines the period of Savannah's high style that was made possible by the high hopes, and higher profits evident in the early decades of the 19th century.*

Wade Spees

Tues.–Sat. 10–5; Sun. 2–5. Closed Mon. Last tour at 4:30.
Admission: Adults $6; seniors and AAA members $5; students $3; children (6–12) $2. (Discounted admission with coupons from other Historic Savannah Foundation properties.)

tains a collection of European and American decorative arts and has a formal garden.

### RALPH MARK GILBERT CIVIL RIGHTS MUSEUM
912-231-8900.
460 Martin Luther King, Jr. Blvd.
Mon.–Sat. 9–5; Sun. 1–5.
Admission: Adults $4; children $2.

Dr. Gilbert, who died in 1956, is considered to be a leader in early efforts to gain educational, social, and political equality for African Americans in Savannah. This new museum features state-of-the-art interactive exhibits focusing on the history of the Civil Rights Movement in Savannah.

### SECOND AFRICAN BAPTIST CHURCH
912-233-6163.
123 Houston St.
Open Mon.–Fri. 10:10–5.
Tours by appointment only.

The church was established in 1802, and was the site of two historic occasions: General W.T. Sherman's reading of the Emancipation Proclamation to the newly-freed slaves and, nearly a century later, Dr. Martin Luther King's delivery of his "I Have A Dream" sermon.

### WORMSLOE HISTORIC SITE
912-353-3023.
7601 Skidaway Rd., Isle of Hope.
Tues.–Sat. 9–5, Sun. 2–5:30.
Admission: Adults $2; children (6–18) $1.

The tabby ruins, an avenue of oaks, and artifacts excavated from the site are all that remain of the colonial plantation built by Noble Jones, a physician and carpenter who came with the first settlers on the ship *Anne* and survived to establish the Georgia colony. An audio-visual show and interpreters of colonial life make the period vivid for visitors.

## MILITARY SITES & MUSEUMS

A strategic upriver location and an abiding sense of history that predates the American Revolution make Savannah rich in military history. The island forts and lighthouses, in particular, recall both the isolation that must have been felt by soldiers stationed there and the efforts they made toward creating community life in a strict and physically confined setting.

## FORT JACKSON

912-232-3945.
1 Fort Jackson Rd., 3 miles from downtown.
Daily 9–5.
Admission: Adults $2.50; seniors and students $2.

The oldest standing fort in Georgia, Fort Jackson saw action during both the Revolution, when an outbreak of malaria forced its abandonment, and the Civil War, when it was central to the Confederate network of river batteries. A self-guided tour takes you to military exhibits in the fort's casemates. Special military history programs enliven the fort several times each year.

## FORT MCALLISTER HISTORIC PARK

912-727-2339.
Hwy. 144, Richmond Hill.
Tues.–Sat. 9–5, Sun. 2–5:30.
Admission: Adults $2; children $1.

The fall of Fort McAllister, on the Ogeechee River, signaled the end of Sherman's "March To The Sea." Unlike other forts in the area, it is not made of masonry; therefore its earthen walls (which could be repaired after a round of fierce bombardment) outlasted the others. There are self-guided tours, rangers on hand, and a good, small museum. Picnicking in the park is popular, but bring insect repellent.

*Massive and moated, Fort Pulaski at the mouth of the Savannah River survived 30 hours of Federal bombardment before succumbing in 1862.*

Wade Spees

## FORT PULASKI NATIONAL MONUMENT

912-786-5787.
Hwy. 80 east, about 30 minutes from Savannah.
Daily 8:30–5:15, to 6:45 in summer months.
Admission: Adults $2; ages 16 and under, free.

A young officer named Robert E. Lee had his first military assignment here, soon after the fort was built. It's a masterpiece of engineering, a huge and heavy brick building, surrounded by a moat, sitting on an unstable marsh. And yet during the Civil War, rifled cannons blasted holes in the masonry of such forts, and they became obsolete. Interpretive programs explain life at the fort during the Civil War, and you are free to roam its ramparts. An excellent selection of books is available at the gift shop.

*The Mighty Eighth Heritage Museum shows off the accomplishments of this celebrated air division.*

Wade Spees

**MIGHTY EIGHTH AIR FORCE HERITAGE MUSEUM**
912-748-8888 /
    800-421-9428.
Bourne Ave., Pooler. (Take
    exit 18 off I-95, then E on
    U.S. 80, then left on
    Bourne Ave.).
Open daily 10–6; last tickets
    sold at 5:15 p.m. Library
    hours are Mon.–Sat. 10–5,
    Sun. 12–5.
Admission: Adults $7.50;
    children (6–12) $5.50;
    under 6 free. Discounts
    for seniors and military
    personnel.

A new museum dedicated to the men and women who served in the "Mighty Eighth" Airforce (formed in Savannah in 1942) during World War II. Various exhibits, photos, film presentations, and a library.

**TYBEE MUSEUM/FORT SCREVEN**
912-786-4077.
30 Meddin Dr., Tybee
    Island, 18 miles E of
    Savannah.
Apr.–Labor Day: Mon.,
    Wed., Thurs., Fri. 10–6,
    Sat.–Sun. 10–4, closed
    Tues. Labor Day– Mar.:
    Mon., Wed., Thurs.,
    Fri. 12–4; Sat.–Sun.

Located within Fort Screven, which was acquired by the Federal government in 1808 and used as a post through World War II, the *Tybee Island Museum* and the *Tybee Lighthouse* (912-786-5801) offer visitors a glimpse of life at a beach outpost over the years. The museum has an assortment of objects, Native American and Civil War weaponry, as well as illustrated newspaper accounts of the Civil War and memorabilia. A lighthouse has marked this site since 1736. Today

10–4, closed Tues.
Admission: Adults $3;
  seniors $2; children $1.

you can climb this 19th-century version (over 150 feet tall) for a wonderful view of the river.

## MUSEUMS

**OATLAND ISLAND
  EDUCATION CENTER**
912-897-3773.
711 Sandtown Rd.
Mon.– Fri. 8:30–5, second
  Sat. of each month
  (special programs) 10–5.
Admission: $1 donation.

Children will love walking the woodland trails of this 175-acre preserve, where they can watch for animals, which are abundant and free to roam in their natural habitat. Sheep, goats, ponies, and swans may cross your path; bald eagles and hawks soar overhead. There is a farmyard, too.

**RIVER STREET TRAIN
  MUSEUM**
912-233-6175.
315 W. River St.
Mon.–Sat. 11–5:30.
Admission: Adults $1.50;
  children $0.50.

Antique model train layouts, including miniature villages and lots of "O" gauge and other train memorabilia.

**SAVANNAH HISTORY
  MUSEUM**
912-238-1779.
303 Martin Luther King, Jr.
  Blvd.
Daily 8:30–5.
Admission: Adults $3;
  children (6–12) $1.75.

Two sight-and-sound presentations, displays, and objects relating to Savannah's history, housed in the old Central of Georgia railway depot train sheds, by the Visitors Center. The Black Soldier exhibit highlights the 1st South Carolina Volunteers and the 178,895 black men who fought in the Civil War.

**SAVANNAH SCIENCE
  MUSEUM**
912-355-6705.
4405 Paulsen St.
Tues.–Sat. 10–5, Sun. 2–5.
Admission: Adults $4.50;
  children $2.50.

If you want to see one of the Southeast's largest collections of amphibians and reptiles, living and dead, comprehensive collections of shells, rocks, minerals, and a wonderful pressed herbarium of indigenous plants — or if someone in your party actually *prefers* this kind of exhibit to a house museum (gasp!) — spend time here. There's a great planetarium, too.

**SHIPS OF THE SEA
  MUSEUM**
912-232-1511.
41 Martin Luther King, Jr.
  Blvd.

Ship models and ships-in-bottles on display tell the exciting story of maritime adventure, war, commerce, and exploration in the world's oceans, from the time of the Vikings forward. Newly

Daily 10–5.
Admission: Adults $4; children $2.

**UNIVERSITY OF GEORGIA MARINE EXTENSION SERVICE AQUARIUM**
912-356-2496.
Diamond Causeway, Skidaway Island, 14 miles from downtown.
Mon.– Fri. 9–4, Sat. 12–5. Closed Sun.
Admission: $1.

located in the William Scarbrough House, a Regency jewel with a lovely garden.

This is a working research lab and facility, but visitors are welcome to visit the aquarium and exhibits, which depict the underwater marine and plant life of coastal Georgia. Fossils of sharks' teeth and whale skulls are prominently displayed. A self-guided visit takes about an hour. Afterward, you can picnic. From here it's but a short hop to *Skidaway Island State Park* (912-598-2300) where you can walk through a maritime forest, birdwatch, and observe the teeming life of the marsh.

## MUSIC

**Savannah Symphony Orchestra** (912-236-9536 / 800-537-7894; 225 Abercorn St.) The orchestra presents regularly scheduled symphony performances; chamber music ensembles often play on Sunday afternoons at the Telfair Academy.

## NIGHTLIFE

**Cross Roads** (912-234-5438; 219 W. St. Julian St., City Market) This place features blues to 3 a.m., nightly except Sunday. Art-students and young Savannah crowd.

**Hannah's East Atop the Pirate's House** (912-233-2225; 20 E. Broad St.) . Great jazz bands and soloists, first set starts nightly at 9 and the crowd disperses about 2 a.m. The patrons know their music — sophisticated but relaxed.

**Kevin Barry's** (912-233-9626; 117 W. River St.) Irish bar serving sandwiches. There's live Irish music most weekends.

## THEATER

**City Lights Theatre Company** (912-234-9860; 125 E. Broughton St.) Productions in a small 75-seat theater; "Shakespeare-in-the-Park" in Washington Square in spring.

**Lucas Theatre** (912-232-1696; 32 Abercorn St.) An old movie palace, just renovated in 1998, features films, musical performances, and theatricals.

**Savannah Theater Company** (912-233-7764; 222 Bull St.) Seasonal productions of contemporary drama, musicals, and comedy.

# RECREATION

## BASEBALL

The area's professional farm team is the *Savannah Sand Gnats* (912-351-9150; Grayson Stadium, 1401 E. Victory Dr.) When at home, they play games weeknights at 7:15, and 2 p.m. Sundays. Admission is $3.75 for adults, $3 for children.

## BEACH ACCESS

*The waves break long, low, and slow at Tybee Beach, offering good opportunities for surfers, skimboarders, and swimmers, who ride the waves right up into the soft sand of the wash.*

Wade Spees

The only accessible beach on Georgia's northern coast, *Tybee Island* lies 18 miles east of Savannah on Hwy. 80, the Islands Expressway.

*Wassaw Island*, located east of Savannah and Skidaway Island, can be reached by private or charter boat arranged through the *U.S. Fish and Wildlife Service*, Savannah Coastal Refuges Office (912-944-4415; 1000 Business Center Dr., Suite 10, Savannah, GA 31405). Within its 10,000 acres, there are more than 20 miles of inland island trails to explore and a seven-mile beach to walk.

## BIRD-WATCHING

The premium spot for birders is the *Savannah National Wildlife Refuge* (912-944-4415; Take I-95 Exit 5 to Hwy. 17 south; 8 miles south of Hardeeville). The refuge consists of 25,608 acres spread across land once used for growing rice. Get a map at the Visitor Center and drive along the 5-mile Laurel Hill Wildlife road for a good introduction to an area which includes fresh-water marsh, river-bottom hardwood swamp, and tidal rivers and creeks. Hiking trails (39 miles in all) are well-marked, many of them following the path of the old rice dikes. A bird watcher could easily arrive at sunrise, when it opens, and spend the day.

## BOATING

Listings or maps which show the locations of public boat landings in Georgia, are contained in the *Historic Savannah Visitor's Guide*, published by the Convention and Visitor's Bureau (912-944-0460; P.O. Box 1628, Savannah, GA 31402). Also, there's an excellent, highly-readable guide to public access points in north coastal Georgia, *A Guide to the Georgia Coast*, by the Georgia Conservancy (912-897-6462; 711 Sundown Rd., Savannah, GA 31410).

## CANOEING AND KAYAKING

Access points along the Savannah River allow you to travel through tidal creeks leading into the *Savannah National Wildlife Refuge* (912-944-4415) For outing ideas, guided tours, and maps, you might call one of the companies listed here. In 1998, the price for three-hour lessons was $75 (group) and $125 (private). Guided trips and workshops on special skills ranged from $45–$85 per person.

**Sea Kayak Georgia** (912-786-8732; P.O. Box 2747, Tybee Island, GA 31328).
**White's Canoe Rentals** (912-748-5858; Bush Rd.).

## SAILING

For beginners, or experienced sailors unfamiliar with local waters, renting a sailboat or having a lesson is a good way to start. Contact *Sail Harbor Academy, Inc.* (912-897-2135; 618 Wilmington Island Rd.). Prices vary according to season, length of sail lesson or charter, and type of boat.

## BOWLING

**Major League Lanes** (912-925-0320; 115 Tibet Ave.).
**Victory Bowling Center** (912-354-5710; 2055 E. Victory Dr.).

## CAMPING

**River's End Campground and RV Park** (912-786-5518 / 800-786-1016; 915 Polk St., Tybee Island, GA 31328) 135 sites, full hookups, water and electric, and tent sites, three blocks from the beach, rec room, groceries, propane.

**Skidaway Island State Park** (912-598-2300; 52 Diamond Causeway, Savannah, GA 31411) A public campground with 88 sites; laundry, pool, bath house, nature trail, water, and electrical hookups.

## DIVING

**Diving Locker and Ski Chalet** (912-927-6604; 74 W. Montgomery Crossroads).

*A dip net, bait, a bucket, and some time are all you need to catch supper.*

Wade Spees

## FAMILY FUN

**Putt-Putt Golf Course** (912-355-4795; 202 Mall Blvd.) Three courses, lit for night play, open to midnight. $4 per round; $8 for three rounds. Play Mon.–Fri. during the day for $5.

**Savannah Skate Inn** (912-238-0000; 3700 Wallin St.) Roller skating, $2.75 per person including rental.

## FISHING

All kinds of fishing are available in the waters off Savannah. Inshore, there's fishing in shallow waters and in narrow creeks when the tide is right; offshore, there are bigger game fish in the Gulf Stream. Saltwater fly-fishing is growing in popularity, and there are charter-boat captains who specialize in this art.

A good place to begin arranging a fishing trip is at a marina (see Chapter Two, *Transportation*), although some sporting goods stores may have recommendations (see the **Shopping** listing at the end of this Chapter). In general, visitors interested in recreational fishing will not need a license: they're not necessary for recreational shrimping and crabbing. If you find you do need one, however, they are sold in most hardware and hunting stores, K-marts, and tackle shops. For further information on licenses, size and catch limits, or to get a brochure on charter services, contact the *Georgia Dept. of Natural Resources* (912-264-7218; One Conservation Way, Brunswick, GA 31523-8600).

A listing of some of the many *Charter Boat Services* available follows. Most boats are fully outfitted with supplies and bait, but check in advance, espe-

*The newly-expanded Tybee Pier offers fishing and a sensational view of the ocean.*

Wade Spees

cially if you have questions about bringing your favorite rod — an option for fly-fishing — or if the length of the trip requires food. Always bring sunscreen, a hat, and a windbreaker. The 1998 prices per person for half-day trips ranged from $75–$125.

**Al Klein's Bottom Line Charters** (912-897-6503; Wilmington Island) 30-foot deep-sea boats; 35-foot Bertram; 60-foot vessel for group charters.

**Chimney Creek Charters** (912-786-9857; Tybee Island) Trips for up to six persons aboard 32-foot craft; for 1–3 persons on smaller Boston Whalers, McKees, and English Dories.

**Miss Judy the Charter Boat** (912-897-4921; 124 Palmetto Dr., Savannah) Deep-sea, bottom fishing, and trolling, Gulf Stream trips.

**Salt Water Charters** (912-598-1814; Landings Harbor, Skidaway) Captain Bob Morrissey. Inshore and deep-sea fishing for bass, grouper and other species by full day or half day.

**The Restless** (912-351-0755; Captain Flash Clark) Inshore fishing (light tackle and fly) by the full day (up to 9 hours) or half-day. Minimum of two passengers.

**Tybee Island Charters** (912-786-4801; Lazaretto Creek) Inshore and deep sea fishing, and sightseeing tours ($60 per hour/six people maximum).

## FITNESS FACILITIES

**Coastal YMCA** (912-354-6223; 6400 Habersham Pkwy.) This excellent facility honors YMCA memberships from other parts of the country and, in any case, your first visit is free. Childcare is available.

**Downtown Athletic Club** (912-236-4874; 7 E. Congress) Step training, aerobics, spa facilities, classes, and fitness machines.

**Islands YMCA** (912-897-1192; 250 Penn Walter Dr.) The same policies apply here as in the Coastal YMCA (see above).

**West Broad St. YMCA** (912-233-1951; 1110 May St.) Recreation center, gym facilities.

## GOLF

**Bacon Park Golf Course** (912-354-2625; Shorty Cooper Drive) Par 72. 27 holes; 6,700 yards. Lighted driving range; putting green. Fees for 18 holes: $21.25 (with cart); $11.75 (without cart.) Pro: Mark Geistweite.

**Henderson Golf Course** (912-920-4653; 1 Henderson Drive) Par 71. 18 holes; 6,700 yards. Lighted driving range; putting green. Fees: $31 (weekdays); $38 (weekends). Cart included.

**Savannah Inn and Country Club** (912-897-1612; Wilmington Island) Par 72. 18 holes; 7,100 yards. Driving range and putting green. Fees: $25–$50 including cart. Pro: Charlie Dobbertin.

**Southbridge Golf Club** (912-651-5455; Southbridge Blvd.) Par 72. Rees Jones-designed 18 holes, 6,990 yards. Driving range, putting green, and a full staff of teaching pros onsite. Fees: $29.50 weekdays; $36 weekends and holidays. Cart included. Pro: Phil Wagoner.

## HORSEBACK RIDING

Local stables can accommodate riders of varying skills, and it's best to call in advance to arrange lessons, trail rides, or workouts in the ring. The 1998 prices ranged from $20–$45 per person for 90 minutes of riding time, depending on the setting. Here are some places to contact for more information:

**Norwood Stables** (912-356-1387; 2304 Norwood Ave.).

**Trelman Farms** (912-236-0559; 1145 Dean Forest Rd.).

## HUNTING

As in other regions of the Lowcountry, land quarry in the Savannah area include a variety of waterfowl, turkey, and various sizes of game. Familiarize yourself with specific hunting seasons, license requirements, and bag limits by visiting an outdoor recreation store (see the listing in the **Shopping** section) or contact the *Game and Fish Division* of the Georgia Dept. of Natural Resources (912-727-2112; 22814 Hwy. 144, Richmond Hill, GA 31324).

Some of the most popular public hunting grounds in the Savannah area are located in the *Webb Wildlife Center and Palachucola* (843-625-3569; Hampton and Jasper Counties), *Turtle Island* and *Victoria Bluff* (843-844-8957; Jasper and Beaufort Counties), and in the *Savannah National Wildlife Refuge* (912-652-4415).

## NATURE PRESERVES

Some of the most accessible, and user-friendly preserves in the Lowcountry are located within 30 minutes of Savannah. They include:

**Pinckney Island National Wildlife Refuge** (843-785-3673; Hwy. 278 at foot of Hilton Head bridge) A 4,053-acre complex of small islands and hammocks set in the marsh. Only Pinckney Island, interwoven with 14 miles of trails, is open to visitors. A good place to spend an hour walking and birding.

**Savannah National Wildlife Refuge** (912-652-4415; Take I-95 Exit 5 to Hwy. 17 south; 8 miles south of Hardeeville) The refuge consists of 25,608 acres spread across land once used for growing rice. Get a map at the Visitor's Center and drive along the five-mile Laurel Hill Wildlife road for a good introduction to an area which includes fresh-water marsh, river-bottom hardwood swamp, and tidal rivers and creeks. Hiking trails (39 miles in all) are well-marked, many of them following the path of the old rice dikes. A naturalist could easily arrive at sunrise, when it opens, and spend the day.

**Victoria Bluff Heritage Preserve** (Sawmill Creek Rd., off Hwy. 278, 3 miles from the Hilton Head bridge) This serenely beautiful parcel of some 1,000 acres on the Colleton River has long been eyed for residential or industrial development, but local residents seem, finally, to have secured its protection as a passive recreation area. Some trails are marked, some hunting is permitted.

## TENNIS

Seven city parks in and around Savannah have a total of 47 courts, and all but ten are lit for night play. The custom at public parks is first-come, first-served. The locations are:

*Bacon Park* (Skidaway Rd.); *Daffin Park* (1500 E. Victory Dr.); *Forsyth Park* (Gaston St. & Drayton St.); *Lake Mayer Park* (Montgomery Crossroad & Sallie Mood Dr.); *Stell Park* (Bush Rd.); *Tybee Memorial Park* (Butler Ave.); *Wilmington Island Community Park* (Lang. St. & Walthour Rd.)

# SHOPPING

There's not much you can't buy in Savannah, from collard greens off a truck to a gilded armoire. There are galleries and craft stores displaying the work of students from the Savannah College of Art and Design; boutiques with unique accessories and household goods that cater to the hip student crowd; bookstores with rare and current volumes; places to buy old prints, sea charts, and maps; and antiques stores by the dozen.

In fact, antiques stores might be considered the city's specialty. The

*Savannah's River Street by day attracts strollers and shoppers; after dark, it's the center of the city's nightlife.*

Wade Spees

Lowcountry habit of preservation has meant that English and American antiques and accessories of an earlier day, purchased during the boom years, have remained in the old houses. Today they are trickling out to local dealers, as tastes change and there are other options for decorating (as heretical as that may sound in an old, classic city). And, of course, the dealers have a market among the owners of the large houses who need authentic furnishings and accessories.

The region's temperate, multi-crop climate means you can buy batches of lettuce, collards, potatoes, tomatoes, watermelon, and peaches most of the year. The man with the bags of boiled peanuts may knock at your door only in summer, but most everyone else can, and does, peddle their goods year round.

There are, too, right in the city and certainly out in the country, stores that are old and vibrant centers of community life, places of shelves that bear small quantities of many things, of dangling fly-paper, squirrel nut candies, pickled eggs, moon pies, single beers, and slushees. Their modest mien guarantees they'll never achieve National Register status; they'll never be etherized, either. Drop in for a local newspaper and a "Co' Cola."

## ANTEBELLUM ARTIFACTS

**Claire West Antiques** (912-236-8163; 413 Whitaker St.) Prints of antebellum life as well as old linens, furnishings, and accessories.

**Pinch of the Past** (912-232-5563; 109 W. Broughton St.) Architectural pieces of the past, including doorframes, columns, mantels, and hardware. Odd nostalgic items, too.

*Many antiques stores are as small as one room, but they overflow with a sense of taste and style.*

Wade Spees

## ANTIQUES

There are antiques of probably every period and style in the city — or a dealer will find you what you want. Whether you live in a sleek, minimalist apartment or a farmhouse, you're likely to find a piece that works. The tradition of acquiring is long-standing here — and so is the tradition of looking, evaluating, and "editing." A man was quoted recently in the paper as saying: "We love old things. It makes life easier because you don't have to like the new ones."

**Alex Raskin Antiques** (912-232-8205; 441 Bull St.) A collection (English and American, 18th and 19th centuries) that has grown steadily in quantity and quality over the years. Primitives and decorative pieces. Preferred by local people.

**Arthur Smith Antiques** (912-236-9701; 1 W. Jones St.) Lots of large antiques, overwhelmingly so. It will help if you know what you want.

**Bohemia Gallery** (912-234-0071; 345 Abercorn St.) An unusual collection of WPA art from the 1930s, such as murals, mixed in with folk and "outsider" art.

**Francis McNairy Antiques** (912-232-6411; 411 Abercorn St.) The loveliest antique shop in Savannah. Fine antiques, many of Southern origin, and many small pieces. If you don't buy one item you can educate yourself here.

**Phillip Dorian Hunter** (912-232-7212; 124 E. Jones St.) Three dealers whose individual styles complement each other in wonderful, often inspired, ways. Donna Terzian's fabrics (17th–20th century) are outstanding.

## AUCTIONS

Besides being a lot of fun, auctions are a total social event in Savannah, after Savannah's fashion. For example, it's not unheard of to attend one where the bidding gets up to five digits and then, all of a sudden, the pot of chili that's been warming on the card table in the back starts smoking, or someone spills their coffee and curses, and people get distracted, and people start smoking, and...

**Kramer & Sadler Auctions** (912-238-1665; 416 E. McDonough St.) There's usually an auction every Monday night, starting at 6:00. No charge to attend; 10 percent auctioneer's commission on purchases. Stays open until everything's gone.

## BOOKS

Savannah has an unusual number of little bookstores, many specializing in certain areas. Don't overlook the small ones.

**Books on Bay** (912-231-8485; 11 W. Bay St.) Good used books, and a coffee bar.

*Esther Shaver will locate the book you came for, and recommend some you may not know.*

Wade Spees

**E. Shaver Booksellers** (912-234-7257; 326 Bull St.) Right downtown and great for browsing. If some topic of Lowcountry history has captured your interest, you'll find it explicated here. Room after room of new and rare books, history, fiction, children's section, and excellent art books. Best in Savannah.

**Printed Page** (912-234-5612; 211 W. Jones St.) A selection of rare and scarce books for bibliophiles and book lovers looking for a special title. By appointment.

**"The Book" Gift Shop** (912-233-3867; 127 E. Gordon St.) Headquarters for *Midnight in the Garden of Good and Evil* fans, the base for tours, a mini-museum of the book that changed Savannah.

**Waldenbooks** (912-352-2750; Oglethorpe Mall) Good selection of popular titles and books of regional interest. Nice children's and nature-oriented titles.

## CLOTHING

There is grunge and retro fashion in Savannah, but it's still the South, after all, and there are plenty of small-scale dress shops (selling more than dresses these days) which are thriving and up-to-date in their sensibility. Mens' styles tend toward the casual and outdoorsy, given the weather.

**Endora's Emporium** (912-232-3030; 35 Montgomery St.) Funky vintage clothing and accessories.

**Gaucho** (912-232-7414; 250 Bull St.) Jewelry, leather, and clothing for women with a rustic, dude-ranch feeling.

**Jezebel** (912-236-4333; 25 E. River St.) Light-hearted and good-looking dresses, casual wear for women.

**John B. Rourke** (912-355-1211; 7135 Hodgson Memorial Dr.) Classic men's suits, accessories, hats and sportswear.

## CRAFTS

**Arts & Crafts Emporium** (912-238-0003; 234 Bull St.) Some 300 American craftspeople have their work for sale here.

**Bull St. Station** (912-236-4344; 151 Bull St.) Model railroad supplies and other accessories, kits, and tools for hobbyists of all kinds.

**Gallery 209** (912-236-4583; 209 E. River St.) A co-op gallery with works of batik, fiber, glass, pottery, and more.

**Palmetto Point Gallery** (912-238-3435; 11 E. Park Ave.) Selective gallery of fine American handicrafts.

**River Works Craft Gallery** (912-236-2012; 105 E. River St.) American crafts featuring pottery and jewelry.

## GALLERIES

**Checkered Moon** (912-233-5132; 422 Whitaker St.) Functional art and wall pieces; jewelry; painted pieces by local artists. Web site: http://www.savannah digital.com/cmoon.

**City Market Art Center** (912-234-2327; 219 W. Bryan St.) Working studios of 35 artists spread through several buildings make this Savannah's art colony.

**Compass Prints, Inc.** (912-234-3537; 205 W. Congress St.) Paintings and prints of golf and traditional maritime scenes by Ray Ellis, perhaps the best-known of Lowcountry artists. Also, books of his work and notecards.

**Exhibit A Gallery** (912-238-2480; 342 Bull St.) A gallery with changing exhibits devoted to the work of students from the Savannah College of Art and Design.

**Southern Images Gallery** (912-234-6449; 132 E. Oglethorpe St.) Photographs, including splendid work by Jack Leigh (highly-regarded for his depictions of the shrimping and oystering life) of the American South. Perhaps his most famous image is the picture in Bonaventure Cemetery that makes the cover of *"Midnight in the Garden of Good and Evil."*

**V. & J. Duncan** (912-232-0338; 12 E. Taylor St.) You could browse through the files and piles of prints, maps, old advertising art and illustrations here for hours. A comprehensive, well-organized collection.

## GIFTS

**The Cottage Shop** (912-233-3820; 2422 Abercorn St.) Linens for bed and table, stationery, lamps, and crystal.

**Davenport House Museum Shop** (912-236-8097; 324 E. State St.) Gifts with a Savannah theme and a Lowcountry flavor in the first house restored by the Historic Savannah Foundation.

**Japonica** (912-236-1613; 13 W. Charlton St.) Small antiques for desktops and bedrooms, jewelry, and cachepots.

**The Little House** (912-232-1551; 107 E. Gordon St.) In business for 70 years, this is a charming shop of the sort that has nearly disappeared. Gifts for children, for weddings, for a special nook at home.

**Twiggs of Savannah Ltd.** (912-356-0027; 5203 Waters Ave.) Fancy needlework pillows and home accessories; elegant baby gifts.

## GOURMET FOOD

**Callaway Gardens Country Store** (912-236-4055; 301 E. River St.) Accessories for the kitchen and Southern goods to stock the shelves — items like grits, grape preserve, and smoked meats.

**Hunter Horn Plantation Co. Store** (912-355-1812; 7202 White Bluff Rd.) The store specializes in spiral-sliced, honey-glazed hams, but also carries baked chickens for take out (the best in the city), and sells many varieties of salads and other deli items by the pound.

**Smith Brothers** (912-234-2204; 2502 Habersham St.) A complete grocery with an excellent butcher and a wide variety of gourmet foods. A longtime Savannah institution.

**Sophisticated Palate** (912-355-6160; 238 Eisenhower Dr.) Gourmet foods including wines, cheeses, canned goods, and coffees; also the tools to make your cooking gourmet, too: pasta machines, coffee grinders, small appliances, and the like.

## HOME FURNISHINGS/KITCHENWARE

**Bob Christian Decorative Art** (912-234-6866; 32 Martin Luther King, Jr. Blvd.) Faux marbeling and painting services offered for a range of decorative pieces.

**D & B Collection** (912-238-0087; 408 Bull St.) Designer accessories for the home, many by local artists.

**Ellis & Co.** (912-236-0111; 15 E. Harris St.) Hand-painted furniture and decorative accessories.

**The Gypsy Moth** (912-232-6800; 311 W. St. Julian St.) Folk art, birdhouses, funky wooden medallions and sculpture, Day of the Dead mementos, wooden animals, and rugs.

**The Mulberry Tree** (912-236-4656; 17 W. Charlton St.) Quilts, replicas of old toys, baskets, and small art objects.

## SPORTING GOODS AND CLOTHING

Most of the following stores not only have athletic equipment and accessories for sale, but they rent equipment, too. Call ahead to check on the availability of rental goods, or to reserve them in advance of your stay.

**Bicycle Link** (912-355-4771; 7064 Hodgson Memorial Dr.).

**Pro Bass Outfitters** (912-354-3377; 6608 White Bluff Rd.).

**Star Bike Shop** (912-927-2430; 127 E. Montgomery Crossroads).

**Thompson's Sports Shop** (912-920-0977; 8110 White Bluff Rd.).

**Wilderness Outfitters** (912-927-2071; 103 E. Montgomery Crossroads).

# CHAPTER FIVE
## *Sea Island Gems*
# BEAUFORT, EDISTO, AND BLUFFTON

*A place that ever was lived in is like a fire that never goes out. It flares up, it smolders for a time, it is fanned or smothered by circumstance, but its being is intact, forever fluttering within it, the result of some original ignition. Sometimes it gives out glory, sometimes its little light must be sought out to be seen, small and tender as a candle flame, but as certain.*

—Eudora Welty, 1944

The fields, creeks, sandy roads, and spreading marshes of the rural Lowcountry, the place where Lowcountry history began, have once again become its center of attention. All along the coast, from Charleston to Savannah, there is an increasing awareness of what the culture of the countryside, expressed in a lifetime of habits and rituals, has meant to the two great cities that bookend the region and present themselves, to today's visitor, like magnificent finished products.

Wade Spees

*Beaufort's cotton boom gave rise to magnificent homes.*

Perhaps the shift in emphasis from urban to rural is simply nostalgic, nourished by a sense that, as the millennium approaches, there is more interest in rediscovering the basics rather than reviewing the complexities. Perhaps it has come because coastal development is accelerating. Typical Lowcountry spaces — fields rimmed by live oaks and stands of pine — are no longer simply evocative "open space" : they are potential building sites. Or maybe the mood has shifted because another shape has emerged from what was a familiar pic-

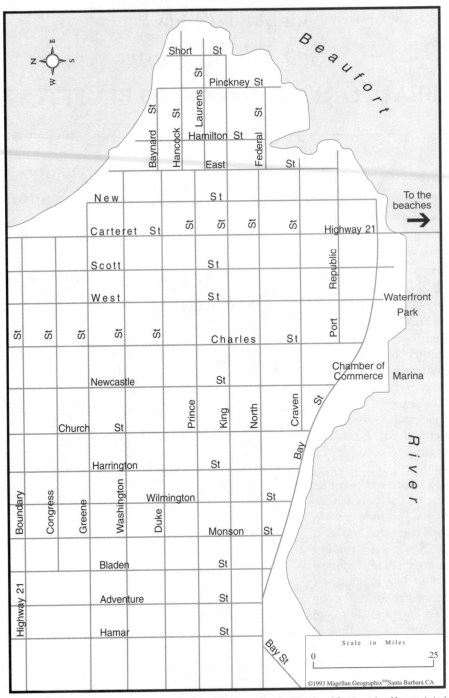

Courtesy of The Greater Beaufort Chamber of Commerce (used by permission)

**BEAUFORT**

ture — like in those clever drawings, where it is sometimes the vase that appears before your eyes, and then it is the facing profiles.

The Lowcountry's alternative view, the rural view, can be seen most clearly in the areas around Beaufort — Lady's Island, St. Helena Island, and Port Royal — on Edisto Island, and in the little village of Bluffton. Before the Civil War they were as imposing, in their own small incarnations, as Charleston and Savannah: they boasted luxurious houses, profitable plantations, hundreds of slaves. Planters sent their children to be educated abroad. But all that changed one day, the day in 1861 that Federal troops arrived to occupy the Sea Islands. All at once, these self-satisfied and self-conscious towns receded from the foreground view into the rural background.

It took years for them to recover, but recover they have. Furthermore, they seem to have done so with a unique sense of the importance of celebrating both views of themselves — the part of them that was prosperous, worldly, and city-like, and the part of them that struggled for decades to make do with the essentials. It comes as no surprise that they are places where vistas, boughs, and fields are valued as much as brickwork, eaves, and intersections.

Today, rather than rely simply on one picture of themselves, these places celebrate the less apparent patterns in their composition: the landscape of "vernacular" homes of farmers and fishermen; the old market roads; the remains of a wharf; the praise houses and plantation neighborhoods; the plantation cemeteries; the creek landings and fishing holes; the "rabbit-box" stores and packing houses. The appreciation of what's plain has brought a proud recognition of how resourceful country people were.

To a visitor, this means that there is more to seek out and understand, and many more chances to do so. The most mundane memories and the most idealized ones are spilling forth from the vault of the past. Their blending is what gives the Lowcountry its dramatic, cohesive, sense of place, a sense that is felt especially (if it is not immediately seen) in the rural Sea Islands.

## BEAUFORT

**B**eaufort has been a small town for a long time. Spanish and French explorers came to the area 100 years before the Pilgrims landed at Plymouth Rock, and they were followed, in due course, by English and Scottish settlers. The city of Beaufort is itself on Port Royal Island, one of the 65 islands that make up Beaufort County. It is the county seat. Other islands include St. Helena, Lady's, Fripp, Hilton Head, Daufuskie, Cat, Harbor, Hunting, Coosaw, Dataw, Polowana, Parris, Cane, Bray's, Lemon, and Pinckney.

Formally founded in 1711, it was a frontier settlement and trading center, attacked at times by Yemassee Indians, beset with illness, and populated by the scrupulous and unscrupulous who made the best of the resources they had. The resources, in fact, were plentiful: Beaufort's outlying lands sustained dense forests, which gave up shipbuilding timber and naval stores; vast tracts of land, suitable for raising cattle and raising crops like corn, potatoes, indigo, rice, and cotton; and rich marshes to feed fowl and game. The maze of waterways provided fish and shellfish in abundance.

Over time, investors spotted Beaufort for what it was and staked their claims. Settlers drifted in from Charleston and Savannah, a parish system of governance was established, and, by the time of the Revolution, Beaufort was bustling. The real boom, however, came immediately after the war. The stability of the newly-independent country, the increase in population (both slave and free), the southward migration of New England merchants and families, and, perhaps above all, the successful cultivation of highly-prized, long-staple Sea Island cotton and the development of the cotton gin lit the fuse. The explosion of wealth that resulted launched Beaufort's heyday. It was a time of building houses and churches in town and developing cotton plantations and plantation households on the islands.

A visitor can see the legacies of this period throughout Beaufort. They include Palladian-inspired doorways and windows, and huge, pillared porches; ornate Adam-style carved moldings and delicately-scaled gardens; churchyards filled with camellias and azaleas, and towered over by steeples. Standing in Beaufort's Waterfront Park, it is easy to imagine a 19th-century scene come to life as dozens of schooners, bateaux, and cottonbox barges, brimming with crops, timber, mail, cotton bales, animals, passengers, produce, and the latest in English fashion and furniture, load or unload goods. There was a lot of activity, for like many societies made newly rich, Beaufort's had a taste for luxury and indulged it.

That, of course, changed abruptly. In another time and place, the shelling of a Federal fort (in this case Fort Sumter) not all that far away, and the Federal response to it, might have produced a shred of hesitation as to the wisdom of the Secessionist rebellion. Not so in Beaufort: it was apparently with great surprise that on November 7, 1861, white Southerners found themselves in flight — leaving hot food on the table, the story goes — from Yankee troops who had just demolished the Confederate port defenses at Bay Point.

Thus the occupation began. Soon the grand old houses were being used as hospitals and headquarters. The area was under military command. Pickets were posted at the outskirts of town and along creeks and boat landings: some on guard duty were able to see the smoke of rebel campfires across the water. Whole plantations were turned over to regiments who appropriated the cows, the liquor, the furniture, the wagons, and the food crops.

By April 1862, the first wave of Northern abolitionists had arrived in town with a mandate to live in and manage the plantations and teach the former slaves to read and write; essentially to "prepare them for freedom." Their enterprise, which was funded by private missionary societies in the north and carried out with the approval of the federal government, came to be called the Port Royal Experiment. In a sense this was an old-time Peace Corps, in which idealistic, mostly young, men and women, volunteered to assist a cause they

There is something very sad about these fine deserted houses. Ours has Egyptian marble mantels, gilt cornice and centre-piece in parlor, and bathroom, with several wash-bowls set in different rooms. The force-pump is broken and all the bowls and their marble slabs smashed to get out the plated cocks. . . . Bureaus, commodes, and wardrobes are smashed in, as well as door panels, to get out the contents of the drawers and lockers, which I suppose contained some wine and ale, judging by the broken bottles lying about. The officers saved a good many pianos and other furniture and stored it in the jail for safe-keeping. But we kindle our fires with chips of polished mahogany, and I am writing on my knees with a piece of flower-stand across them for a table, sitting on my camp bedstead.

— Edward S. Philbrick to his wife in Brookline, MA,
from Beaufort, March 9, 1862

believed in, at some personal risk and under conditions of definite hardship. Their efforts had an impact on the lives of freedmen which resonates today, in particular at Penn Center on St. Helena Island, which has remained a center for teaching native islanders.

*From the end of the Civil War right up to World War II, farmers brought their cotton to market in ox-drawn wagons.*

Courtesy of The Charleston Museum, Charleston, South Carolina

In the years following the Civil War, promises made were often promises broken. Some former slaves were given land; some bought tracts communally; some worked the old fields under a new owner. A nascent phosphate mining industry provided jobs for a while, but it eventually collapsed. The terrible hurricane of 1893 which soured Sea Island soil for fine cotton plants, and the scourge of boll weevil in the 1920s finally dimmed the last hope of large-scale cotton production. For most people, living returned to subsistence level farming and fishing. Photographs from the early 1900s and those taken even as late as 1936 by employees of the Farm Security Administration — Walker Evans and Marion Post Wolcott among them — showed islanders dressed in rags and living in shacks with matted palmetto fronds for a roof. In 1969, Beaufort County was still one of the poorest counties in the United States, the focus of a Hunger Tour by several U.S. Senators. In town, these were the years of unpaved roads and bare feet, when white people were "too poor to paint, too proud to whitewash."

As in many other parts of the South, it took the American entry into World War II to improve the economy. The United States Marines had been a presence in Beaufort since the turn of the century, and at this point their role was expanded. While not exactly prosperous, Beaufort benefited from slow, steady growth. Commercial farming of tomatoes and other vegetables, and seafood processing, became healthy industries. By the mid-1960s, with the development of resort islands like Hilton Head and Fripp, and with the first wave of retirees flocking to its shores, Beaufort's economic future was assured.

It is hard to believe that the downtown Beaufort of today ever suffered reverses. The paint doesn't dare peel. It has become a destination for tourists, a second home to people from the north and west, and a first home for young families who are looking for an ideal, charming, "small town" in which to raise their children. It has been turning up on "Best Small Town" lists for several years. It has even become a character in Hollywood movies: two of native son Pat Conroy's novels have been filmed here, *The Great Santini* and *The Prince of Tides*, as well as *The Big Chill* and *Daughters of the Dust*. Parts of *Forrest Gump, Something To Talk About*, and *The Jungle Book* were shot here, too. Ron and Natalie Daise's acclaimed television series for children, "Gullah Gullah Island," is set in Beaufort and its environs, and features many well-known local residents in its cast.

Having come as far as it has in this century, it will take a lot more than Hollywood to turn Beaufort's head. The problems associated with regional planning and zoning, improved education, traffic and water service, the preservation of resources, and economic development seem pressing here, as they do on the other Sea Islands. Having spent the better part of this century becoming what it is today, Beaufort, it turns out, is still a work in progress.

## LODGING

The WPA Guide, *South Carolina, A Guide to the Palmetto State*, first published in 1941, indicates the presence of three hotels in Beaufort, and a number of "tourist homes" where guests could stay. Then as now, the preferred season was spring, although there was, beginning in the 1920s, an informal "winter colony" of artists, playwrights, and others who found the laid-back town to their liking. Quite a few of them returned every year for an extended stay in rooms at "Tidalholm," an elegant antebellum house in the neighborhood known as "The Point."

In those days, the comings and goings of visitors were duly reported in the

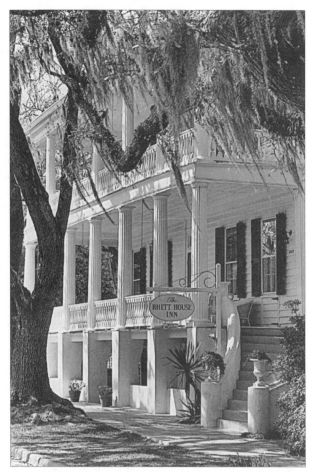

*Beaufort's 19th-century prosperity is revived in its grand old homes now open for guests.*

Wade Spees

local paper — perhaps an indication of what made news in this sleepy town. Other seasonal arrivals included sportsmen from the north who hunted and fished in several vast private preserves which, by the 1940s, claimed up to one-third of the acreage in Beaufort County.

Today, the visitor in the next room might be a painter or a fly-fisherman, a movie director scouting locations or a honeymooning couple. It's unlikely the newspaper will pay any attention at all.

### Rates

| | |
|---|---|
| Inexpensive | Up to $50 |
| Moderate | $50 to $110 |
| Expensive | $110 to $180 |
| Very Expensive | $180 and up |

These rates do not include room taxes or special service charges that might apply during your stay.

### Credit cards

| | |
|---|---|
| AE — American Express | DC — Diner's Club |
| CB — Carte Blanche | MC — MasterCard |
| D — Discover Card | V — Visa |

**BAY STREET INN**
Innkeeper: Peter Staciak.
843-522-0050 / 800-256-9285.
www.bbonline.com/sc/
  baystreet/
601 Bay St., Beaufort, SC
  29902.
Price: Moderate to
  Expensive.
Credit Cards: AE, D, MC, V.

The Lewis Reeve Sams House, built in 1852 and most recently the filming location for scenes in *The Prince of Tides* (it's where Lila lived with Reese Newbury) is the site of the inn. This three-story building with double porches overlooks the Beaufort River. From most of its nine guest rooms you can watch the boats cruise the Intracoastal Waterway or line up and wait for Beaufort's old swing-span bridge to let them pass. There are fireplaces in every room but one, window air-conditioning units, private baths, and loads of light. A library filled with books, on the first floor, is a great place for settling down. Full breakfast is included, served in a formal dining room; tea in afternoon; wine and cheese in evening.

**BEAUFORT INN**
Innkeepers: Rusty and
  Debbie Fielden.
843-521-9000.
809 Port Republic St.,
  Beaufort, SC 29901-1257.
Price: Expensive to Very
  Expensive.
Credit Cards: AE, D, MC,
  V.
Handicap Access: Yes; full
  ramp, some rooms.

To look at from the outside, it's a three-story clapboard building with bays and porches jutting here and there, trimmed in vines, trees, and flowering shrubbery. There's nothing but luxury inside, including an elevator (actually one of a handful in Beaufort), long hallways covered in plush carpet, chandeliers, and a vivid decorating style characterized by antiques, patterned wallpapers, draperies and soft curtains, and carefully-hidden modern amenities. Each of the 11 rooms is named for a notable Lowcountry plantation whose story you will learn.

**CUTHBERT HOUSE INN**
Innkeepers: Gary and
  Sharon Groves.
843-521-1315 / 800-327-9275.
Fax: 843-521-1314.
1203 Bay St., Beaufort, SC
  29902.

The Cuthbert House has seen its share of excitement over the last 185 years, and its architecture tells the tale. Moved from its original site in 1810, embellished with fine Federal-period woodcarving, and enlarged with Victorian additions (sun porches and bays), it is renovated for modern

Price: Expensive.
Credit Cards: AE, D, MC, V.
Handicap Access: One
room.
Note: Children over 12
welcome; no smoking
inside.

comfort. It was the headquarters of Union General Rufus Saxton during the Federal blockade. Accommodations include two one-bedroom suites on the ground level (one is wheelchair accessible), and parlor suites. Its great site on the Beaufort River bluff makes the full Southern breakfast, afternoon tea, evening coffee, or simply lounging a pleasure.

**OLD POINT INN**
Innkeepers: Joe and Joan
Carpentiere.
843-524-3177.
Fax: 843-525-6544.
www.oldpointinn.com
212 New St., Beaufort, SC
29902.
Price: Moderate.
Credit Cards: AE, MC, V.

There are four guest rooms tucked away in this little turn-of-the-century Victorian, and the coziest of them are up under the eaves, lit by dormers and skylights. If you sit on the upstairs porch, you will feel embowered, lofted in the treetops, and very much a resident of Beaufort's "Point," one of its Historic District neighborhoods. There's also a nice back patio. Each room has a private bath; full breakfast is included.

**RHETT HOUSE INN**
Innkeepers: Steve and
Marianne Harrison.
843-524-9030 / 888-480-9530.
Fax: 843-524-1310
www.innbook.com/rhett.
html
1009 Craven St., Beaufort,
SC 29902.
Price: Expensive to Very
Expensive.
Credit Cards: AE, MC, V.
Handicap Access: Two
rooms.

The Harrisons left their careers in New York's fashion business for good when they came to Beaufort, but they brought along their sophisticated taste and a meticulous attention to detail. Indeed, they've lavished it on their 10-room inn and 7-room annex just a stone's throw away. The inn is a beautiful old place, circa 1820, full of sunlight and breezes (only steps from the waterfront), furnished with antiques and comfortable chairs, prints, and vases of fresh flowers, flanked in the back by a garden and on the side by a courtyard fountain. Many of the rooms have fireplaces or Jacuzzi tubs; all have private baths and color televisions with cable service. The porches, upstairs and downstairs, are dreamy places to have afternoon cookies and tea, or read and rest — there's even a hammock. The rooms in the annex have private porches and entrances, mini-bars, and 6 have gas fireplaces. Full breakfast, including homemade breads and muffins, is included and picnic baskets can be made up.

**TWOSUNS INN**
Innkeepers: Carrol and
Ron Kay.
843-522-1122 /
800-532-4244.

This six-room inn faces the Beaufort River at one of its prettiest points, just as it turns the bend and heads away from town, making for exceptional views from the Bay Street bluff or from the

1705 Bay St., Beaufort, SC 29902.
Price: Moderate.
Credit Cards: AE, D, MC, V.
Handicap Access: One room.

inn's own front porch. If you sit a while, you'll see a steady stream of bicyclists and walkers going by, just as they might have in 1917 when the house was built. If you would like to be among them, you can borrow a bicycle, ask for a picnic and go exploring. On your return you may find Carrol Kay working at her loom in the front room, or guests enjoying the "Tea and Toddy Hour." The rooms are individually decorated to reflect Victorian, Oriental, and country themes, and enlivened by cozy, personal touches. Rates include a full breakfast.

**SEA ISLAND INN**
(Best Western).
843-522-2090 / 800-528-1234.
1015 Bay St., Beaufort, SC 29902.
Price: Moderate.
Credit Cards: AE, CB, D, DC, MC, V.

Conveniently located on Beaufort's main street, the locally owned and operated 43-unit motel has a pool, exercise room, and outdoor patio tables. Continental breakfast is served in the lobby. An excellent budget choice.

## *Beaufort Area Islands*

**DATAW ISLAND** (843-838-3838 / 800-848-3838; One Club Rd., Dataw Island, SC 29920) Dataw is a beautifully planned and maintained private 870-acre residential community, about 20 minutes from Beaufort on the way to the beaches. It has limited accommodations, but if you are interested in viewing sales property (homesites or homes) you may call to make arrangements for an overnight or weekend stay.

**FRIPP ISLAND RESORT** (843-838-3535 / 800-845-4100; One Tarpon Blvd., Fripp Island, SC 29920) Fripp is a private, 3,000-acre island bordered by an ocean beach about 35 minutes by car from downtown Beaufort. It's a residential community with two golf courses, tennis facilities, miles of biking trails, resort shops, pools, a beach club, and marina. Activity programs in the summer keep children busy. You can stay in homes accommodating 20 or in one-bedroom villas: there are more than 300 listings. In 1998, the cost of a weekly home rental in summer (sleeps six) ranged from $1,050–$2,300.

**HARBOR ISLAND SALES AND ACCOMMODATIONS** (843-838-2410; / 800-809-2410 2 Harbor Drive, Harbor Island, SC 29920) Fully furnished villas and homes for rent on Harbor Island, a small private community with pool, tennis courts, and 2.5 mile beach. Oceanfront/oceanview two-bedroom homes and villas start at $750 for a week in summer.

**ROYAL FROGMORE INN** (843-838-5400; 863 Sea Island Pkwy., St. Helena Island, SC, 29920) A modest 50-room inn located midway between Beaufort and the beaches, with rates beginning at $47 per night. Credit cards accepted; coffee in the lobby. The Gullah House restaurant next door serves breakfast on the weekends.

National chain motels are also well-represented in Beaufort. A list of some of them is below. It's a good idea to make reservations in advance, for they are often booked by family members of the graduating classes (many each year) of "boot camp" recruits from the Parris Island Marine Corps Recruit Depot. Most of these motels are located on Hwy. 21 between the Marine Corps Air Station and the National Cemetery.

**BATTERY CREEK INN** (843-521-1441; Hwy. 802 near the main gate of Parris Island).

**BEST INN HOTEL** (843-524-3322; Hwy. 21, Beaufort).

**COMFORT INN** (843-525-9366; Hwy. 21, Beaufort).

**DAYS INN** (843-524-1551; 1660 S. Ribaut Rd., Beaufort).

**HAMPTON INN** (843-986-0600; Hwy. 21, Beaufort).

**HOLIDAY INN** (843-524-2144; Hwy. 21 at Lovejoy St., Beaufort).

**HOWARD JOHNSON** (843-524-6020; Hwy. 21, Beaufort).

# DINING

No matter how popular Beaufort and the Sea Islands are becoming, they are still, at heart, small towns, and in their restaurants you are likely to find small town specialties derived from old recipes — or "receipts," as the local spelling sometimes has it.

Some of these dishes may have been passed down in families or borrowed from a favorite cook; some may be extremely simple, a result of necessity, price, and the fact that the fresh ingredients are hard to improve on; some may be adaptations to suit the local taste and the local harvest.

Thus, there will be grits and tiny creek shrimp fixed in many ways — with a spicy tasso sauce, with cheese, in soufflés, or served beside fried eggs. The same goes for greens (mustard, collard, kale, and dandelion), a crop which is available fresh nearly all year long, and crab, which appears in soft or hard shell, in soups and salads, as a stuffing or a sauce. Tomatoes are a prominent cash crop in late spring and early summer, and are featured in many ways at

*Locals celebrate special occasions at Beaufort's elegant Anchorage House.*

Wade Spees

that time. (The Sea Islands have a "window" for selling tomatoes on the national market for about three weeks in May, when migrant workers and local people harvest the fields and work in the packing houses well into the night.)

Many other local specialty foods flourish from late March through May, before the relentless summer heat warms up the creeks and dries out the soil. These include shad roe from the Edisto River, soft shell crabs, strawberries and blueberries, kiwi fruit, and oysters. Game birds, such as dove and marsh hen, and venison are cooler weather treats.

The best place to sample these local offerings is, of course, in local restaurants, but if you find something you especially like, buy a cookbook. The most popular one in the Beaufort area is *Sea Island Seasons*, a collection published by the Beaufort County Open Land Trust. It is available in stores, or by contacting the Trust (P.O. Box 75, Beaufort, SC 29902). Within its covers you'll find out how to make such Lowcountry dishes as Frogmore Stew (sausage, corn-on-the-cob, potatoes, and shrimp in broth); shrimp paste (a spread that retains the delicate, sweet flavor of fresh shrimp); bread-and-butter pickles; and lemon chess pie (the secret ingredient is cornmeal).

As the island communities have grown and are attracting lots of visitors, the variety of dining options has increased dramatically. You can choose among fancy and plain places, bars that serve tapas, or lunch counters that offer fried chicken and fish. The point is to experiment: go ahead, try okra.

### Dining Price Code

|  |  |
|---|---|
| Inexpensive | Up to $10 |
| Moderate | $10 to $20 |

Expensive      $20 to $30

Very Expensive      $30 or more

## *Credit Cards*

AE — American Express      DC — Diner's Club

CB — Carte Blanche      MC — MasterCard

D — Discover Card      V — Visa

**THE ANCHORAGE HOUSE**
843-524-9392.
1103 Bay St.
Closed Sun.
Price: Moderate to Expensive.
Cuisine: Continental.
Serving: L, D.
Credit Cards: AE, D, MC, V.

Located in an 18th-century mansion overlooking the Beaufort River, the Anchorage has both cozy and formal rooms. The back bar is a quiet place for a nightcap; residents sometimes choose the front rooms for business entertaining at lunch or dinner. Southern exposure fills the place with light and brightens the dark Victorian paneling and intricate plasterwork of a late 19th century renovation. The shrimp creole was featured in *Gourmet Magazine* — and other seafood dishes are excellent, too.

**BANANA'S**
843-522-0910.
910 Bay St.
Open daily.
Price: Inexpensive.
Cuisine: American.
Serving: L, D.
Credit Cards: D, MC, V.

Banana's has a loose and tropical feel. The floors are bare wood, ceiling fans whir overhead, and baskets of hanging flowers sway in the breeze. The menu is mostly sandwiches, local seafood, and burgers — prime rib is the weekend special — but lots of locals go for a beer or frozen drink and homemade potato chips after work. Live entertainment on the weekends.

**THE BANK BAR AND GRILL**
843-522-8831.
926 Bay St.
Open daily.
Price: Inexpensive to Moderate.
Cuisine: American.
Serving: L, D.
Credit Cards: AE, D, MC, V.

Located in a well-restored former bank building dating from the early 20th-century, the restaurant's theme is "banking" — you get your bill in a dollar-sized envelope, as if it had come from the teller — and the food is American: local seafood, burgers, salad, and pasta. Patio dining.

**BEAUFORT INN AND
  RESTAURANT**
843-521-9000.
809 Port Republic St.
Open daily.
Price: Expensive.
Cuisine: American and
  Continental.
Serving: D, Sun brunch.
Credit Cards: AE, D, MC, V.

A quiet, white-linen tablecloth place, but casual enough to relax for a long meal. The presentation is beautiful — drizzled sauces, crisp vegetables arranged on the edge of oversized dinner plates — but not precious.

**BISTRO DE JONG**
843-524-4994.
205 West. St.
Closed Mon.
Price: Moderate to
  Expensive.
Cuisine: Continental.
Serving: L, D.
Credit Cards: All major.

Peter de Jong, a local chef with a loyal following, has artfully converted a storefront on a side street into a European-style cafe. Open for business in early 1998, its bar and small tables are jammed at night. Chicken or fish with Peter's sauces are especially good; or pate, sausage, and she crab soup from the appetizer list make a meal. A wonderful addition to town.

**DAD'S PLACE**
843-522-2737.
2127 Boundary St.
Closed Sun.
Price: Inexpensive to
  Moderate.

In a most unprepossessing location, next to the K-Mart in Jean Ribaut Square, Dad's is where the locals go for a big bowl of spaghetti, an antipasto platter, or specialty lasagna. It's friendly and family-oriented, with sports memorabilia tacked to the

---

### Gathering and Corn-Shelling, St. Helena Island

When they go into the field to work, the women tie a bit of string or some vine round their skirts just below the hips, to shorten them, often raising them nearly to the knees; then they walk off with their heavy hoes on their shoulders, as free, strong, and graceful as possible. The prettiest sight is the corn-shelling on Mondays, when the week's allowance, a peck a hand, is given out at the corn-house by the driver. They all assemble with their baskets, which are shallow and without handles, made by themselves of the palmetto and holding from a half a peck to a bushel. The corn is given out in the ear, and they sit about or kneel on the ground, shelling it with cleared corn-cobs. Here there are four enormous logs hollowed at one end, which serve as mortars, at which two can stand with their rude pestles, which they strike up and down alternately....They separate the coarse and fine parts after it is ground by shaking the grits in their baskets: the finest they call corn-flour and make hoe-cake of, but their usual food is the grits, the large portion, boiled as hominy and eaten with clabber.

— Harriet Ware (a young abolitionist and teacher from Boston,
who lived and taught at Coffin Point Plantation,
St. Helena Island) to her parents, May 22, 1862.

Cuisine: Italian.
Serving: L, D.
Credit Cards: MC, V.

**11TH STREET
    DOCKSIDE**
843-524-7433.
1699 11th St., Port Royal.
Open daily.
Price: Moderate.
Cuisine: American;
    Seafood.
Serving: D.
Credit Cards: AE, D, MC,
    V.

**EMILY'S RESTAURANT
    AND TAPAS BAR**
843-522-1866.
906 Port Republic St.
Closed Sun.
Price: Moderate to
    Expensive.
Cuisine: Continental.
Serving: D.
Credit Cards: AE, D, MC,
    V.

**OLLIE'S BY THE BAY**
843-522-3000.
822 Bay St.
Closed Sun.
Price: Moderate to
    Expensive.
Cuisine: American.
Serving: L, D.
Credit Cards: All major.

**PLUMS**
843-525-1946.
904 1/2 Bay St.
Open daily.
Price: Inexpensive to
    Moderate.
Cuisine: American.
Serving: L, D.
Credit Cards: D, MC, V.
Special Features:
    Homemade ice-cream;
    Sunday brunch.

walls and good, quick service. Great after a hot day at the beach.

A casual restaurant, excellent for families, right on Battery Creek, where shrimp boats tie up and the sunsets pour color in the sky. The menu offers fried and broiled seafood specialties, as well as steak and pasta. Before dinner, work up your appetite by a visit to the town of Port Royal's marsh boardwalk and observation tower located at "The Sands," a beach to the east of the port terminal at the foot of Paris Avenue. Sharp eyes can find lots of fossilized sharks' teeth here.

At Emily's you can settle on one entree or put together a meal from "tapas" items — small dishes of hot and cold appetizers, which may have light sauces or seafood stuffing. The small restaurant is dark and cozy, attracting local lawyers, young business people, new downtown residents, and sailors cruising through on the Intracoastal Waterway. A good place for a light, late meal: tapas served to 11 p.m.

Seafood platters, including lots of shellfish, and large salads of tender mixed greens. The restaurant is long and narrow, so the best seating is at either end: out on the patio overlooking the Waterfront Park and the Beaufort River, or in the colorful nook by the front door.

Plums, with its checkerboard floor, pale wood banquettes, and narrow, covered, outdoor porch, has been a runaway success ever since it was started by two local women. It could use a facelift, but it's so popular you wonder where the owners would find the time. Hot sandwiches like grilled turkey or reubens, and multi-layered clubs, are lunchtime stars; there's peanut butter and jelly for kids. The dinner menu features more elaborate entrees, though lots of people still choose larger

*Plums' ice cream factory in Port Royal supplies the downtown restaurant of the same name with sweet desserts, and offers local passersby the rich treat in a casual setting.*

Wade Spees

versions of the excellent luncheon salads. The soups are homemade and so are the desserts. (Plums has its own ice-cream factory in Port Royal.) Full bar service is available.

**SHRIMP SHACK**
843-838-2962.
Hwy. 21, St. Helena Island, about 11 miles south of Beaufort on the way to the beach.
Closed Sun.
Price: Inexpensive.
Cuisine: Seafood.
Serving: L, D.
Credit Cards: None.

Fresh seafood from the family dock — you can see the shrimp boats from the porch — accompanied by slaw, red rice, hush puppies, and beans. Deviled crab and shrimp burgers (ground, seasoned shrimp on a bun) are specialties. You can eat upstairs on the screened-in porch or in an adjacent gazebo. It's laid back and local, and the hard work of the Upton family keeps the standards high.

**THE STEAMER**
843-522-0210.
Hwy. 21, Lady's Island.
Closed Sunday.
Price: Moderate to Expensive.
Cuisine: Lowcountry.
Serving: L, D.
Credit Cards: AE, D, MC, V.
No Reservations.

Consistently the most popular spot in Beaufort, Steamer's boasts a clientele that is a curious — though congenial — mix of transplanted northerners and locals. (The Beaufort-made bumper sticker that reads "I Don't Give A Damn How You Did It Up North" is often seen on pickup trucks parked in this lot.) There's usually a line for dinner, so be prepared to wait. A place at the bar can be hard to find, too, although the addition of adjacent space at Steamer's Pub helps the crowd move along.

*Frogmore Stew at The Steamer gathers the best of land and sea: sausage, corn, potatoes, slaw, and all that firm, pink shrimp.*

Broiled local seafood and shellfish platters are the main dishes; there's steak if you wish. It's noisy, crowded, and very informal (toss your empty oyster shells into a bucket at the center of your table). If you're curious about Frogmore Stew, an indigenous dish that features sausage, corn on the cob, shrimp, and potatoes, in a spicy broth, this is the place to try it.

**WHITEHALL PLANTATION RESTAURANT**
843-521-1700.
Hwy. 21, Lady's Island, just over the Woods Bridge.
Closed Mon. Sun. brunch only.
Price: Moderate to Expensive.
Cuisine: Continental.
Serving: L, D, Sun. brunch.
Credit Cards: MC, V.
Reservations recommended.

A wonderful setting under a canopy of live oaks by the river, and a dining room that has windows on three sides, makes eating here so relaxing and enjoyable that it's usually the place local people bring their visiting guests. It has a nicely settled-in feeling. No one seems to be in a big hurry. The menu offers some surprises: roast lamb, lightly-sauced sliced veal, and broiled fish are worth trying.

# FOOD PURVEYORS

## BAKERIES/COFFEE BARS

**Camelo's Coffee Co.** (843-521-3055; 81 Sea Island Pkwy.) Dozens of varieties of coffee from around the world, served up "plain" or in specialty drinks.

**Firehouse Books & Espresso Bar** (843-522-2665; 706 Craven St.) Coffees, cappuccino, latte, juices, muffins, and sweets, set amidst an excellent two-story bookshop.

## CANDY AND ICE CREAM

**Chocolate Tree** (843-524-7980; 507 Carteret St.) A family-owned emporium selling many different kinds of chocolates, truffles, and dipped fruits made right on the premises, plus candy-making accessories, gift boxes, jelly beans, cards, and gifts.

## DELIS AND FAST FOOD

**Bay Towne Grill** (843-522-3880; 310 West St.) If you see a crowd at the edge of a parking lot, you're here: a tiny building with outdoor tables and stools marks the spot. Burgers, vegetarian sandwiches, salads, subs, and soups. Good chow at low prices, and lots of character.

**Blackstone's Deli & Cafe** (843-524-4330; 915 Bay St.) Best breakfast in town; deli items for lunch. Wines and specialty foods for sale, as well as locally-produced paintings and furniture. Good place to sit with the morning paper.

**Fuji Teppanyaki Restaurant** (843-524-2662; Lighthouse Center, Hwy. 21, Lady's Island) Seafood, chicken, steak, and vegetables, each tossed on the hot griddle, served with rice and salad with ginger dressing, about covers the choices. The food is excellent, plentiful, and for lunch, less than $5.

**Maryland Fried Chicken** (843-524-8766; 1100 Ribaut Rd.) Best fried chicken in town, by the piece, box, or bucket, as well as side orders like fried okra, mashed potatoes, slaw, and catfish. Drive-thru window.

**Upper Crust** (843-521-1999, Lighthouse Center, Hwy. 21, Lady's Island) Pizza, salads, subs, beer, and wine. A slice of the super-deluxe house pie and iced tea goes a long way towards satisfaction. Conveniently located across the street from the movie theater and near the marina.

# CULTURE

In all the ways Beaufort has grown in the last ten years, none is more dramatic than the development of cultural activities, both home-grown and imported. The museums and the annual house tours have gained a professional thoroughness in their presentations; the bookstores sponsor signings and readings; there is a new exhibit and performing space at the University of South Carolina's Beaufort branch; late night music prospers; art galleries seem to be as active and as numerous as restaurants, and there are several venues for live theatre and dramatic readings. It may be enough to sit and watch the tide go by on a Friday at dusk, but you don't have to in Beaufort anymore.

For information about cultural organizations in town, a walking tour of artists' studios and galleries, or upcoming events, write or call: *The Arts Council of Beaufort County,* 801 Carteret St., Beaufort, SC, 29902; (843-521-4144). For events more specifically focused on African-American heritage there's a web site at: www.GullGeeCo@aol.com/ or http://users.aol.com/ queenmut/ GullGeeCo.html.

## FILM

**Lady's Island Cinema** (843-986-5806; Sea Island Parkway, Lady's Island).

**Plaza 8 Theaters** (843-524-9468; Beaufort Plaza, Hwy. 170).

**Plaza 21 Drive-In Theatre** (843-846-4500; Hwy. 21).

## HISTORIC HOMES, GARDENS & RELIGIOUS SITES

**BAPTIST CHURCH OF BEAUFORT**
843-524-3197.
601 Charles St.

This is an 1844 Greek Revival beauty. The ceiling plasterwork and ornamented cornices seem to match — in their absolute, solid mass of decoration — the abundant self-confidence of the prosperous little town of Beaufort in its heyday.

**CHAPEL OF EASE**
Martin Luther King, Jr. Drive, St. Helena Island.

The ruins of this planters' church, built in the 1740s to serve worshippers far from town, are of brick and *tabby*, a construction material that blends oyster shells with lime, sand, and water. The site is a wonderful place for photographs.

**JOHN MARK VERDIER HOUSE**
843-524-6334.

Built circa 1790 for a local merchant according to the plan and Adam-influenced decoration of the day, this house includes a formal parlor and

801 Bay St.
Mon.– Sat. 11–4; last tour at
3:30
Admission: Adults $4;
children $2.

ballroom, ornamental fireplace friezes, carved moldings, and antiques that are original both to the family and to the period of the house. Head-quarters of the Historic Beaufort Foundation.

**OLD SHELDON
CHURCH RUINS**
Secondary Rd. 21, off Hwy.
17, NW of Beaufort.

**B**eautiful brick columns, fragile arches, and sill slabs remain from a church that was burned twice, first by the British in 1779 and then by the Union Army in 1865. A little temple in the woods.

**PENN CENTER**
843-838-2432.
Martin Luther King, Jr.
Drive, St. Helena Island.
York W. Bailey Museum
Mon.– Fri. 11–4.
Admission: Adults $4;
children $2.
Weekend hours by
appointment only.

**F**ounded in 1862 by two Pennsylvania women as a school for the newly freed slaves, Penn has remained a vital institution to promote education, self-sufficiency, and cultural expression among native islanders. In the days of segregation, it was one place where blacks and whites could meet together, as they did when the Rev. Dr. Martin Luther King planned his march on Washington. The York W. Bailey Museum (843-838-8540) holds a collection of cultural artifacts, African objects, and paintings. Community sings featuring gospel choirs and spirituals, a cherished island tradition to which visitors are welcome, take place in Frissell Hall on the third Sunday of each month from September to May at 7:30 p.m. The entire campus is a National Historic Landmark.

*The 19th-century interior of St. Helena's Episcopal Church in Beaufort offers 20th-century worshippers serenity and a sense of history.*

Wade Spees

**ST. HELENA'S
EPISCOPAL CHURCH**
843-522-1712.

**T**his church, built of brick from England in 1724, is adorned inside with graceful columns, upstairs galleries, and tall, multi-paned windows

507 Newcastle St.
Mon.– Sat. 10–4.

on the deep sills of which rest buckets of blossoming magnolia, daffodils, or narcissi in season. Its shaded, walled churchyard makes for a lovely stroll.

**TABERNACLE BAPTIST CHURCH**
843-524-0376.
907 Craven St.

A lovely, white clapboard building with bell tower; in its churchyard lies the grave — and stands a fine bust — of Robert Smalls, who was born a slave, engineered a daring ship capture during the Civil War, and was later a congressman.

## MILITARY SITES

**PARRIS ISLAND MUSEUM**
843-525-2951.
War Memorial Building.
Marine Corps Recruit Depot.
Daily 10–4:30; except on Thursdays to 7 p.m. and Friday mornings at 8 a.m.
Admission: Free.

The museum is a showcase for the history and development of the area on which the famous "boot camp" stands, from its earliest settlement through contemporary recruit training. (Artifacts have been recovered from the Spanish village of Santa Elena, which dates from 1566, and from Charlesfort, a French outpost established by Jean Ribaut in 1562. Excavation continues at these sites, located near the depot golf course.) Exhibits of uniforms, personal items, weapons, drawings, and documents trace the history of the Marine Corps in its worldwide engagements. Maps for a self-guided driving tour around the depot are available. If you're interested in observing morning colors or a graduation, contact the Visitor Center (843-525-3650). You may also picnic in designated areas or eat at a base restaurant.

**NATIONAL CEMETERY**
Hwy. 21, Beaufort.

Created by President Lincoln in 1863 for victims of Southern battles, this is the final resting place of some 9,000 Union soldiers and more than 100 Confederates. It is still in service.

## MUSEUMS

**BEAUFORT MUSEUM**
843-525-7077.
713 Craven St.
10–5; closed Wed. and Sun.
Admission: Adults, $2; children $0.50.

Located in the old Beaufort Arsenal, an ochre-colored bastion with a courtyard, the museum is redefining itself from what might once have been called Beaufort's "attic" to a center of local history and culture.

*The old Beaufort Arsenal (circa 1798) has become the Beaufort Museum.*

Wade Spees

**NORTH ST. AQUARIUM**
843-524-1559.
608 North St.
Thurs.–Sat. 10–6.
Admission: Adults $2;
    children $1.
Call ahead for group rates.

The aquarium features a collection — in this case, 600 species of sea creatures, some in "touch tanks" — and a knowledgeable "curator" in Bob Bender, who introduces visitors to Lowcountry marine life in a relaxed and interesting way.

## MUSIC

**Hallelujah Singers** (843-986-9688; 2201 Boundary St., Beaufort, SC 29901). The group of singers under the direction of Marlena McGhee Smalls, a talented vocalist who has earned a national reputation for her singing and her acting (she was Bubba's mother in the movie *Forrest Gump*) performs throughout the year, often in a downtown church at the time of annual house tours; weekly during the summer at various sites. Call or write for specific schedules.

*Community sings held monthly at Penn Center keep the heritage of spirituals and gospel music alive.*

Wade Spees

**Penn Center Community Sings** (843-838-2432; P.O. Box 126, St. Helena Island, SC 29920). Community groups, quartets of senior citizens, gospel choirs, spur-of-the-moment vocalists, and soloists who deacon out lines of spirituals to the audience perform at 7:30 p.m. on the third Sunday of every month, from September to May, in Frissell Hall on the historic Penn Center campus. The popularity of the sings and the feelings of dignity and fellowship that characterize them are a moving testament to the pride of Sea Islanders in their culture and heritage. Contributions are welcome.

## NIGHTLIFE

**Banana's** (843-522-0910; 910 Bay St.) Jazz combos on the weekends.

**Johnson Creek Tavern** (843-838-4166; Hwy. 21, Harbor Island.). A modest beach bar about 25 minutes from town, where you'll find campers from Hunting Island State Park, young couples, and "after-party" groups who come for the last set. A variety of music is offered on the weekends, from bluegrass to rock.

## THEATER

**Beaufort Little Theater** (843-522-2000; P.O. Box 1422, Beaufort, SC 29901). Beaufort's popular community theater performs well-known works — musicals, comedy, and drama — several times each year.

*A newly-rehabilitated church serves multiple purposes.*

Wade Spees

**Port Royal Playhouse** This refurbished church serves a variety of purposes. The interior provides an intimate space with good accoustics.

**The Shed** (843-525-0968; 809 Paris Avenue, Port Royal) A large space in Port Royal dedicated to theatre education and performances, both local and regional.

**The "Spirit of Old Beaufort"** (843-525-0459; 210 Scott St.) Ensemble group presents the story of Beaufort's history. Seasonal. Call for tickets.

## RECREATION

For at least 200 years, Lowcountry people have depended for nourishment on the reliable bounty of land and sea. They became so accustomed to going forth to gather and returning home with full baskets that the *work* of gathering and the *pleasure* to be had in it were easily interchanged. These days the sportsman, the naturalist, and the Sunday painter take to the outdoors in equal numbers — and often with equal results: going in seriousness, returning with, at the very least, a day of pleasure to their name. Such is the natural abundance of the Lowcountry, and the dozens of opportunities to explore it — by power boat, kayak, windsurfer; with fishing pole, crab net, paintbrush, or pup tent — that visitors still have this experience today.

Beaufort, in particular, claims the advantage over Charleston and Savannah of having its rural recreational opportunities close at hand. Informally, resi-

of having its rural recreational opportunities close at hand. Informally, residents and visitors can fish or throw cast nets for shrimp at bridges off *Hwy. 21 at Cowan Creek and Village Creek,* from the *Waterfront Park,* and at the fishing pier at the *Broad River Bridge,* among other spots. *Hunting Island State Park* is located off Hwy. 21, about a 30 minute drive north of town. At the north end of Hunting Island is *Paradise Pier* (843-838-7437), at 1,120 feet, the state's longest. There are dozens of public boat landings within easy reach. Launching is free, and so is parking, but you're on your own — no attendants, telephones, or rest rooms. For locations, inquire at marinas or sporting goods stores or write: *Lowcountry Resort Islands and Tourism Commission* (800-528-6870; P.O. Box 615, Yemassee, SC 29945).

In addition, the development of Beaufort's downtown and nearby coastal resorts has created opportunities for recreation of a more studied sort. There are fine golf courses, tennis complexes, marinas, boat tours, and fishing expeditions of all kinds.

Perhaps the most significant resource for those who love the outdoors and savor its hidden beauty, is the consolidation of some 350,000 acres of marsh, creek, sound, and forest to the north, east, and west of Beaufort in the *ACE Basin Preserve* — the crescent of landscape that encompasses the forested, inland shore of the Ashepoo, Combahee, and Edisto Rivers and their small tributaries. And not all the activity is on the water, either: from points on dry land, birders have identified more than 256 species of resident and migratory birds. *ACE Basin Tours* (843-521-3099) will take you on a 3-hour pontoon boat trip in the ACE. The boat leaves from Coosaw Island at 10 a.m. Weds. and Sats. (Adults, $25; Children 6–12, $15.00; under 6 free when accompanied by a parent.) Call for reservations and directions. Tours may be scheduled on other days, with a minimum 8 passengers.

So here are some options. If your recreational pursuits require clothing or equipment you didn't bring with you, see the shops listed in the **Shopping** section under "Sporting Goods and Clothing."

*There is never a "best time" for bicycling in Beaufort — and that's because there's never a bad time to do so.*

Wade Spees

## BEACH ACCESS

**Hunting Island State Park** (See entry under **Camping**.) Sunrise – sunset; $3 per car.

## BICYCLING

**Low Country Bicycles** (843-524-9585; 904 Port Republic St.) A shop filled with the latest mountain, cruising, high performance, and kid's bikes, maps, and accessories. John Feeser, the owner, is a great source for routes and ideas. Bikes for rent by the hour ($5 adults; $3 children) and day ($20 adults; $12 kids), as well as racks for the car ($10), and helmets, locks, etc.

## BOWLING

**Ribaut Lanes** (843-524-3111; 1140 S. Ribaut Rd.)

## CAMPING

**Hunting Island State Park** (843-838-2011; 2555 Sea Island Pkwy., Hunting Island, SC 29920) on Hwy. 21, about 30 minutes from Beaufort. 200 sites, 15 cabins, nature trails, picnic sites, showers and dressing rooms, a store, water, and electrical hookups. The 19th-century Hunting Island lighthouse offers an expansive view of the confluence of ocean waters and St. Helena Sound.

**Kobuch's** (843-525-0653; Hwy. 302, Burton, minutes from Marine Corps Recruit Depot at Parris Island). 15 sites, full hookups.

**Tuc In De Wood Campground** (843-838-2267; 22 Tuc In De Wood Lane, St. Helena Island, SC 29920) 74 sites with city water, electricity, and cable television connections; 30 sites with full hookups.

## CANOEING AND KAYAKING

**The Kayak Farm** (843-838-2008; 1289 Sea Island Pkwy., St. Helena Island) Jea Chapman, a British Canoe Union certified (Level II Coach) instructor, offers half or full day accompanied tours, or she will teach you the basics on land, rent you kayaks and equipment, and load them on your car for your own trip. Group tours traveling locally (to Hunting Island and nearby creeks); longer trips to ACE Basin sites. Custom expeditions and overnight tours by arrangement. Rates from $25 per day per kayak to $65 for a full day outing including lunch.

Wade Spees

*Kayaking is a simple, quiet way to get eye-level with the marsh.*

**Tullifinny Joe's Outpost** (843-726-4545; I-95 frontage road at Coosawhatchie) A sea-kayaking, saltwater fly fishing, and touring company, located about 35 minutes from Beaufort, offering numerous guided expeditions, instruction, and equipment rental.

### DIVING

**Dive Masters** (843-524-9372; Lady's Island Marina); and **Dive Junction** (843-522-9430; Forest Pointe Plaza) offer scuba lessons by certified instructors, repair service, equipment, and rentals.

### FISHING

Fishing was and is such a common, pleasurable pastime in the Lowcountry, so thickly woven into the fabric of local life, that in describing it one is likely to end up talking about the entire culture itself: the way its residents cook, the stories they choose to tell, the skills they wish to pass on, where they live, what they do on weekends, what kinds of politicians they elect, how they judge character, what their values are for their children. Like the Myth of the Old South and Old Families, the lore of fishing confers a kind of lineage by which people know themselves. And where the Old Families might have Old Houses, people who fish have Old Cars, "fishing cars" as they are widely known — dinged-up rustbuckets that make it to the boat landing (not much further) with the faithfulness of a hunting hound.

In fact, the opportunities for fishing are so numerous, the catches still plentiful, the waterways still generally pristine, the tradition so revered, that a book written in 1856, *Carolina Sport By Land and Water* by William Elliott, can be read as a nearly modern account.

Today's enthusiast can choose freshwater or saltwater sites, fishing from piers, bridges, boats or banks, from the beach, or by trolling an artificial off-shore reef. Saltwater fly fishing is a new and popular specialty. ***Paradise Pier*** (843-838-7437) is located on Hunting Island near Beaufort and open 24 hours. The fishing fee is $4. The catch can range from small bream, porgy, and spot — of the family commonly known as "sailor's choice" — to flounder, to big game fish like wahoo, drum, shark, and cobia. In general, the best part of the season extends from April through November, but small panfish remain active beyond those dates.

Licenses are required for freshwater fishing and for saltwater fishing under certain conditions. Most visitors interested in recreational fishing will not need one; they're not necessary for recreational shrimping and crabbing. Licenses are sold in many hardware and hunting stores, K-Marts, and tackle shops. For further information on licenses, and size and catch limits, contact the ***South Carolina Wildlife and Marine Resources Dept.*** (843-795-6350; P.O. Box 12559, Charleston, SC 29412).

For a comprehensive map indicating recreational fishing facilities in the Lowcountry, including marinas, boat landings, bridges and catwalks, shellfish grounds, and offshore reefs, write the ***Lowcountry Resort Islands and Tourism Commission*** (800-528-6870; P.O. Box 615, Yemassee, SC 29945).

## SPORT-FISHING CHARTERS

A sport-fishing charter can take you to the Gulf Stream or to any of the dozen or so artificial reefs offshore. Over 150 years ago, the first artificial reefs used in this area were approximately 6 feet high, log, hut-like structures

*Paradise Pier reaches across Fripp Inlet, where dozens of species run with the tides.*

Wade Spees

that were sunk to attract sheepshead; today's reefs are far more elaborate affairs that attract dozens of species. Given that much of the sea floor off the coast is sandy, these reefs provide the hard substrate necessary to create a "live bottom" of invertebrates, small fish, coral, crabs, and sponges. They are active feeding stations for the big fish, and experienced guides know them well. Trips of this sort generally take a full day. Trips closer to shore, in smaller boats, can be easily enjoyed by the half-day.

A listing of some of the many **charter boat services** available follows. Others may be available at marinas listed in the *Transportation* Chapter. Rods, reels, bait, and tackle are provided; lunch or snacks are usually available, but you should check in advance; boats are equipped with safety equipment and licenses; all but the smallest have heads. It is wise to bring sunscreen, windbreakers, and a towel.

Many charters will design a trip to suit your particular interest or prepare a boat for a fishing tournament. If bad weather is forecast, call ahead to confirm that the trip is on. Also check the reservation, deposit, and cancellation policies of each charter. The 1998 prices per person for half-day trips ranged from $50 to $100.

**Bay Street Outfitters** (843-524-5250; 815 Bay St.) Visitors who are experienced in the art of fly fishing, as well as those who are rank beginners, can find experienced guides, instruction, and a full line of Orvis outfits, accessories, and specialty rods here. In 1998, full-day guided charters (for 2 anglers), including lunch, cost $350; $250 for a half-day. Licenses are not required on the charters; drinks and equipment are provided. Private fly casting lessons (by the hour) are $50. One- and two-day casting and fly fishing schools begin at $150 per person. It's best to reserve in advance and see what the season has to offer.

**Capt. David Murray** (843-525-6820; 100 Grayson St., Beaufort). David Murray is an experienced fisherman in many types of water, a guide, an Orvis fly-fishing instructor, and an advocate of Lefty Kreh's modern method of fly-casting. For one or two persons, his fees are $225 for a full day; $175 for a half-day, including lunch and beverages, aboard a 16' Hewes Bonefisher.

**Capt. Eddie Netherland** (843-838-5661; Fripp Island Marina). Offshore and inshore trips by day and half-day on a 25-foot Grady-White Sailfisher. King mackerel a specialty.

**Lou Too Sportfishing** (843-838-9122; Fripp Island). Captain Robbie Gilbert offers the beginner or advanced fisherman lots of expeditions to choose from, aboard a 32-foot boat with many of the comforts of home. Just wear soft-soled shoes and bring your picnic. For up to 6 passengers, six hours of fishing costs $450; for up to 30 miles offshore (8 hours) is $550; a full day and then some (10 hours) is $750; and 12 hours of big game, blue water, Gulf Stream fishing is $950.

**Low Country Fishing** (843-522-8066; Beaufort). Captain Doug Gertis. Light tackle inshore fishing for jack crevalle, trout, tarpon, and other species on a 19-foot Maverick Master Angler. Tag and release fishermen get a discount.

**Sea Wolf V** (843-525-1174; Port Royal Landing, Beaufort). Captain Wally Phinney, Jr. USA, Ret. Deep sea fishing, diving, cruising, by day or half-day aboard 32-foot boat.

## FITNESS FACILITIES

**Fitness Galleria** (843-522-1400; 1013 Charles St.) A variety of workouts are available here, from yoga to dancing, as well as personal training by instructor Cherry Newton.

**Ray's Gym** (843-524-8351; Hwy. 170) Complete gym, fitness training, body-sculpting, Nautilus, weights, fitness machines.

## GOLF

The presence in the Lowcountry of so many golf courses, public, private and semi-private — so many beautiful ones, and so many that are consistently ranked by golf professionals as among the top 100 in the world — means that visitors can and do spend every day for a week playing one or two courses without ever repeating themselves. The Lowcountry probably has more golf courses per person than any other region in the country, and probably more courses with holes offering expansive ocean or marsh views, or such scenic hazards as deer, heron, and the occasional alligator.

Whether you're a duffer or scratch golfer, the pleasure you can derive from simply being on a course — early in the morning as the heavy dew dries and the temperature rises, or late in the day as the chuck will's widows commence their plaintive call — is worth the planning and expense that today's golf excursions require. Lowcountry weather allows for year-round play and (in the summer) late-afternoon starting times. The high-season months are in fall and spring, so it is wise to schedule your playing time well in advance.

On some courses carts are required at peak playing times. For resort play, it is usually necessary to be an overnight guest. Golf packages that include lodging are numerous, so ask about them. Club rentals and instruction are available at all courses. Greens fees/cart rentals reflect 1998 prices.

### *Public and Semi-Private Courses*

**Country Club of Beaufort** (843-522-1605 / 800-869-1617; 8 Barnwell Dr., Lady's Island) Russell Breedon design, 18 holes, par 72. Four sets of tees:

4,753 yards, 5,416 yards, 6,112 yards, and 6,506 yards. Pro: Craig Fischer. Greens fees including cart $40.

**Fripp Island** (843-838-1576 / 800-933-0050; Fripp Island) Set on the rim of the Atlantic and Fripp Inlet, **Ocean Point Golf Links** is an 18-hole, par 72, George Cobb–designed course, from 4,951 yards to 6,556 yards. The **Ocean Creek Course**, the first designed by Davis Love, III, is a par 71, winding through the marshes and interior wetlands. Yardage from 4,884 to 6,510. Walking is an option at both courses. Since they lie within a gated community, you must call ahead to reserve tee times and a visitor's pass. Fees are $49–$59 per person.

**Lady's Island Country Club** (843-524-3635; Lady's Island) Pines Course, par 72, 7,003 yards; Marsh Course, par 72, 5,929 yards. Pro: Jack Kolb. Greens fees including cart $40.

**South Carolina National Golf Club** (843-524-0300 / 800-221-9582; 8 Waveland Ave., Beaufort) George Cobb's last design, par 71. Four sets of tees: 4,933 yards, 6,150 yards, 6,610 yards, and 6,625 yards. Pro: Charlie Bohmert. Greens fees including cart $49 plus tax according to season.

## HORSEBACK RIDING

Dorinda Mark's *Broomfield Stables* (843-521-1212), *D&L Quarterhorses* (843-521-0467) and *Shalimar Horse Center* (843-521-0419) welcome inquiries from visitors seeking instruction within the ring.

## TENNIS

Public courts, some of which are lit for night play, are located on *Boundary Street* across from the National Cemetery; on the corner of *Battery Creek Rd. and Southside Blvd.*, and in the *Port Royal Park* on *Paris Ave.* in the village of Port Royal. Free. No reservations required.

# SHOPPING

## ANTEBELLUM ARTIFACTS

**Palmetto Art Gallery** (843-522-2110; 492 Laurel Bay Rd.) Civil War items and autographs, prints, relics, and reproductions.

## ANTIQUES

**Bellavista Antiques & Interiors** (843-521-0687; 206 Carteret St.) Large scale furniture and vases, stone ornaments, English pine furniture.

**Chitty & Co.** (843-524-7889; 208 Carteret St.) Fine European, American, and Oriental antiques, silver, porcelain, lamps, chandeliers, and sconces.

**Consignor's Antique Mall** (843-521-0660; 913 Port Republic St.) A little bit of everything from primitive furniture and quilts to prints and salt-and-pepper sets.

**Der Teufelhund** (843-521-9017; 13B Marina Blvd., near Parris Island) Military books, antique gear, insignias, trunks, and other ephemera of 20th century warfare.

**Legacy & Whimsey** (843-524-2685; 208B Carteret St.) Architectural elements like gates, columns, and doors are a specialty.

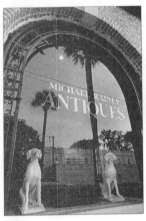

*A fine antique store in a restored building draws customers to downtown Beaufort.*

Wade Spees

**Michael Rainey Antiques** (843-521-4532; 702 Craven St.) A beautiful gathering of antiques, many of them from New England and Pennsylvania. Baskets, boxes, benches, and paintings, too.

**Past Time Antiques** (843-522-8881; 205 Scotts St.) Collectibles, charming old household ware, and country furniture.

**Village Hut Antiques** (843-521-1436; 707 Paris Ave., Port Royal) A special collection of platters, china, glassware, silver, and some small pieces of art.

## BOOKS

**Bay St. Trading Co.** (843-524-2000; 808 Bay St.) Best-sellers, books-on-tape, excellent children's section, comprehensive local and regional history, and many fine photography books. The staff is very knowledgeable, which makes this store the best place to browse downtown.

**Beaufort Bookstore** (843-525-1066; Jean Ribaut Sq.) A large selection and wide variety of books from best-selling fiction and non-fiction to military and Lowcountry favorites.

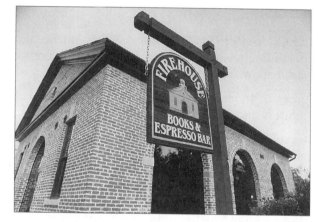

*Locals, kids, and visitors find a hot drink, books, and sweets at the Firehouse*

Wade Spees

**Firehouse Books and Espresso Bar** (843-522-2665; 706 Craven St.) A charming book store with an excellent magazine selection and a coffee bar.

**Lady's Island Bookstore** (843-524-0444; Island Square, Lady's Island) Paperback classics, good non-fiction, history, and biography.

**McIntosh Book Shoppe** (843-524-1119; 917 Bay St.) It's easy to miss this bookstore, which carries rare and old volumes, but seek it out. Some books on South Carolina you'll find no where else. It's at the Port Republic Street end of the Old Bay Market Place, Beaufort's little mall.

## CLOTHING

**Beaufort Men's Shop** (843-524-7118; 723 Bay St.) Casual clothing with a classic look, outdoor wear, tuxedos.

**Deal's** (843-524-4993; 724 Bay St.) Cotton sweaters, khakis, shirts in natural fibers, and imported Irish apparel, all at discounted prices.

**Jasmine** (843-524-6660; 919 Bay St.) A women's boutique with dresses, separates, and colorful accessories.

**Lipsitz Department Store** (843-524-2330; 825 Bay St.) A family-owned and family-run business for nearly 100 years. Everyday wear and shoes in all sizes, superior friendly service.

**Plumage** (843-522-8807; 104 West St.) Evening clothes with glittering accessories and distinctive casual outfits, including a fine small selection for kids.

## CRAFTS

**The Craftseller** (843-525-6104; 818 Bay St.) Local and regional artists' work, including jewelry, benches made of old wood from local buildings, fabric art, handmade paper, wind-chimes.

**Stones & Bones** (843-521-1185; 909 Bay St.) Minerals, stones, Native American pottery and crafts, jewelry.

**Sweetgrass Baskets** made by local artists can be found on Hwy. 21, at a roadside stand by the Red Piano Too Gallery, and at two additional stands further along, between the Gallery and the turn for Coffin Point at Seaside Road. The baskets, which incorporate palmetto frond, pine needle, and rush with the pale grass, come in many shapes and sizes, with individual variations inspired by the utilitarian shapes used in the past. They require enormous amounts of labor and skill and are useful as well as beautiful.

**TwoSuns Handwovens** (843-522-1122; 1705 Bay St.) Wearable art, table linens, and beaded jewelry. The weaver is Carrol Kay, an artist and innkeeper who works on large floor looms in her parlor.

## GALLERIES

**Bay Street Gallery** (843-522-9210; 719 Bay St.) Original works by Lana Hefner and Sandra Baggette — accomplished and quite stunning. Hefner's pastels of marsh scenes are moody and impressionistic; Baggette's watercolors have light bursting forth. There is a fine collection of Sea Island baskets on hand for sale, too.

**Cole Studio** (843-521-1880; 165 Pleasant Point Drive, Lady's Island) Original watercolors and prints in a home/studio about eight miles from Beaufort. Best to call ahead.

*Coiled sea grass baskets laid out on street corners attract viewers and buyers.*

Wade Spees

**Fern House Studio/Gallery** (843-986-0631; 909 Bladen St.) The work and gallery space of oil painter Pat Boquard is open by appointment or chance.

**Gloria Dalvini Watercolors** (843-521-0221; 101 Scott's St.) A wonderful, tiny building by the Waterfront Park houses dozens of watercolors of Lowcountry houses, gardens, and landscapes.

**Indigo Gallery** (843-524-1036; 809 Bay St.) Limited and open editions of many of the best-known Lowcountry artists, as well as serigraphs, original art, and framing.

**Juxtaposition** (843-521-1415; 301 West St.) A talented local artist who grew up in Beaufort has transformed a former shoe-repair shop (itself a local landmark) into an exciting gallery full of painting, ceramics, glass, jewelry and fine art.

**Longo Gallery** (843-522-8933; 103 Charles St.) Suzanne and Eric Longo, husband and wife, are proficient and playful artists. Her ideas find their expression in clay and concrete sculpture; his, in brightly-colored, whimsical paintings (sometimes on old roof tin, or boards) and found-object constructions. Their work is on display and for sale at both their home and downtown galleries.

**The Red Piano Too** (843-838-2241; 853 Sea Island Parkway, St. Helena Island) Located just 15 minutes from Beaufort, this gallery has a superior collection of folk art and outsider art by many artists — including St. Helena native Sam Doyle — sea grass baskets, quilts, books, furniture, beads, African objects, and prints. It also serves as something of a community center, in the sense that the owners and patrons are particularly interested in the preser-

*The Red Piano Too Art Gallery is unique in the Lowcountry, featuring an excellent collection of outsider art, antiques, quilts stitched on St. Helena Island, paintings by local artists, books, and beads.*

Wade Spees

vation of St. Helena Island as a special rural place, not just a suburb of Beaufort. Fine framing is available. Definitely not to be missed — the gallery represents the best of the Lowcountry.

**Rhett Gallery** (843-524-3339; 901 Bay St.) Prints and watercolors of the Lowcountry by Nancy Ricker Rhett — works that seem to capture the Lowcountry light just right — as well as antique first-edition prints and maps, Civil War and nautical materials, and hand-colored engravings. Custom framing and shipping available.

**Shipman Art Gallery** (843-524-7722; 904 Bay St.) Watercolor artist Barbara Shipman offers some 70 of her paintings in collectible print editions, as well as originals. She captures the Lowcountry in both intimate and grand ways — from one crab or one blossom to an entire coastline scene.

**Susan Graber Studio** (843-524-4353; 805 London Ave., Port Royal) Commissioned portraits in oil, works-in-progress, still-life paintings, and expressive interior scenes painted on shaped wood panels fill this artists' studio. Her use of warm colors and blending techniques makes her work stand out. By appointment or chance.

## GIFTS

**Beaufort Butterfly Company** (843-986-0555; 928 ¹/₂ Bay St.) Everything you'll need to attract, observe, identify, catch, and collect butterflies, as well as books about natural history and tee shirts with nature themes.

**Boombears** (843-524-2525; 501 Carteret St.) Fancy toy stores may have become a cliché in cities and upscale malls, but this one, founded and run by a local family, is probably the very best you've ever seen. It is ingenious, unpretentious, and filled with items of the highest quality: toys, books, dolls, games, tin soldiers, stuffed animals, tool kits, racing cars, and kits of all kinds.

**Fordham Hardware** (843-524-3161; 701 Bay St.) Everything from hammocks to waste baskets, fireplace tools to floor wax. A Beaufort institution.

**Precious Cargo** (843-525-1075; 904 Bay St.) Needlework pillows with saucy sayings, folk art, accessories for the bar, collectibles from around the world.

**Rossignol's** (843-524-2175; 817 Bay St.) Two dozen selections of fine china patterns, silver and gold jewelry, stationery, and expensive stemware — all suitable for wedding gifts — as well as platters, picture frames, and tea towels that would make good house presents.

**Thorndike Williams Antiques and Collectibles** (843-524-7688; 308 Scotts St.) Located in a little green and white cottage that looks nearly tropical, you'll find items decidedly un-cottagelike: fine reproduction furniture, prints, lamps, china, brass, fabrics, and antiques. The shop also offers interior design service.

**Waterside Place** (843-524-0201; 308 Charles St.) Linens, specialty food items, and special little things for interiors.

## GOURMET AND HEALTH FOOD

**Blackstone's** (843-524-4330; 915 Bay St.) A small gourmet grocery and an informal "chandlery" for sailors coming through on the Intracoastal Waterway. (see **Deli** listing, too.)

**Cravings By the Bay** (843-522-3000 / 800-735-3215; 928 Bay St.). Savor Lowcountry flavors as well as memories by ordering soups, condiments, sauces, and specialty books by mail. Shrimp, oysters, clams, scallops, and soft-shell crab can be delivered overnight. Drop by for more information.

**Vita Villa Ltd.** (843-522-0583; Hwy. 21, Lady's Island Square) Herbs, grains, candies, books, vitamins, local honey, and sugar-free and preservative-free health foods.

**W.H. Gay Seafood** (843-521-5090; 2242 Boundary St.) Fresh fish, shellfish, and shrimp from local waters, packed in ice to last on the road. Utensils, shirts, and "shrimp boots," in the classic white, low-cut style.

## HOME FURNISHINGS/KITCHENWARE

**The Cook's House** (843-524-6198; 706 Carteret St.) If there's something you need for the kitchen, from an ergonomic can opener to a baguette pan, you'll find it here, in rooms that are stocked floor to ceiling. A stationery store for chefs — or anyone who loves the tools of the trade.

**Out of Hand** (843-522-8525; 207 West St.) A tiny storefront imaginatively decorated and stocked with very special treats for the home: glassware, painted benches, candles, and linens.

## SPORTING GOODS AND CLOTHING

**Barefoot Bubba's** (843-838-5431; Hwy. 21, Harbor Island) The best in surf wear and accessories, toys for the beach, boards, and rafts.

**Bay Street Outfitters** (843-524-5250; 815 Bay St.) A full line of high-end sportswear from Orvis and Barbour, as well as fishing gear, reels, binoculars, and books.

**High Tide Surf Shop** (843-524-2334; 905 Bay St.) Comfortable clothes for the 90s, like corduroys, clogs, Doc Marten's, cool sneakers, and pullovers, as well as swimwear and wet suits, boards, and surfing accessories.

**Island Outfitters** (843-522-9900; Hwy. 21 Lady's Island) Headquarters for serious gun and bow hunters, campers, and fishermen. Rods, coolers, bait, hooks, ammunition, and a big selection of rugged outdoor camouflage and boots. The expert advice is free.

# EDISTO ISLAND

Like the Sea Islands around Charleston and Beaufort, Edisto's history is characterized by a culture of Native American settlement, followed by rice, indigo, and cotton cultivation, slavery, the occupation of Federal troops, and from the end of the Civil War, isolation. Small farming and fishing operations have remained constant over time. However, unlike the other Sea Islands, Edisto remains something of a backwater, lively in the summer season, due to the scads of modest rental homes on Edisto Beach, and the presence of Edisto Beach State Park, quiet the rest of the time. The residents seem to prefer it that way: a newly established preservation land trust seeks to protect and enhance vistas and procure land and easements. Development is undoubtedly going to occur, but with good planning and cooperation, it may reflect the Edisto that has survived thus far. If you're looking for a few days of peace and quiet, enlivened by beachcombing, a good meal, and perhaps a kayak or boat tour, your choice will probably be Edisto.

The island lies about 45 miles south of Charleston by road, and about 80

*Life at Cassina Point Plantation on Edisto Island takes its sweet, meandering time as the late-afternoon sun warms up the broad piazza, and the old porch rockers.*

Wade Spees

miles from Beaufort — of course far less by water. From Hwy. 17, take Hwy. 174 (signs alert you to Edisto) the island's main travel route. A variety of creeks and rivers irregularly indent Edisto, so that today, as in the past, there are roads that cross the marsh or wind through the woods in what seems to be the long way around. Original sections of the King's Highway, laid out in the early 18th century, remain in use today. The main road dead ends at the Atlantic Ocean.

For a visitor, Edisto is the least immediately knowable of the Sea Islands. What remains of its "Golden Age," the period between the Revolutionary and Civil Wars, is mostly hidden, tucked away along secondary roads that wind through fields and patches of scrub oak, and meander by the North and South Edisto Rivers and their tributaries. Historic sites that are listed on the National Register of Historic Places (27 so far) do include churches, but consist primarily of private plantation homes and gardens.

A good overview of the island's history and culture, from the time of its Native American inhabitants, is provided by the Edisto Island Historic Preservation Society's *Museum* (Hwy. 174 at Chisolm Plantation Rd.; Hours are 1–4 Tues., Thurs., and Sat. Admission $2; free to children 10 and under.) Island artifacts such as baskets, clothing, farm tools, letters and documents, uniforms, and furniture are displayed in several small rooms. There are old photographs and explanatory remarks. The little gift shop sells a nice variety of natural history items for kids — good to use to explore and collect on their own — as well as a series of excellent reprints of booklets you're not likely to find anywhere else on your travels. They include *"Edisto Island in 1808," "Indigo in America," "Gullah,"* and *"She Came To the Island,"* the Edisto diary of Mary Ames, a Northern abolitionist whose account of teaching and living among the newly-freed slaves during the Civil War is among the most poignant of the genre.

If you're interested in a closer look and more explanation than what the museum exhibits can provide, contact *Island Tours* (843-869-1937 / 843-869-2683) a service which provides two-and-a-half hour guided van tours of Edisto. Cost is $12 per person. The *Annual Tours of Edisto* generally take place on the second Saturday in October. Contact the *Edisto Island Historic Preservation Society* (843-869-1954; P.O. Box 393, Edisto Island, SC 29438) for information. In 1998, tour prices were $20 for adults; $5 ages 6–16. If you want to stay in an old house (circa 1847), contact *Cassina Point Plantation Bed & Breakfast* (843-869-2535; P.O. Box 535, Edisto Island SC 29438; www.bbon-line.com/sc/cassina). There are four guest rooms with fireplaces and half-baths; the price is moderate. The house is set back from the creek and salt marsh, accessed by a sandy lane. The innkeepers, Bruce and Tecla Earnshaw, also offer canoe and kayak rentals on Westbank Creek (from $15 for guests; from $20 for non-guests). Dinner at the *Old Post Office Restaurant* (843-869-2339; Hwy. 174 at Point of Pines Rd.) would round out a fine day. Meals are moderate to expensive, and include grilled and sautéed entrees that represent a change from the fried food popular at other island spots. The setting is cozy. Hours are 5 p.m.–10 p.m., Tuesday–Saturday.

Edisto Beach, the curve of Edisto that faces the Atlantic then turns to embrace the inner marsh, has been for years the summer destination of South Carolina families — both as day trippers to the state park or as vacationers who stay for one or more weeks. Families take up residence in the plain, two-story houses which line the boulevards for about three dozen blocks, and spill across adjacent avenues. Absolutely nothing fancy here: it's informal, full of kids riding bikes and loaded minivans parked in the sand. Shopping is done at the local *Red & White Grocery* (843-869-1144; Hwy. 174) or, for special treats, at *Geechee Gourmet* (843-869-1000; 143 Jungle Rd.). A high point of the day is watching the shrimp boats come in. Many of these houses are for rent by the week, and several rental agencies list them, including:

**The Atwood Agency** (843-869-2151 / 800-476-0126).

**Edisto Sales and Rentals** (843-869-2527 / 800-868-5398).

**The Lyons Co.** (843-869-2516 / 800-945-9667).

A small resort, *Fairfield Ocean Ridge* (843-869-2561 / 800-845-8500; 1 King Cotton Rd., Edisto Island, SC 29438) also offers rentals and its 300-acre grounds includes amenities such as tennis, golf, swimming, a restaurant, and a kid's summer program. *Edisto Beach State Park* (843-869-2156; 8377 State Cabin Rd., Edisto Island, SC 29438) offers 75 camping sites for tents and RVs, (two are designated for handicapped visitors) as well as five two-bedroom cabins for families. Some sites are available by advance reservation. There's a boat ramp and general store, trails, showers, water and electrical hookups, and interpretive programs. The beach is a wonderful place to hunt for fossils and shark's teeth.

*In a campground clearing, your "bed" will be soft and sandy, and your bedtime music the rustle of the wind in the dry palmetto fronds.*

Wade Spees

Because of its location at the confluence of the North and South Edisto Rivers, the Atlantic, and St. Helena Sound, Edisto Beach offers probably the easiest access to the ACE Basin. If you're touring on your own, and want maps and information for sightseeing and bird-watching, contact the *ACE Basin National Wildlife Refuge Headquarters* (843-889-3084) or write: ACE Basin NERR, P.O. Box 12559, Charleston, SC 29422-2559; 843-762-5437. From Edisto, take SC Hwy. 174 north over the Dawhoo River Bridge to the intersection with the flashing light. Turn left on to Willtown Rd. Two miles further on, turn left on Jehossee Island Rd. (S-10-346) at the sign reading "The Grove."

If you want to tour the ACE Basin by water from Edisto, contact the guide services below. Some of these operators also offer beachcombing tours on uninhabited islands, inshore and offshore fishing charters, parasailing, pontoon boat tours, and boat, kayak, or waverunner rentals:

**Edisto Essentials** (843-869-0951).

**Edisto Watersports and Tackle** (843-869-0663).

**Miss Bohicket Charter Sailboat** (843-869-3025).

**Ugly Duckling Charters** (800-303-1580).

## BLUFFTON

The most common mistake made when visitors reach Bluffton, and it is often made, is to make too much of the place, to think that you've missed something that was "there." Well, if you spent an hour along its quiet, small grid of streets looking through the bramble and old fences at some of its wonderful 19th-century houses, visited the church and gazed out across its bluff, stepped into a few shops, perhaps hit the dead-end that is actually the ramp to the town boat landing, you've done it. Really.

Why bother? For one thing, Bluffton is one of the Lowcountry's last, true cul-de-sacs. It ain't going nowhere. It is absolutely not bothered by your coming or going, either. There are a couple of "Historic" this-and-that signs nailed up, it is true, but what you thought it ought to have been and whether or not it ever becomes that scrubbed-up, idealized version of itself is of no matter. Tiny Bluffton has all the charm of a wonderful, barefoot kid who is not going to live up to some schoolmarm's idea of his "potential" — it's as imaginative, sassy, and good-looking, too. It makes Hilton Head look like the teacher's pet.

### VISITING BLUFFTON

From Beaufort (about 35 minutes) follow Hwy. 21 to Hwy. 170 and continue as if you were going to Hilton Head, across the Broad River Bridge until the intersection with Hwy. 278. Turn left on Hwy. 278 and about four miles ahead, exit right at the Hilton Head sign and loop around. After a couple of miles, you will see Hwy. 46 marked as a right turn. Take it into Bluffton.

From Hilton Head, cross the bridge on Hwy. 278. Turn left on Hwy. 46 and follow it to Calhoun Street.

Bluffton was a summer community of island planters, and in 1863 it was nearly burned to the ground by Union troops. Ten antebellum buildings remain; another 16 or so houses were built after the Civil War. Taken together, they give a view of classic Lowcountry village life. Far from extravagant, they are nonetheless suffused with a sense of form appropriate to the landscape and to their function as seasonal dwellings belonging to families who had most likely seen better days. It is worth the trip alone to see the *Church of the Cross* on Calhoun St., an unpainted wooden church (circa 1857) with beautiful interior detailing, original pews, and Gothic-style windows.

A complete, self-guided walking tour takes about two hours — houses are marked by plaques, but not all are visible from the street. One book will help you appreciate them. It is: *No. II A Longer Short History of Bluffton, South Carolina and its Environs* produced by the Bluffton Historical Preservation Society (843-757-3650; P.O. Box 742, Bluffton, SC 29910). The price is $9.95. It includes historic essays and descriptions of homes, a map, and wonderful photographs. The biggest day of the year is the Saturday before Mother's Day:

Bluffton's Village Festival, a loose gathering of vendors of all sorts and fine local artists.

Some sites of interest in Bluffton are the working studio of potter *Jacob Preston* (843-757-3084; Church St. off Hwy. 46; Tues.–Sat. or by appointment) and the large gallery at *Crossroads Fine Art & Framing* (843-757-5551; #8 Town Center) which features work in many media by local and regional artists. *Eggs 'n Tricities* (843-757-3446; Calhoun St.), which is located in an old filling station, has funky furniture outside and inside, and sells everything from 1940's era lamps and linens, to contemporary tableware. *The Store* (843-757-3855; Calhoun St.) covers some of the same ground with similar esprit. *Antiques and The Garden* (Hwy. 46) offers prints, porcelain, silver, rugs, and furniture — some American, some English — chosen with a sense of what fits in the big new houses at the resorts as well as the real old ones. The shop represents the second generation of the old *Stock Farm Antiques* (843-757-8046) and Laura Barrett, whose firm, May River Designs (843-757-6630) offers complete design services and, more casually, excellent design advice. If you'd prefer to dig for your treasures, try your luck at *The Bluffton Trading Barn* (843-757-4247; Hwy. 46); *Toy Closet/Bluffton Antique* (843-757-7488; Hwy. 46); or *Another Man's Treasure* (843-757-8498), consignment / antique shops that carry a little bit of everything. *The LaRoche Collection* (843-757-5826; 51 Pine View Rd., May River Plantation) is located on the outskirts of the village; if you're interested in Southern contemporary folk art, call for an appointment. Louanne LaRoche is a private dealer who has been collecting in the field for more than 20 years.

Locals eat at the *Squat & Gobble* (843-757-4242; Hwy. 46 and at the *Copper Kitchen* (843-815-4557; Hwy. 46) for homestyle meals. Another restaurant nearby, though hardly in the same category, is *Cafe at Belfair* (843-757-7818; Sheridan Park, Hwy. 278). Lunch and dinner is served daily except Sunday. (Dinner begins at 5:30, which is a bonus for travelers who have been touring all day). An excellent meal for two at lunch, with beverage runs about $30. Grilled seafood, duck confit, chicken livers, sweetbreads, and elegant pastas are among some of the entrees. Reservations highly recommended.

# CHAPTER SIX

# Courts, Courses, Sails, and Sand

## HILTON HEAD

The Hilton Head Island that a visitor sees today is a far different place from what it was 25 years ago. It represents a startling change — in landscape, population, commerce, and traffic — to those who, in the past, were accustomed to seeing growth in their region come slowly — if it came at all. It is the Lowcountry's boom town, envied for its tax base, business opportunities, recreational resources, and political muscle, scrutinized as an example of the balance

Wade Spees

*The Harbour Town lighthouse and marina at Sea Pines are the symbols of the widely copied "resort- plantation" culture of Hilton Head Island.*

between careful planning and stupendous growth. Its popularity caused the mayor to remark recently: "We're just trying to keep from getting run over."

Unlike the rest of the Lowcountry, Hilton Head is a place of condensed pleasure: in one day, a visitor can enjoy a range of activities that might have taken a week's vacation to savor in the past, had even the possibilities existed. The island is twelve miles long and five miles wide, shaped like a boot. It's on the Intracoastal Waterway, so there's river, ocean, and marsh access, and a mild year-round climate. Shops, tennis courts, golf courses, and restaurants prosper and proliferate. It's a pretty place, too, with groomed and glossy neighborhoods. The commercial districts are discreetly screened from view and even the busiest thoroughfare, Highway 278 (a.k.a. William Hilton Parkway), lacks neon signs. It's easy to understand why more than 1.8 million visitors come every year.

Until about 1960, soon after a bridge linked Hilton Head to the mainland, the island's history resembled that of its Sea Island neighbors. First settled by

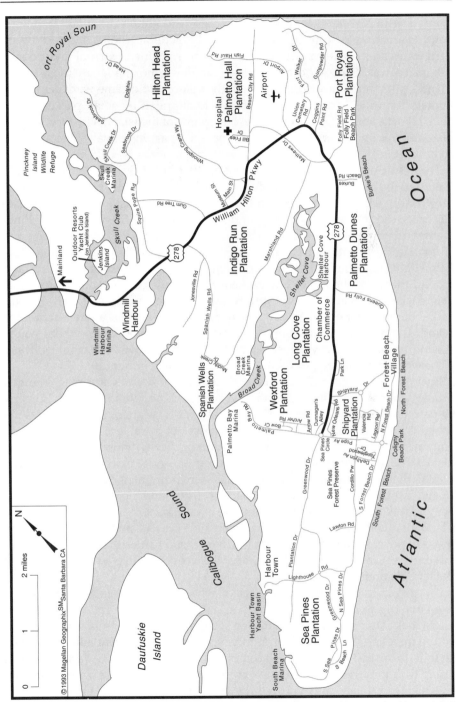

Courtesy of The Hilton Head Island Chamber of Commerce (used by permission)

# HILTON HEAD ISLAND

planters with slaves who raised rice, indigo, and cotton on about 16 plantations, later occupied during the Civil War by Federal troops, and faced with hard times and isolation after that, the island remained as rural and poor as any place was. The African-American families who made up most of the island's population farmed and fished; the visitors who came were gentleman hunters from the north. Transportation was supplied by small packet steamers, sailboats, and barges. (For the best overview of the island's history, stop by *The Museum on Hilton Head Island* where a 4-part historical videotape runs continuously.)

The resort and residential development that began in earnest in the early 1960s led to the "plantation" layout that orders the island's geography today. Most resort activities are based in those original subdivisions, which are usually accessed by security gates and called private. They are: Sea Pines Plantation, Shipyard Plantation, Palmetto Dunes, Port Royal Plantation, and Hilton Head Plantation. Others include Spanish Wells Plantation, Indigo Run, Palmetto Hall, Windmill Harbour, Long Cove, and Wexford. Within and around them are the dozens of golf courses, tennis courts, and marinas that define island recreation. Stores and restaurants are usually gathered in malls and shopping centers; many smaller residential areas lie scattered across the island. If you venture more than a short bike ride away from where you're staying, be sure to carry an island map. It's easy to overlook a turn-off in a place where strict design standards keep signage to a minimum.

Even as the geography has changed (much of it literally sculpted into golf courses), so have the island's residents. Today the population by race is nearly 90 percent white, by age nearly 30 percent over 60 years old. There are established schools and churches that didn't exist 30 years ago, and an excellent daily newspaper, *The Island Packet*. Continuing development and a changing cast of visitors give Hilton Head the feeling of a new place. In addition, Del Webb's Sun City Hilton Head, a new 6,500-acre retirement community just off-island, is making an enormous impact on the island's economy, traffic, and demographics. For a contrasting sense of timelessness, you must seek out the island's authentic Lowcountry character: its vistas of marsh and ocean, the flocks of pelicans that dive for fish, the loggerhead turtles that lay their eggs in the dark, the whistling songbirds, and the groves of live oak and pine that shelter deer and dove.

As you plan, you might want to decide what, if any, particular quality you'd like your trip to have. If you think you only want to play golf or tennis, you might look into options in the **Lodging** section for "stay-and-play" packages. If you're traveling with friends or family, you may want to rent a house or villa (a fully-furnished unit in a condominium complex). If you decide upon a resort, you may not need a car — most resort amenities are within walking and biking distance, and you will be fetched at the airport. An island-wide bike trail system continues to be expanded and upgraded.

The high season starts with the big tennis and golf tournaments hosted at Sea Pines Plantation in March and April. May and early June can be a quiet time before the crowds of summer, as can the fall, right up to Thanksgiving. When the island is crowded, however, you can expect traffic tie-ups and lines everywhere. Inter-island trips can take easily three times as long, and getting off-island during morning or evening rush-hour is a war of nerves. Some of the congestion has been alleviated by the Cross Island Expressway, a new toll road.

## LODGING

*Oceanfront hotels dominate some sections of the beach: the convenience, view, and cool breezes can't be beat.*

Wade Spees

The development boom on Hilton Head Island has brought more variety to lodging choices. Whatever your budget or the size of your group, you will find a place that suits.

There are more than 3,000 hotel and motel rooms and 6,000 rental units, including cottages, houses, and villas scattered across the island, from sites on or near the beach to those around golf courses, marinas, lagoons, in residential subdivisions or low-rise housing complexes, even on the main highway. Another 1,000 units are dedicated to "timeshare" arrangements and may be available for rent, too. Some "vacation ownership" properties offer weekend packages to attract potential purchasers: *Disney's Hilton Head Island Resort* (843-341-4080 / 800-341-2616) and *Marriott's Vacation Club International Grande Ocean Resort* (843-686-7394 / 800-473-6674) are among the newest.

Your accommodations may be elegant or simple; offer as much or as little privacy as you wish; come with or without kitchens; lie within walking distance, or not, from the beach and recreational amenities.

Rates vary from as little as $60 per night (off-season) for an economy motel room to as much as $6,000 per week for a luxurious oceanfront home with a swimming pool. The range reflects differences in size and location — oceanfront is premium; resort privileges add to the price — and also the time of year: summer is the most expensive season, followed by spring (especially late March and April, the time of the *Family Circle Tennis Tournament* and the *MCI Heritage Golf Classic*). The fall brings ideal golfing conditions, so prices can stay high through mid-October. In the winter months, rates can be half what they are in the high season. Like many resort areas, Hilton Head adds an accommodations tax to lodging bills, and some establishments place a surcharge on credit-card payments. Ask for an estimate of your total bill when you are booking.

Whatever accommodation you choose, inquire about special rate packages or coupons offered for restaurants, health clubs, or shops. Many hotels have discounts for golf and tennis; some have family plans, including activities for kids. In larger hotels, children often stay for free. Lodgings that are not located in private resorts often have arrangements to allow you access to some of their recreational facilities.

The easiest way to make reservations in a hotel or motel is to call directly. To inquire about home and villa rentals, call a property management company. Central reservation agencies can give you a sense of the whole picture, and they may be especially helpful in designing a package tailored to your specific interests. If you're interested in camping, look into the two recreational vehicle parks listed under **Recreation**, later in this chapter. If you're staying on a boat, see the section on Marinas, also in the **Recreation** listings.

The following rates are for one night's stay, per person, double occupancy. They do not include taxes, surcharges, or any special recreation/entertainment discounts. Prices quoted are for high season accommodations. Note that the rates for Luxury Accommodations are *at least* in the "Very Expensive" category: they can easily run to $260 per night.

### Rates

| | |
|---|---|
| Inexpensive | Up to $55 |
| Moderate | $55 to $75 |
| Expensive | $75 to $150 |
| Very Expensive | $150 and up |

### Credit Cards

| | |
|---|---|
| AE — American Express | DC — Diner's Card |
| CB — Carte Blanche | MC — MasterCard |
| D — Discover Card | V — Visa |

## LUXURY HOTELS

**CROWNE PLAZA
RESORT**
843-842-2400 /
800-334-1881.
In Shipyard Plantation.
Price: Very Expensive.
Credit Cards: All major
cards.
Handicapped Access: Yes.

A recently renovated 340-room oceanfront luxury hotel with full concierge service, two restaurants, and a popular lounge for evening entertainment. Pools, golf course and putting green, tennis courts, health center, sailing, and water sports all on site.

**HILTON RESORT**
843-842-8000 /
800-845-8001.
In Palmetto Dunes.
Price: Very Expensive.
Credit Cards: All major
cards.
Handicapped Access: Yes.

A luxury hotel that claims the largest rooms on the island — 560 sq. ft. each — with private balconies and kitchenettes. At the oceanfront setting there's an adults-only pool and a family pool, whirlpools, and a fitness center. Activities for kids (4–16) can be arranged for an additional charge — even at night. Restaurants and nightclubs within the complex.

**HYATT REGENCY**
843-785-1234 /
800-233-1234.
In Palmetto Dunes.
Price: Very Expensive.
Credit Cards: All major
cards.
Handicapped Access: Yes.

The largest hotel on the island, with 505 rooms, indoor pool, Olympic-sized outdoor pool, and children's pool. Health club available to guests, as are tennis and golf privileges, sailboat and bicycle rental, and lots of beachfront. Several restaurants offer both formal and casual poolside dining. Children's program (additional fee) available weekends year-round; daily in summer.

**MAIN STREET INN**
843-681-3001 / 800-471-3001.
2200 Main St.
Price: Very Expensive.
Credit Cards: All major
cards.
Handicap Facilities: Yes.

Probably the only place on Hilton Head (except a private home) that is high-end, quiet, and not a beach resort. It offers 34 luxury rooms, an outdoor lap-pool and hot tub, and lounge areas with fireplaces, where, depending on the time of day, breakfast, tea, dessert, and coffee are laid out. The European spa offers skin-care treatments and more. The rates, which are among the island's highest, are reduced from mid-November to March.

**WESTIN RESORT**
843-681-4000 / 800-937-8461.
http://www.westin.com
At Port Royal Plantation.
Price: Very Expensive.

Often considered the most luxurious of the island's oceanfront resort hotels, Westin Resort is praised for its Sunday brunch, the elegant decorations hung for the annual "Twelve Days of Christmas" celebration, the rooms with balconies,

Credit Cards: All major
    cards.
Handicapped Access: Yes.

and a good childrens' program. By day, there are all the standard excellent amenities; by night, light entertainment and dancing.

## SMALLER HOTELS

**BEST WESTERN OCEAN
    WALK SUITES**
843-842-3100 /
    800-528-1234.
36 S. Forest Beach Drive.
Price: Expensive.
Credit Cards: All major
    cards.
Handicapped Access: Yes.

A 140-room hotel featuring rooms with kitchenettes, mini-refrigerators, and cable television. Complimentary Continental breakfast, two pools, and beach access directly across the street.

**HAMPTON INN**
843-681-7900 /
    800-752-3673.
1 Dillon Rd.
Price: Moderate.
Credit Cards: All major
    cards.
Handicapped Access: Yes.

Most convenient motel to the airport; 124 rooms; shopping nearby at Port Royal Plaza. Swimming pool, complimentary breakfast, and fitness room.

**HOLIDAY INN
    OCEANFRONT**
843-785-5126 /
    800-423-9897.
Forest Beach Dr. at Coligny
    Circle.
Price: Expensive.
Credit Cards: All major
    cards.
Handicapped Facilities:
    Yes.

The island's most popular public-access beach is at your doorstep, and there's plenty of people-watching at the beachside snack bar. Outdoor pool and rock music during the summer months.

**RADISSON SUITE
    RESORT**
843-686-5700 /
    800-333-3333.
12 Park Lane, in Central
    Park.
Price: Expensive to Very
    Expensive.
Credit Cards: All major
    cards.
Handicapped Facilities:
    Yes.

Each of the 156 suites features a fully-equipped kitchen and some suites have wood-burning fireplaces. Complimentary Continental breakfast buffet. A recreation area includes basketball, volleyball and tennis courts, pool, Jacuzzi hot tub, jogging trails, and a playground. Free shuttle to the beach four times daily.

**SOUTH BEACH MARINA INN**
843-671-6498 /
800-367-3909.
In Sea Pines Plantation.
Price: Expensive to Very
Expensive.
Credit Cards: AE, D, MC,
V.

Located in a New England-style marina village in Sea Pines Plantation, this 17-room inn sits above waterfront shops and restaurants. The rooms are condominium suites with living and dining rooms and kitchenettes, overlooking the courtyard or marina. The inn has a Cape Cod feeling: throw rugs, brass beds, hardwood floors. Tennis, water sports, restaurants, and the beach close by.

## BUDGET CHOICES

Each of these national chain motels of approximately 100 rooms has a swimming pool and is close to inexpensive restaurants or shopping areas.

**FAIRFIELD INN** (843-842-4800 / 800-228-2800; 9 Marina Side Dr. at William Hilton Parkway south of Palmetto Dunes Resort).

**HOLIDAY INN EXPRESS** (843-842-8888 / 800-465-4329; 40 Waterside Dr.).

**RED ROOF INN** (843-686-6808 / 800-843-7663; 5 Regency Parkway).

**SHONEY'S INN** (843-681-3655 / 800-367-3909; Hwy. 278 at Main Street Village).

## VACATION PROPERTY RENTALS

Most vacation rental properties are concentrated on the south end of the island in Sea Pines Plantation, Shipyard Plantation, South Forest Beach, and Palmetto Dunes Resort. Several villa rental complexes are located mid-island on or near Folly Field Beach. The northern half of the island is geared mainly to permanent residents; the island's other private communities do not generally permit short-term rental programs.

Villas and homes usually rent by the week, but nightly rates are available. The least expensive summer rates are about $595 per week, which can buy you a small villa outside a plantation more than one-half mile from the beach. In 1998, about $3,000 per week in the summer would secure an oceanfront home with pool. From November to March, rates drop substantially.

Most rental companies manage properties in a variety of sizes, shapes, and locations. A desirable vacation rental would offer free swimming, free or discounted tennis, discounts on golf, and should be within walking distance of the beach. Some offer dining and shopping discounts, too. Before you make your final decision, you might consider where you want to be and what it is you wish to do. You need not pay premium oceanfront prices if you're going to be on the links all day.

Before you sign a rental agreement, make sure you understand policies regarding deposits, refunds in the event of cancellation, times of arrival and departure, and charges, if any, for cleaning services. If you have special needs — handicap-accessible or non-smoking rooms, cots or cribs for children — alert the agent from the start. The agencies listed below are just some of many.

**Hilton Head Island Beach and Tennis Resort** (843-842-4402 / 800-475-2631) Located at Folly Field, a 200-unit oceanfront villa complex with 10 tennis courts, two pools, restaurant, and pool bar.

**Island Getaway Rentals** (843-842-4664 / 800-476-4885) Beachfront and ocean-oriented homes and villas, mostly in Palmetto Dunes. Golf packages for more than 20 courses. Website: http://www.islandgetaway.com.

**Lancaster Resort** (843-686-6008 / 800-845-7017) This established independent management company has more than 200 rental properties from Sea Pines to mid-island. Fairway views in Sea Pines, oceanfront homes on residential North Forest Beach and in Palmetto Dunes. Website: http://www.hhisland rentals.com.

**Palmetto Dunes Resort** (843-785-1161 / 800-845-6130) Manages more than 500 villas and homes throughout the Palmetto Dunes Resort, including Shelter Cove Marina condominiums.

**Sea Pines Resort** (800-732-7463) One- to six-bedroom accommodations in private homes and villas in the island's most exclusive and well-known resort. Website: www.seapines.com.

**Shoreline Rental Co.** (843-842-3006 / 800-334-5012) More than 200 villas and homes, mostly ocean-oriented except for those at Sea Pines' Harbour Town. Website: http://www.shorelinerentals.com.

**Trident Rentals at Palmetto Dunes** (843-785-3447 / 800-237-8306) One- to four- bedroom villas and four-bedroom oceanfront homes, fairway, and harborfront villas included among 150-plus listings.

**Worthy Rentals** (843-785-5577 / 800-476-9674) Longtime family-owned property management company with about 350 homes and villas listed in Sea Pines Plantation. Golf discounts on 23 island courses.

## RESERVATION SERVICES

The following services can assist you with making reservations in advance of your trip:

**Condo Hotline** (843-785-2939 / 800-258-5852).

**Hilton Head Accommodations and Golf Hotline** (843-686-6662 / 800-444-4772).

**Hilton Head Central Reservation** (843-785-9050 / 800-845-7018). http://www.hiltonheadcentral.com.

**Vacations on Hilton Head** (843-686-3500 / 800-232-2453).

### RECREATIONAL VEHICLE PARKS

**Outdoor Resorts Motor Coach Resort** (843-785-7699 / 800-722-2365; 19 Arrow Rd.) Full hookups, 401 sites, six tennis courts, pool, man-made lake, shuffleboard, horseshoes, basketball, playground, laundry, bathrooms with tubs and saunas.

**Outdoor Resorts RV Resort, Marina, and Yacht Club** (843-681-3256 / 800-845-9560; Jenkins Island, north end of Hilton Head) Full hookups, 200 RV sites, bath houses, two pools, three tennis courts, laundry, exercise room, sauna, and whirlpool.

## DINING AND NIGHTLIFE

The restaurants included in the listing below are just some of the hundreds of places to eat or relax and listen to music. There are selections in every price category. Where you go may depend on whether you're traveling with children or not (if you're at a resort, ask the concierge about baby-sitting ser-

*Many Hilton Head restaurants capitalize on a sublime view and local, catch-of-the-day cuisine.*

Wade Spees

vices), whether you like rock bands, acoustic guitar, jazz or dance music, where on the island you're staying, and your budget. Fast-food and moderately-priced, national chain restaurants are well represented on Hilton Head, too.

The nightspots following the restaurant listings are, also, some of many. They deserve special mention at Hilton Head because they are so numerous and so much a part of its resort culture. Of course, what is popular one year may be B-list the next, but the descriptions are an attempt at an overview. Very few have cover charges; most serve at least finger food.

The price categories are the same described elsewhere in the guide, and represent per person expenses estimated without tax, tip, or bar beverages. In general, dining out is more expensive on Hilton Head than in similar restaurants elsewhere, although there are savings to be found in eating before the crowd (early-bird specials) or on a particular evening when the restaurant has an advertised special.

| Inexpensive | Up to $10 |
|---|---|
| Moderate | $10 to $20 |
| Expensive | $20 to $30 |
| Very Expensive | Over $30 |

**CAFE EUROPA**
843-671-3399.
Harbour Town.
Open daily.
Price: Expensive to Very
  Expensive.
Cuisine: Continental.
Serving: B, L, D.
Credit Cards: All major.

**L**ocated at the base of the Harbour Town Lighthouse, this longtime island restaurant looks over the island's classiest setting. The menu reflects high-style continental cuisine: veal, duckling, beef, and seafood. Lunch, featuring great omelettes, is especially nice outside in the marina setting. Reservations recommended.

**CAFE AT WEXFORD**
843-686-5969.
Village at Wexford.
Open daily.
Price: Expensive to Very
  Expensive ($7 minimum
  per person).
Cuisine: Country French.
Serving: L, D.
Credit Cards: All major.

**A** charming place that feels like Provence: interior brick walls, open kitchen, windows with real "cafe-curtains," accents of dried herbs and flowers. There's a small alcove just off the parking lot for al fresco dining. Brunch replaces lunch on the weekends.

**CHARLIE'S L'ETOILE
  VERTE**
843-785-9277.
1000 Plantation Center.
Open Tues.– Sat.
Price: Expensive to Very
  Expensive.
Cuisine: Continental.

**C**harlie Golson, a Savannah native, never went to cooking school and spent vacations in quiet Bluffton, but his years abroad amidst friends (who were mostly French chefs) seem to have fed his talent. His restaurant is often called the best on Hilton Head. Dinner features a dozen fish dishes (the pompano is a usually a sell-out) as well as a beef

Serving: L, D.
Credit Cards: All major.

and veal choice. Soup stocks are made up from scratch; the country bread is baked on bricks every day in the open kitchen; most of the wine list is French. The wait staff is knowledgeable without showing off. The two connecting dining rooms can be noisy when full. Share a gorgeous salad at lunch and don't pass up homemade desserts. Reservations highly recommended.

**GIUSEPPI'S**
843-785-4144.
Shelter Cove.
Open daily.
Price: Inexpensive.
Cuisine: Italian.
Serving: L, D.
Credit Cards: AE, MC, V.

Creative pizza (tomato-less sauce, two dozen toppings), beer and wine, table service indoors or out. Locally very popular. Also offers island delivery.

**HILTON HEAD BREWING COMPANY**
843-785-2739.
Hilton Head Plaza.
Open daily.
Price: Moderate.
Cuisine: American.
Serving: L, D.
Credit Cards: AE, MC, V.

The island's only microbrewery, with a good selection of bar food and pizza. Tends to be a later-night kind of place, with crowds coming after 8 p.m. No reservations. Hearty, friendly atmosphere.

**HILTON HEAD DINER**
843-686-2400.
Open daily, 24 hours.
Price: Inexpensive.
Cuisine: American.
Serving: B, L, D.
Credit Cards: All major.

Recently opened, the diner updates the classic American roadside eatery. Breakfast is served all the time — but there are big sandwiches, dinner entrees (with potato, salad, and vegetable) and beer and wine available, too. Coffee, of course, and desserts from the cold case.

**HUDSON'S SEAFOOD**
843-681-2772.
Squire Pope Rd.
Open daily.
Price: Moderate.
Cuisine: Seafood.
Serving: L, D.
Credit Cards: AE, DC, MC, V.

Large, informal family restaurant, one of the first ones on the island, in a rustic setting overlooking the Intracoastal Waterway on the docks at Skull Creek. Lunch is served in the Oyster Bar. Entrees include fresh local seafood like crab, shrimp (fried, sautéed, boiled) and blackened and stuffed specials, and even a steak for landlubbers. No reservations — it can get crowded on summer nights.

**JULEP'S**
843-842-5857.
Gallery of Shops, near Sea Pines Circle.

A kind of restaurant made popular by young New South professionals, who flock here. Basic southern foodstuffs meet Continental tradi-

Open: daily.
Price: Expensive to Very
　Expensive.
Cuisine: Upscale Southern.
Serving: D.
Credit Cards: AE, MC, V.

tion: bourbon and beef, peanut and roast pork, cornmeal pancakes. Formal setting with white tablecloths and fresh flowers. Reservations recommended.

**MARKET STREET**
843-686-4976.
Coligny Plaza.
Open daily.
Price: Inexpensive.
Cuisine: Mediterranean.
Serving: B, L, D.
Credit Cards: AE, MC, V.

If on a starry summer night you've decided to walk the beach near the Coligny Beach access point and hear Greek music, you must be nearby. Come back after your walk to enjoy informal grill food — gyros, pita wraps — or Greek specialties like moussaka, dolmati, and spanakopita.

**MIKIM'S**
843-842-2455.
71 Pope Ave.
Closed Sunday.
Price: Inexpensive.
Cuisine: American.
Serving: B, L.
Credit Cards: All major.

Robust salads and specialty sandwiches are loaded up with the best quality meat and fresh mozzarella. Save room for homemade desserts and milkshakes or Hilton Head Ice Cream. For a hearty deli, it has a tidy, comfortable, tea-shop quality to it.

**OLD OYSTER FACTORY**
843-681-6040.
Marshland Rd.
Open daily.
Price: Moderate to
　Expensive.
Cuisine: Seafood.
Serving: D.
Credit Cards: All major.

One of the best locations for a restaurant on Hilton Head, overlooking Broad Creek and extensive marshes. Large bar area and very relaxed, seaside feel. Come here for happy hour (5 p.m. to 7 p.m.) when there are specials on oysters and crab legs. Very popular. No reservations.

**SAN MIGUEL'S**
843-842-4555.
Shelter Cove Marina.
Open daily.
Price: Inexpensive to
　Moderate.
Cuisine: Mexican.
Serving: L, D.
Credit Cards: All major.

After twenty years on Hilton Head, this cafe remains a reliable favorite. The patio, facing Shelter Cove Harbour, is friendly and informal, with live music on most nights. Superb place to watch the sunset and sip margaritas. It's popular, so you may be in for a wait.

**SIGNE'S HEAVEN
　BOUND BAKERY &
　CAFE**
843-785-9118.
Closed Sunday.
Price: Inexpensive.
Cuisine: American.

Founded in 1972 by an enterprising cook, nationally recognized many times since, and a regular stop for returning visitors and for residents who appreciate fresh, healthy, food. Here are salads and soups, many kinds of homemade bread and muffins, fabulous pastry, and desserts. The French

Serving: B, L.
Credit Cards: MC, V.

**STELLINI**
843-785-7006.
15 Pope Ave. Executive
   Park.
Closed Sunday.
Price: Moderate to
   Expensive.
Cuisine: Italian.
Serving: D.
Credit Cards: All major.

**TRUFFLES CAFE**
843-671-6136.
71 Lighthouse Rd.
Open daily.
Price: Inexpensive to
   Moderate.
Cuisine: American;
   Continental.
Serving: L, D.
Credit Cards: All major.

**WILD WING CAFE**
843-785-9464.
72 Pope Ave.
Open daily.
Price: Inexpensive.
Cuisine: Spicy American.
Serving: L, D.
Credit Cards: All major.

toast is probably an inch thick; the brownies and blondies even thicker. The cafe itself is very modest — it's the bakery display cases that aren't.

A top choice for transplanted New Yorkers and East Coast urbanites who miss their city's own Little Italy. Not a fancy setting, though nicely hidden, not a place to wear jeans. The emphasis is on the meal and conviviality. Two appetizers could be dinner, or choose from pasta, veal, chicken, or seafood prepared in a classic Italian way: Marsala, Piccata, Fra Diavolo, etc. Very good wine list. Reservations recommended.

Casual atmosphere, homemade soups, huge salads, great French bread sandwiches, fresh vegetables, and grilled entrees. Light meals like black bean cakes or smoked salmon are inexpensive, and you can order them at any time — there's continuous serving. The market is full of gourmet items; take-out, too. If you're staying anywhere in Sea Pines, Truffles will deliver.

Noisy and casual by design. Popular with the college crowd, and, if your kid will eat it, families, who like to come early. (There are un-spicy choices like roast chicken and hamburgers.) There are more than a dozen sauces for wings, very hot and less so, 35 brands of beer, a variety of munchies to share. Open to 2 a.m.

## NIGHTLIFE

The beat goes on and on at Hilton Head, and especially in summer, the crowds jam the dance floor. Check ahead for cover charges or drink minimums. The legal drinking age is 21; bars close at midnight Saturday unless special liquor licenses are in hand. The style is supremely casual.

**Big Rocco's** (843-785-9000; Central Park) A huge place, with a deli in one section, a lounge in another, and a large restaurant. Brightly colored walls give it a glamorous, big-city, feel. Live jazz nightly from 8:30. Known for dancing and the late-night bar food.

**Callahan's** (843-686-7665; New Orleans Rd.) Late-night pool and sports bar with 20 televisions and lots of patrons.

**Castaways** (843-686-2526; 55 New Orleans Rd.) Raw bar with dozens of kinds of fish and shellfish, including conch and alligator, if you're feeling adventurous.

**Cheryl's Piano Bar** (843-842-7227; 13 Heritage Plaza) A cafe/cabaret featuring local talent. Nice place to dance for an over-30 crowd.

**Coconuts Comedy Club** (843-686-6887; Heritage Square) The nation's best comedians perform here. Four to eight shows weekly starting at 9:30 p.m. After the acts, there's often a blues or jazz session, too. Cover charge.

**Frank's Clubhouse** (843-686-3388; Palmetto Bay Rd.) A sports bar that won't quit: darts, pool, shuffleboard, horse shoes, volleyball, etc.

**The Lodge** (843-842-8966; Hilton Head Plaza) It had to happen — a cigar bar on Hilton Head. Plus billiards, single-malt scotch, wines by the glass. Open daily to 2 a.m.

**Monkey Business** (843-686-3545; Park Plaza) Big, upscale dance club with nights devoted to 60's music, beach tunes, rock 'n roll, etc. Civilized atmosphere and bar scene.

**Quarterdeck** (843-671-2222; Harbour Town) Laid-back waterfront lounge which deserves to be called the island classic — since 1970. Peak periods include late afternoon, suppertime (kids welcome), and late night. Outdoor rocking chairs make sunset viewing a treat. Upstairs and downstairs bars; great nightly dancing to beach music and contemporary hits.

**Reilly's** (843-842-4414; Hilton Head Plaza) Irish pub in feel, sports-talk in the air. Very popular Friday happy hour for weary locals. Friendly, neighborhood-bar atmosphere.

**Two Eleven Park Wine Bar & Bistro** (843-686-5212; 211 Park Plaza) Close to the movies, so it's a great place for a late meal, including eggs and grits. Dozens and dozens of wines by the glass.

## CULTURE

As Hilton Head has grown, so has its arts community. It is infused with energy from new, young residents and cultivated by the many retired people hoping to recreate in their adopted home the range of cultural activities that interested them in the cities and towns they left behind. Check the Arts &

Entertainment section of *The Island Packet* for weekly listings.

A new addition to the cultural landscape is the *Self Family Arts Center* (William Hilton Pkwy., Shelter Cove; 843-842-2787), a top-notch visual and performing arts facility. Residents and visitors alike benefit from its 350-seat theater, gallery space, classrooms for continuing education, and offices, which gather under one roof the diverse elements of the arts community. Another is the month-long *Native Islander Gullah Celebration* (888-856-4982) which offers visitors a glimpse of African-American heritage by way of tours, art exhibitions, performances, and lectures.

## ART

**Hilton Head Art League** (843-671-9009; Sea Pines Center) A gallery with regularly scheduled shows of work by members and others.

**Self Family Arts Center** (843-686-3945; Shelter Cove).

## CINEMA

**Coligny Cinemas** (843-785-4468; Coligny Plaza) One screen.

**Main Street Cinemas** (843-785-5001; Park Plaza) Five screen complex.

**Northridge Ten Cinemas** (843-342-3800; 435 Wm. Hilton Pky.) Ten screens.

## DANCE

**Hilton Head Dance Theater** (843-785-5477; 24 Palmetto Business Park Rd.) Talented students from local schools and visiting companies perform on the Hilton Head Playhouse stage and at the Self Family Arts Center.

## HISTORIC SITES

Several sites dating as far back as the time of Native American settlements and covering the period of the Civil War are accessible to visitors. For more information and location maps, contact *Coastal Discovery, Museum on Hilton Head Island* (see address and hours below).

**Baynard Ruins** (Sea Pines Plantation) The remains of a plantation house and outbuildings first constructed circa 1800 can be seen on a short, self-guided walk. A well-written brochure available on site gives a fine introduction to its history and construction, and to cotton cultivation. The ruins are made of tabby, a popular homemade Lowcountry building material that resulted from the burning of oyster shells (to make lime), which were then mixed with whole shells, sand, and water. This is one of few sites where you can still see it.

**Coastal Discovery, Museum on Hilton Head Island** (843-689-6767; 100 William Hilton Parkway, Hilton Head Island, SC 29925) Recently established in its own building at the north end of the island, near the bridge, **Coastal Discovery** is an enormous addition to a place where so much is new. Archaeological digs have yielded a collection of more than 75,000 artifacts relating to the island's history and culture, some of which are on display in a small exhibition space. Efforts to record island life through oral history interviews are ongoing; solid scholarship produced a fine four-part videotape (which is shown at the museum) documenting early habitation, the years of slavery, Reconstruction and the decades of small farming, and the fishing, oystering, and timbering industries. The gift shop offers the widest and best selection of books on the Lowcountry of any place on Hilton Head Island. Call for reservations for any number of excellent off-site programs, including walking tours of the marsh, the beach, and other natural areas including historic sites; marine study cruises; bird-watching; and science and nature study for children. Museum hours are Mon.– Sat. 10–5, Sun. 12–5. Museum admission is a $2 donation. For the outdoor programs, a fee is charged, depending on the event. Call to reserve places.

**Fish Haul Plantation** (off Beach City Rd., near the county baseball complex) Only the chimneys of slave dwellings remain of what was once a thriving Sea Island cotton plantation. Federal troops camped here from the time of Union occupation in November, 1861.

**Fort Howell** (Beach City Rd.) A large earthwork built by the Union troops in 1864 to strengthen the defense of Mitchelville.

**Fort Mitchel** (Hilton Head Plantation) An earthwork fortification circa 1862, constructed as part of the island's defense system.

**Indian Shell Ring** (Sea Pines Forest Preserve) Native Americans occupied Hilton Head and other Sea Islands some 4,000 years ago, and left their mark in huge rings and shell middens. It is thought that this site represents the refuse of oyster shells piled behind each of many huts that stood in a small circle.

**Zion Chapel of Ease** (William Hilton Pkwy. at Mathews Dr.) A small chapel, built circa 1786 for the convenience of worshippers who lived too far from the Episcopal church at Beaufort, once occupied this site. The **Baynard Mausoleum**, circa 1846, within its cemetery is the largest antebellum structure extant on the island.

## MUSIC

**Hilton Head Jazz Society** (843-842-4457) The group sponsors formal and informal performances at various island sites on the first Sunday of each month.

**Hilton Head Orchestra** (843-842-2055; 10 Office Park Rd.) Performances of symphonic and popular music throughout the year, held in the First Presbyterian Church, 540 William Hilton Pkwy.

## THEATER

**Port Royal Clubhouse Dinner Theatre** (843-689-4653; Port Royal Plantation) Look here for performances by the Hallelujah Singers, a troupe that celebrates Gullah life on the Sea Islands.

**Self Family Arts Center** (843-842-ARTS; 888-860-ARTS; 14 Shelter Cove) The venerable Hilton Head Playhouse has evolved into a multifaceted arts center, which, in addition to theatrical performances, offers a performing-arts series with visiting artists, a visual-arts gallery with national exhibitions, community outreach programs, and more.

# RECREATION

In the last 15 years, Hilton Head has come into its own as a town that services full-time residents, but its identity still rests on its reputation as a place where visitors come to pursue golf, tennis, fishing, and water sports, and to enjoy the beach. The following listings offer some sense of the amazing range of activities the island has to offer.

## BEACH ACCESS

Twelve miles of gently sloping beaches define the island's ocean edge. They can be as wide as 600 feet at low tide, providing a hard surface for fat-tired bicycles. (For tidal information, tune into island cable television or check *The Island Packet*.) Although many entry points to the beach are restricted — behind private resort plantation gates — there are several public beach access points. The most popular are *Coligny Beach Park* (located at the end of Pope Ave.), *Folly Field Beach Park* (off Folly Field Rd.), and *Dreissen's Beach Park*

*Despite Hilton Head's popularity, its beaches are often uncongested spots for bike-riding and strolling.*

Wade Spees

(off Bradley Beach Rd.) All offer metered parking spaces ($.50 to $1 per hour) and Coligny and Dreissen have long-term lots where you can park for $4 a day. *Alder Lane* (off South Forest Beach Drive) and *Burke's Beach,* on the north end of the island near Folly Field, have limited parking. Within the plantations, the beaches are accessible by marked footpaths.

On some summer nights, it is possible to watch the amazing loggerhead turtle, an endangered species, crawl ashore and lay its eggs in nests it digs on the beach; or to see hundreds of loggerhead hatchlings make their way back to the ocean. Volunteer groups monitor the beach and sometimes move the eggs to higher ground or protected sites, away from tides and hungry raccoons. The turtles are slow-moving and docile, but chary: do not disturb them with light, or touch the nests. Just seeing these huge creatures is magical.

Dogs are not permitted on the beach from 10 a.m. to 5 p.m. from the beginning of Memorial Day weekend through Labor Day weekend. Motor vehicles, alcohol, glass containers, and nudity are not allowed. Fishing, boating, surfing, ball-playing etc. is prohibited in designated swimming areas. The beaches are patrolled by sheriff's deputies.

## BEACH ACTIVITIES: DOING THE DUNES

If you haven't brought your beach equipment with you, you can stock up at these shops near the Coligny and Alder Lane beach access points: *Coligny Kite and Flag Company* (at Coligny Plaza), *Great White Surf Shop* (at Heritage Plaza), *Heat Wave* (70 Pope Ave.). Larger items such as boogie boards, chairs and umbrellas, floats, Hobie Cat boats, bikes, and aqua cycles can be rented at the beach from *Shore Beach Service* (843-785-3494).

*Coastal Discovery,* a series of educational programs sponsored by *The Museum on Hilton Head Island* (843-689-6767), offers guided walks several days per week on the island's beaches. Each tour lasts about 90 minutes and explains the island's ecology, flora and fauna. Children will like learning about shells and hunting hermit crabs. In 1998, the prices were $8 adults, $5 children (free for those under 6). Call in advance to purchase tickets.

## BICYCLING

*Though it's adjacent to Hilton Head, the Pinckney Island Wildlife Refuge seems to be in another world: restful and quiet, a place of subtle shadings and natural textures.*

Wade Spees

You can rent bikes of all varieties in many locations, and most outlets offer island-wide pick-up and delivery. If you're traveling with youngsters, you'll be able to get baby-carriers, helmets, bikes with training wheels, baby "trailers" that hook on the back of bikes, and jogging strollers.

Public bike paths extend from the tip of North Forest Beach to the end of South Forest Beach, along Pope Ave., and up William Hilton Pky. to Squire Pope Rd. Bike paths also thread through the plantations. If it's not too windy, riding on a hard-packed beach is an exceptional pleasure.

Rental charges for bicycles vary by the hour, half-day, full day, or week. In 1998, you could expect to pay $5–$6 per hour; $10 per day or $20 to $30 per week. For information check the following outlets:

**All American Bikes** (843-842-4386).

**Bikes Plus** (843-671-5588).

**Harbour Town Bicycle** (843-785-6233).

**Hilton Head Bicycle Company** (843-686-6888).

**Island Cruisers** (843-785-4321).

**Pedals** (843-842-5522).

**South Beach Cycles** (843-671-2453).

## BIRD-WATCHING

Hilton Head still has some very quiet places for birds to nest and feed. According to the island's Audubon Society chapter, some 200 species of birds regularly visit, and in the last 10 years, more than 350 species have been sighted. Among the most distinctive "frequent flyers" are the snowy egret, great blue heron, white ibis, and osprey. Catch a glimpse of them for yourself during daylight hours at the following sites:

**Newhall Audubon Preserve** (Palmetto Bay Rd.).

**Sea Pines Forest Preserve** (843-842-1449; entrances at Greenwood Dr. and Lawton Dr. in Sea Pines Plantation; $5 admission per car to enter Sea Pines Plantation) This 400-acre site offers a self-guided walking tour, which takes 1–2 hours. There are also picnic areas with grills.

**Whooping Crane Conservancy** (Hilton Head Plantation) features a boardwalk and self-guided nature trail.

*Coastal Discovery* (843-689-6767) offers guided walks of the Forest Preserve and has a birding exhibit on display at its headquarters in the *Museum on Hilton Head Island* (100 William Hilton Parkway) For nearby, off-island sites, see the **Nature Preserves** heading in the *Savannah* and *Beaufort* Chapters.

## BOATING AND WATER SPORTS

For sailboat charters and bare-boat rentals, contact the companies listed below and also check the **Marina** section in this chapter. If you want to nurture a wilder streak, look into renting a jet ski, floating with a parasail, riding a wave-runner, or "sledding" on a rubber tube. Some companies have special lessons for kids, so ask.

**Action Watersports** (843-785-7368; Palmetto Bay Marina) Waverunners, motor boats (17 feet to 19 feet) and pontoon boats for rent.

**Breakwater Adventures** (843-689-6801; Hudson's Landing, Squire Pope Rd.) Runabouts, pontoon boats, and cruisers equipped with appropriate fishing gear, charts, and safety equipment. Licensed guides available. For the daredevil, there's parasailing, waterskiing, and waverunning. Also, kayak tours and dolphin-watch expeditions.

**Commander Zodiac** (843-671-3344; South Beach Marina) Sunfish, Hobie Cat and Prindle sailboats for rent, private lessons, and rides. Sailing school for youngsters to age 16. Visit the dolphins or Daufuskie Island in engine-powered rubber rafts.

**Harbour Town Powerboats** (843-363-2628; Sea Pines) Small pleasure craft (15 feet to 22 feet) for rent.

*The Intracoastal Waterway near Hilton Head Island is a main path for pleasure and transit and sheer beauty.*

Wade Spees

**H2O Sports Center** (843-671-4386; Sea Pines) Rentals for, and instruction in, parasailing, waverunning, kneeboarding, hydrosliding, waterskiing, and skurfing.

**Island Watersports** (843-671-7007; South Beach Marina) Power and sail boats for as many as 14 passengers, by the hour, half-day, or day. Guided private cruises, sailing lessons, sunset sails. Wave-runners and skis for rent.

## BOWLING

**Main Street Lanes** (843-681-7750; Main Street Village).

## CANOEING AND KAYAKING

Explore miles of Lowcountry waterways in a canoe or kayak, on your own or with a guided tour. No experience is necessary; all safety equipment and basic instruction is provided; kids are welcome. You may end up paddling out to a sandbar or into the web of coastal marshlands, along the *Okatie River* or in the waters around *Pinckney Island Wildlife Refuge*. *Awesome Expeditions* (843-842-9763; Shelter Cove Marina); *Breakwater Adventures* (843-689-6800; Hudson's Landing); *Cool Breeze Kayaking* (843-816-5959); and *Outside Hilton Head* (843-686-6996 / 843-671-2643) all offer a nice way to leave the world behind.

In 1998, a half-day rental and basic kayaking lesson cost about $30; rentals by the day about $55. Two-hour guided tours of local waters like Broad Creek, where you are likely to see lots of birds and fish in action, start at $35 per person; $17.50 for kids 12 and under; $48 for half-day tours; $60 for full-day. Longer tours run about $80–$100 per person, depending on the arrangements, food, and car travel time. The best place for information is: www.outside-hiltonhead.com.

## CRUISES

**Adventure Cruises** (843-785-4558; Shelter Cove Harbour) has several sightseeing outings, including trips to Daufuskie Island (land tour of historic sites costs extra), 90-minute "dolphin watch" cruises, evening shark trips, and sunset dinner cruises. In 1998, the cost for the Daufuskie cruise was $15 for adults, $7.50 for children; the daytime dolphin watch was $16 for adults, $6 for kids.

**Calibogue Cruises** (843-785-8242; Freeport Marina) A big, two-level, fully outfitted power boat (snack bar on board) travels to Savannah or Daufuskie Island for day trips — leaving you on land for four hours of exploring, or even a Daufuskie cookout. Land transportation and tours are available, at extra cost.

**Cheers** (843-671-1800; Shelter Cove Harbour) Two-hour cruises daily and at sunset aboard a 47-foot luxury sailing yacht. In 1998, prices were from $18 for adults; from $12 for children. Sunset cruises are $20 for adults, $15 for children under 12.

**Drifter Excursions** (843-363-2900; South Beach Marina) Sunset cruises; a morning kid's cruise in which children throw a cast net for shrimp, pull crab pots, and spot dolphins; and a fully-narrated dolphin watch cruise. Trips last approximately two hours. Prices in 1998 started at $15 for adults, $7 for kids. Reservations required.

**Eco-Adventures** (843-785-7131; Palmetto Bay Marina) Dolphin watch tours, kayak tours, boat-and-kayak trips to outlying islands (including a buffet lunch), and sunset/fireworks cruises. Emphasis on interactive experience and understanding. Adults $10–$58; kids $10–$30.

**Flying Circus** (843-686-2582; Palmetto Bay Marina) is a fast-moving catamaran offering 2-hour daylight and sunset cruises for a maximum of six passengers. Tickets are $25. **Pau Hana,** a larger catamaran, can carry 49 passengers. Prices are $13–$15 for kids under 12; $18–$20 for adults.

**Spirit of Harbour Town** (843-842-7179; Harbour Town) Narrated cruises, an enclosed dining room, air conditioning— a deluxe way to spend a sunset dinner, a commute to Savannah or evening fireworks. Reservations required. Adults: $39–$55; kids $20–$30.

**Sport Crabbing and Dolphin Watch** (843-689-6558; Shelter Cove Marina) Take a two-hour trip on the comfortable, covered, *Crabber J II* and cast for crabs in the calm waters of Broad Creek. Adults $14; kids $10.

**Stars & Stripes** (843-842-7933; Harbour Town) This is the 12-meter America's Cup yacht, 65 feet long and powered by the wind in 2,000 square feet of sail. A unique cruise.

**Vagabond Cruises** (843-842-4155; Harbour Town Marina) Dolphin-watch, sightseeing, sunset, and dinner cruises; kids' nights, and Daufuskie tours, on a big double-decked powerboat. Depending on the cruise, 1998 prices were adults, $10–$25; children $6–$15.

## FAMILY AMUSEMENTS

*To the Ducklings: "Make Way For People!"*

Wade Spees

If you're coming with your children to Hilton Head, a place richly endowed with simple pleasures, activities like beachcombing, bike-riding, flying a kite, taking a walk after supper, or taking in free child-oriented entertainment may make a great family vacation. *Island playgrounds* are located at **Harbour Town** (in Sea Pines; $5 admission), **Shelter Cove Harbour**, and the **Island Recreation Center** (20 Wilborn Rd. at the north end of the island) The Rec Center features a handicapped-accessible area with a swing for wheelchairs. Check newspaper listings to confirm schedules or find special family-oriented events. Some of the following listings may be of help on a rainy day, too.

**Coastal Zone Education Center** (843-837-4848; Sawmill Creek Rd., Bluffton) Call ahead for information about scheduled beach and marsh walks, and mini-classes in nature and ecology studies.

**Island Recreation Center** (843-681-7273; 20 Wilborn Rd.) A year round activity center with camps, clinics, and sports programs organized by the day, week, and month for children, teens, and adults. Check to see if events like bike races, fishing tournaments, rollerblading races, water carnivals or craft classes (among others) might coincide with your visit. Call ahead: registration may be required.

**Main Street Golf & Games** (843-689-3866; 4101 Main St.) It's all here, including: mini-golf, batting cages, basketball shoots, air hockey, pool tables, foosball, Ping Pong, arcade bowling, and table shuffleboard. You'll probably spend two hours trying everything out, then another hour getting everyone to leave. Cost of admission, which includes all games, is $5.95.

**Summer Concerts:** In the evening, family entertainers gather large audiences for free concerts and shows. Check the local paper for listings, and plan to arrive early to secure parking. In *Sea Pines Plantation* (under the Liberty Oak at Harbour Town) singers and guitarists perform nightly from 8 to 10 except Saturday. The audience sits on benches and kids are encouraged to participate. Family sing-alongs also take place Tuesday through Saturday at *Shelter Cove Harbour*, and once a week, usually Tuesday, there are fireworks. Various musicians, puppeteers, and clowns also turn up at *Coligny Plaza* (off Pope Ave.) each night to entertain families. At *South Beach Marina* (Sea Pines Plantation) you can enjoy music while the sun sets over the docks.

**Waterfun Park** (843-842-8108; 2 Tanglewood Dr.) Putt-putt golf course, three waterslides, arcade games, and a toddler's pool.

## FISHING

If you want to go fishing, it's easy to do, but have in mind the kind of experience you're looking for. There are many options: size of the boat, length of the day, level of challenge, location, number of anglers, type of catch, and, of course, the probability of success. (All but the last can be provided.) Fly fishing, the Lowcountry's up-and-coming sport, is also available. Boats are fully equipped with tackle, etc., and depart from several marinas for inshore waters, flats, artificial reefs, and the Gulf Stream. Potential catches include tarpon, marlin, and sailfish in the Gulf Stream; amberjack, shark, king mackerel, and bluefish closer to shore; and flounder, red drum, sea trout, and sheepshead in the coastal flats. In 1998, prices for four to six passengers for a half-day of fishing ran from about $250 to $325. Here are some suggestions.

**A Fishin' Mission** (843-785-9177; 45 Squire Pope Rd.) Join the Captain on one of four boats (from 20 feet to 45 feet) that are suited for all types of local fishing — from flat-water to the Gulf Stream.

**Atlantic Fishing Charters** (843-671-4534; Harbour Town Yacht Basin) Five large boats rigged with fish-finding equipment; fish at night for shark.

**Blue Water Charters** (843-671-3060; South Beach Marina) Trophy fishing and taxidermy services.

**Captain Fuzzy Davis** (843-689-5873; 145 Squire Pope Rd.) A well-known island fisherman and angling authority takes you on inshore and tarpon-catching charters.

**Desert Storm Fishing Charters** (843-681-3236; Skull Creek) Capt. James R. Maples offers half-day, most-of-the-day, and full-day trips on a 28-foot boat; catch-and-release is okay, too.

**Drifter** (843-363-2900; South Beach Marina) Four- and five-hour trips from $30 per person, with $5 discount for kids under 12. Shorter evening shark-fishing trips. The boat carries some 60 people; families welcome.

**Lowcountry Outfitters** (843-837-6100; Moss Creek Village, just off-island) A fine hunting and fishing (and cigar) emporium where serious practitioners often gather and swap stories. Guided fly-fishing and light tackle expeditions for one or two passengers on an open 18-foot boat are available. Equipment provided (or you can bring your own) as you search for redfish and speckled trout (late-October through late-April) or, at other times, ladyfish, spanish mackerel, jack crevalle, and bluefish. In 1998, prices for a half-day started at $200 per boat; $400 for a full day.

**Skipper** (843-785-4558; Shelter Cove Marina) A big boat for fishing or partying — or some of both. Offshore trips, specialized shark fishing, and shorter half-day trips available. In 1998, prices for adults started at $25; for kids, $20.

**Tammy Jane** (843-681-3922; Hudson's Landing) Trawl for shrimp with 40' nets and share the catch (boat carries 21 passengers.) Trips last about 4 hours; kids welcome. An experience popularized by Forrest Gump. Adults $25; under age $6, $20.

## FITNESS CENTERS

**Downtown Athletic Club** (843-842-4001; 22 Arrow Rd.).
**Hilton Head Health Institute** (843-785-7292; 14 Valencia Rd.).
**Island Nautilus Center** (843-681-5321; Northridge Plaza).
**Ladies Workout** (843-686-4930; Shipyard Galeria.).

## GOLF

There are more than 30 courses in the Hilton Head area; of these 22 are on the island itself. Most of the area's courses are open to the public and resort guests, though some are for members (and their guests) only. Even so, except for a handful of courses off the island, they are not public in the traditional sense of the word. They are located within private communities like Sea Pines and Shipyard Plantations, Palmetto Dunes Resort, and Port Royal Plantation, and may have dress codes and time limits. For courses in and around Beaufort — all of them less than an hour's drive from Hilton Head — check that chapter.

Reservations to secure tee times are important — some courses accept reservations from non-resort guests up to 90 days in advance, others just 30 to 60 days in advance. (It gets crowded — 800,000 rounds of golf are played annually at Hilton Head.) Unless noted, all courses are 18 holes. Appropriate dress calls for shirts with collars for men and no blue jeans, gym shorts, or jogging shorts.

### *Price Codes:*

Prices include greens and cart fee unless mentioned otherwise. Walking is permitted on several courses — check ahead for caddy help. Reduced rates available for resort guests. The rates listed, and range of price if there is one, are the two-tiered high-season rates — spring and fall. Summer fees are slightly less. By the low season — winter months — prices can drop by 40 percent. Rates are lower for afternoon or twilight play. Rates are lower for some combination-course or two-day golf packages. For an island golf guide, call 1-888-GOLF-ISLAND.

| | |
|---|---|
| Inexpensive | Up to $50 |
| Moderate | $51 to $64 |
| Expensive | $65 to $80 |
| Very Expensive | Over $80 |

### *Hilton Head Plantation*

**Country Club of Hilton Head** (843-681-4653) Par 72. Range: 5,373-yard ladies course to 6,919-yard champion course. Pro: Tim Eckstein. Price: Expensive.

**Oyster Reef Golf Club** (843-681-7177 / 800-728-6662) Rees Jones course. Par: 72. Range: 5,288 ladies course to 7,027 champion course. Pro: Mike Bartholomew. Price: Expensive to Very Expensive.

### *Indigo Run*

**Golden Bear Golf Course** (843-689-2200) Par 72. Range: 4,974-yard ladies course to 7,014-yard championship course. Pro: Bob Thomas. Price: Moderate to Expensive

### *Palmetto Dunes Resort*

**Arthur Hills Course** (843-785-1140) Par 72. Range: 4,999-yard ladies course to 6,651-yard champion course. Pro: Clark Sinclair. Price: Very Expensive.

**George Fazio Course** (843-785-1138) Named one of *Golf Digest's* 100 top American courses. Par 70. Range: 5,273-yard ladies course to 6,873-yard champion course. Pro: Bobby Downs. Price: Expensive.

**Robert Trent Jones** (843-785-1136) The lagoon system is a factor in 11 holes here. Par 72. Range: 5,425-yard ladies course to 6,710-yard champion course. Pro: Ken Conroy. Price: Expensive.

### *Palmetto Hall Plantation*

**Arthur Hills Course** (843-689-4100) Par 72. Range: 4,956-yard ladies course to 6,918 champion course. Pro: Bob Faulkner. Price: Expensive.

**Robert Cupp Course** (843-689-4100) Par 72. Range: 5,220-yard forward course to 7,079-yard tour course. Pro: Bob Faulkner. Price: Expensive.

### *Port Royal Plantation*

**Barony Course** (843-689-4653 / 800-234-6318) Par 72. Range: 5,253-yard ladies course to 6,530-yard champion course. Pro: Mike Beverly. Price: Moderate to Expensive.

**Planter's Row Course** (843-689-4653 / 800-234-6318) Par 72. Range: 5,126-yard ladies course to 6,520-yard champion course. Pro: Mike Beverly. Price: Moderate to Expensive.

**Robber's Row Course** (843-689-4653 / 800-234-6318) A Pete Dye renovation of a George Cobb course near what was Fort Walker, a Civil War camp. Par 72. Range: 5,000-yard ladies course to 6,642-yard champion course. Pro: Mike Beverly. Price: Moderate to Expensive.

### Sea Pines Plantation

*The world's pro golfers play the course at Sea Pines during the MCI Heritage Golf Tournament every spring.*

Wade Spees

**Harbour Town Golf Links** (843-363-4485 / 800-955-8337) The Heritage Golf Classic is played on this course, designed by Jack Nicklaus and Pete Dye, rated among the top 25 in the world. Par 71. Range: 5,019-yard ladies course to 6,912-yard "Heritage" course. Pro: John Farrell. Price: Very Expensive.

**Ocean Course** (843-363-4485 / 800-955-8337) First course on the island, redesigned in 1995 by Mark McCumber. Par 72. Range: 5,325-yard ladies course to 6,906-yard champion course. Pro: John Richardson. Price: Expensive to Very Expensive.

**Sea Marsh Course** (843-363-4475 / 800-955-8337) Par 72. Range: 6,619-yard ladies course to 6,515-yard champion course. Pro: John Richardson. Price: Expensive.

### Shipyard Plantation

**Shipyard Golf Club** (843-689-4653 / 800-234-6318) Par 72, 27 holes. A favorite of the senior PGA Tour. Range: 5,391-yard ladies course to 6,830 champion course. Manager: Ted Ketchum. Price: Expensive.

### Off-Island

**Executive Golf Club** (843-837-6400; Hwy. 278, Bluffton, at entrance to Hilton Head National) Nine holes, par 30, lit for night play. Range: 1,452-yard "grey" course and 1,656-yard "maroon" course. Price: Inexpensive.

**Hilton Head National** (843-842-5900; Hwy. 278, Bluffton) Par 72, Gary Player-designed course. Range: 4,649-yard course to 6,779-yard champion course. Pro: Jeff Osler. Price: Moderate.

**Island West Golf Club** (843-689-6660; Hwy. 278, Bluffton) Par 72. Range: 4,948-yard ladies course to 6,843-yard champion course. Dir. of Golf: Arthur Jeffords. Price: Inexpensive to Moderate.

**Old South Golf Links** (843-785-5353 / 800-257-8997; Hwy. 278, Bluffton) Par 71/72. Range: 4,776-yard ladies course to 6,772-yard champion course. Pro: Brady Boyd. Price: Inexpensive to Moderate.

**Rose Hill Country Club** (843-842-3740; Rose Hill Plantation, Hwy. 278, Bluffton) Par 72. Range: 5,099-yard ladies course to 6,808-yard champion course. Pro: Matt Minasi. Price: Inexpensive to Moderate.

**Sun City/Okatie Creek Golf Club** (843-705-4653 / 800-978-9783; Sun City Hilton Head, Hwy. 170). The first of three planned courses at this new resort, designed for the over-55 crowd. Five sets of tees per hole accommodate the skilled and less-skilled golfer. Par 72. Range: 4,763-yard forward course to 6,734-yard Okatie course. Director of Golf: Jeff Seman. Price: Inexpensive to Expensive.

## HORSEBACK RIDING

Call ahead for reservations. Small groups and families are welcome; all equipment is provided.

**Happy Trails Stables** (843-842-7433; Bluffton — behind Old South Golf Links) In 1998, 90-minute rides in and around the golf course and forest preserve were $25 for adults; $20 for ages 12 and under. Reservations suggested.

**Lawton Stables** (843-671-2586; 190 Greenwood Dr., Sea Pines) Seventy-minute walking trail rides for adults and kids over eight years old (unless they've had riding experience) through the 600-acre Sea Pines Forest Preserve are $30 per person; pony rides for the younger set are $5. Lessons (all levels) are $35 per half-hour and include preparation of the horse.

**Sandy Creek Stables** (843-689-3423; 102 Jonesville Rd.) Boarding, lessons, and trail rides along the edge of the marsh and in the woods.

**Sea Horse Farms** (843-681-7746; 34 Mitchelville Rd.) Unique, one-hour beach rides leave four times per day except Sunday. Riders must be 7 years old or older. $30 per person.

## IN-LINE SKATE RENTALS

**Outside Hilton Head** (843-686-6996; Shelter Cove or 843-671-2643; South Beach Marina) Individual and group lessons for beginners through advanced skaters from $20 per person; rentals $12–$20.

**Player's World** (843-842-5100; 105 Market Place) Rent Bauer skates for recreation, roller hockey, or trick skating, at $9 per hour or $15 per day. Safety equipment included.

## MARINAS

The Hilton Head area has 13 marinas that offer numerous boat rental facilities, transient berths, fishing charters, and services, such as dry-dock storage, launching ramps, fuel, showering facilities, ship's stores, and repair shops. The nine that are open to the public are listed below. Cost for berthing ranges from $.25–$1.50 per foot; or fees by the month. Charter fishing boats, small powerboats, sailboats, and yachts as long as 150 feet are berthed side by side, offering a striking example of the myriad ways residents and visitors choose to enjoy the water.

**Freeport Marina** (843-785-8242 / 800-398-7687; Daufuskie Island) The gateway to Daufuskie for large tour boats and the island touring headquarters. Golf-cart rental for transportation, restaurant, cookouts, gift shop, and marina store. Low tide draft: 15 feet.

**Harbour Town Yacht Basin** (843-671-2704 / 843-671-4534; Sea Pines Plantation) 85 slips accommodating boats up to 150 feet. Marina store, various types of boats for rent; tours, instruction, and cruises available. Near shops and restaurants in Harbour Town. Low tide draft: 8 feet.

**Hilton Head Marina** (843-681-3625; 18 Simmons Rd., off Marshland Rd.) 33 slips accommodating boats up to 100 feet. Ship's store with boat cleaning supplies and equipment. Charters and sightseeing, sailing instruction, and kayaking available. Low tide draft: 15 feet.

**Outdoor Resorts Yacht Basin** (843-681-3256; Jenkins Island at northern tip of Hilton Head) 101 slips, maximum boat length 70 feet. Amenities of Outdoor Resorts RV Park (see **Lodging** listing in this chapter) as well as charters, waterski rentals and instruction, ship's store. Low tide approach depth: 8 feet; 20 feet at dockside.

**Palmetto Bay Marina** (843-785-3910 / 800-448-3875; 164 Palmetto Bay Rd.) 140 slips, maximum length 85 feet. Marina store, boat repair, fishing and sailing charters, parasailing, and youth sailing program. Low tide draft: No limit.

**Schilling Boathouse** (843-681-2628; 405 Squire Pope Rd.) Dry stack only; maximum 33 feet. Ship's store; near restaurants.

**Shelter Cove Harbour** (843-842-7001; Palmetto Dunes Resort) 170 slips, maximum length 155 feet. Fish and tackle store, charters, cruises, rentals; rod and reel rental. In village-like area of shops and restaurants. Low tide draft: 9 feet.

**Skull Creek Marina** (843-681-4234; Hilton Head Plantation) 180 slips, maximum length 200 feet. Sailing charters and night fishing, restaurant and lounge, courtesy bike and van transportation. Low tide draft: 10 feet.

**South Beach Marina** (843-671-3577; Sea Pines Plantation) 100 wet slips, 20 dry slips, maximum length 35 feet. Tackle and bait shop, boat and motor repair, rentals, cruises, instruction, and junior sailing school. Restaurants and shops at the marina village. Approach depth at low tide: 3 feet.

## MINIATURE GOLF

A half-dozen courses (par 40 to par 65) featuring water-hazards, dog legs, and sand traps laid out in realistic settings. A great way to spend two hours. Most lit for night play. From $5.95 per adult.

**Island Putt & Drive** (843-842-9990; William Hilton Parkway at Folly Field Rd.).

**Legendary Golf** (Two locations: 843-686-3399; 900 William Hilton Pky. and 843-785-9214; 80 Pope Ave.).

**Main Street Golf & Games** (843-689-3866; 4100 Main St.).

**Pirate's Island Adventure Golf** (843-686-4001; William Hilton Parkway and Marina Side Dr.).

**Waterfun Park and Mini Golf** (843-842-8108; 2 Tanglewood Dr.).

## SCUBA DIVING

**Island Scuba Dive & Travel** (843-689-3245; 130 Mathews Dr.) Scuba gear, rentals, and instruction.

## TENNIS

There are more than 300 tennis courts — hard, clay, and even grass surfaces — on Hilton Head, spread through 19 clubs. Seven of them are open for public play: they are listed below. Call ahead for reservations — the staff may even be able to set you up with a game. Pros on site offer lessons, daily stroke clinics, and intensive camps year round; fully-stocked shops provide stringing services and sales of equipment, clothing, and accessories. Court rental fees in 1998 ranged from $15 to $22 per hour — usually with discounts for resort guests or visitors renting villas within the plantation. Many places offer reduced walk-on rates for midday play (12 to 4). Notable tournaments are the *Family Circle Magazine Cup* (for women, early April) and clay court championships for juniors and seniors.

*Tennis is a year-round sport at Hilton Head, where resorts feature clinics, national tournaments, and top-ranked professionals.*

Wade Spees

**Hilton Head Island Beach and Tennis Resort** (843-785-6613; 40 Folly Field Rd.) 10 hard, lighted courts.

**Palmetto Dunes Tennis Center** (843-785-1152; Palmetto Dunes Resort) 23 clay, 2 hard courts. Hard courts and six clay courts are lighted for night play.

**Port Royal Tennis Club** (843-681-3322; Port Royal Resort) 10 clay, 4 hard, 2 natural grass courts. Night play available on six courts.

**Sea Pines Racquet Club** (843-363-4495; Sea Pines Plantation) 23 clay, 5 hard. Hard courts are lighted for night play. Exhibition matches are frequently held during the season, and the Family Circle Magazine women's pro tournament held here.

**South Beach Racquet Club** (843-671-2215; Sea Pines Plantation) 11 clay courts, 2 lighted.

**Van der Meer Tennis Center** (843-785-8388 / 800-845-6138; DeAllyon Rd.) 28 courts: 25 hard, 3 clay. Night play available on 8 courts. The center is internationally-known for its rigorous teaching programs and camps for kids and pros, as well as serious players. The island's top youngsters often train here.

**Van der Meer Tennis University/Shipyard Racquet Club** (843-686-8804 / 800-438-0793; Shipyard Plantation) 20 courts: 11 clay, 9 hard. Night play on 8 courts.

## TOURING

If you're interested in exploring more of Hilton Head and the surrounding area, here are some suggestions. The towns of *Bluffton* and *Beaufort* are

*Hilton Head's neighbor, Daufuskie, still bears witness to the way Sea Island life used to be before the resorts.*

Wade Spees

easy day trips. (For detailed information on these destinations, see Chapter Five). Each has a historic area of old houses, as well as shops and restaurants. *Daufuskie Island* is served by tour boat operators who offer cookouts and on-shore touring options (see **Cruises** in the **Recreation** section). *Savannah* is about an hour away, and in a day you could tour the historic district, shop, have at least one meal, and be back in time for sunset over the marsh. A trip to *Charleston* requires a bit more time and planning, including approximately four hours by car round trip.

**Camelot Limousine and Tours** (843-842-7777) On and off-island transportation, personalized tours, maximum of six people per vehicle.

**Discover Hilton Head** (843-842-9217) Daily tours of the island by car.

**Executive Air Ltd.** (843-681-4705) can make arrangements for private flights over the area for up to five passengers. priced according to air time and destination.

**Gullah Heritage Trail Tours** (843-681-7066) Two-hour tours through 10 neighborhoods and to sites prominent in the island's African-American culture.

**Low Country Adventures** (843-681-8212 / 800-845-5582) Island and off-island tours in a 14-passenger tour van or 21-passenger bus, including day trips with a tour guide to the historic area of Charleston ( $65 per person). Door-to-door shuttle service to Savannah International is $24 one way, $44 round trip.

## SHOPPING

A s Hilton Head has grown, it has tried to minimize both the visual and physical impact of strip development along its major thoroughfare Hwy. 278 — the William Hilton Parkway. (You have to look hard to spot the fast-food outlets, for though they exist, their signs are required to be more tasteful here than elsewhere.) As a result of this wish to maintain some degree of natural landscape, the small shopping centers and larger, well-designed malls that have sprung up to serve 1.5 million visitors per year are self-enclosed destinations. They have their own plentiful parking, and a mix of tenants that includes restaurants, pizza and ice-cream counters, supermarkets, and boutiques. Here are some highlights.

*Harbour Town*, in Sea Pines Plantation, remains the only shopping area with a unique village character — in its case, rather Mediterranean in feel, located around the harbor basin, clustered near the lighthouse. It is worth paying the $5 per car entrance fee to Sea Pines to wander and browse, if not buy.

*Roadside fruit and vegetable stands on the road to Hilton Head provide the freshest, native grown, peaches, melons, greens, and cucumbers in the Lowcountry.*

Wade Spees

The *Mall at Shelter Cove* is a more conventional shopping center, anchored by big department stores. National chains like Banana Republic, Ann Taylor, Talbot's, and Polo/Ralph Lauren are represented. There is a food court and the mall is enclosed, making it a good rainy-day outing.

*Main Street Village* (north island, near Hilton Head Plantation), the *Village at Wexford, Sea Pines Center,* and *Shelter Cove Harbour* are smaller areas you might explore if you are staying in accommodations nearby. *South Beach Marina Village* and *Coligny Plaza* are especially good spots for finding beach-related souvenirs and inexpensive resort-wear.

In addition, there are three outlet malls: ***Shoppes on the Parkway*** and ***Pineland Mill Shops*** are on Hilton Head; just off the island is the ***Hilton Head Factory Stores 1 & 2***. Stores here offer bargains in every category, including housewares, toys, shoes, eyeglasses, children's clothing, linens, high fashion, and sportswear. Their inventories are large and well-organized; there's plenty of parking. Dozens of name-brand manufacturers are represented.

The tourist-based economy has also allowed many smaller specialty shops to flourish as they might not in a place where the permanent population numbers under 30,000. As a result, shopping trips can yield both the obvious and the offbeat: golf clubs and gifts as well as original art and collectibles. Here are some ideas.

## ART AND ANTIQUES

Some galleries have limited hours but welcome visitors by appointment. If you're interested in more than browsing, call ahead to check.

**Altermann & Morris** (843-842-4433; 38 New Orleans Rd.) A large selection of 19th and 20th century American representational art, including painting and sculpture. The gallery has locations in the South and West — large inventory.

**Antiques of Hilton Head** (843-785-3696; Village Exchange; Palmetto Bay Rd.) All sorts of small things, prints, quilts, furniture, and Victoriana. A good place to dig around.

**Barry Honowitz** (843-842-2400, ext. 7655; Crowne Plaza Resort, Shipyard Plantation) This artist creates the annual MCI Classic / Heritage of Golf lithograph, as well as many other golf-related lithographs and Lowcountry sketches.

**Blue Heron Gallery** (843-785-3788; Coligny Plaza) Sculptures in brass, copper, and verdigris; regional art with seaside themes; works on paper.

**Decorator's Wholesale Antiques** (843-681-7463; 1 Cardinal Rd.) Stripped pine furniture from Europe favored by the "shelter" magazines for beach houses. Also antiques with polished metal details.

**Endangered Arts Ltd.** (843-785-5075; South Island Square) The featured artist, Wyland, is responsible for murals of whales and dolphins that can be seen on the sides of buildings in cities across the country. His originals and limited editions, in many forms, are available here, as well as work of other artists specializing in natural landscape and wildlife themes.

**The Gilded Age Antiques** (843-750-7766; Hwy. 278) High-end antiques and many small Georgian and Edwardian era boxes.

**Guggenheim's** (843-785-9580; 20 Dunnagan's Alley) Antiques and collectibles, on consignment. A place you could get lucky.

**Harbour Art Gallery** (843-785-2787; Shelter Cove Harbour) Paintings and limited edition works of Beaufort, Savannah, and island scenes by artist R. Bolton Smith.

**Joe Pinckney Art Enterprises Ltd.** (843-681-5661; 15-I Airport Rd.) Original portraits and wildlife art.

**John Stobart Gallery** (843-671-2739; Harbour Town) Limited edition maritime prints; original oils, and watercolors. Ship models and sculptural sea animals.

**Moonshell Gallery and Artist Studio** (843-671-2262; 224 S. Sea Pines Dr.) Varied collection of works and styles, from impressionistic Lowcountry scenes to children's portraiture. Three artists work on site; others are represented by the gallery.

**Red Piano Art Gallery** (843-785-2318; 220 Cordillo Parkway) Lowcountry landscapes, sculpture, and fine art from the 19th and 20th centuries. A regular stop for collectors.

**Swan House Antiques** (843-785-7926; 7 Bow Circle) Quality rugs, china, silver, paintings and prints, small objects, and furniture. The best of the consignment shops.

## BOOKS AND MUSIC

**Audubon Nature Store** (843-785-4311; Village at Wexford) Field guides, children's guides on local flora and fauna.

**Author's Cafe & Bookstore** (843-686-5020; The Village at Wexford) A place to read and sip.

**Book Warehouse** (843-689-9419; Festival Centre) Remainders and contemporary books discounted in all categories.

**Christian Book Store** (843-681-3868; 5 Thompson St.) Religious and inspirational literature.

**Disc Jockey** (843-842-2844; Mall at Shelter Cove) Music in all formats; music videos, movies and accessories.

**Island Bookseller** (843-671-3773; Sea Pines Center) Adult and children's titles, local authors.

**Paperback Exchange** (843-842-5614; Village Exchange, Palmetto Bay Rd.) A wide and constantly changing selection of used books.

**Port Royal Bookstore** (843-689-9996; Port Royal Plaza) Big selection of books, tapes, CDs, magazines.

**Waldenbooks** (843-785-4301; Mall at Shelter Cove) Books for beach reading, children's section, history, cooking, and coffee-table books.

## CLOTHING

**A Shore Thing** (843-686-2330; South Beach Marina) Silk-screened tee-shirts and resort wear.

**Camp Hilton Head** (843-842-3666; Shelter Cove) Fun, casual beachwear embossed with unique logo of Camp Hilton Head. Locations at Harbour Town and Coligny Plaza, too.

**Carriage House** (843-689-6200; 1405 Main St. Village) Traditional women's clothing, dresses, swimwear.

*Shops on Hilton Head offer an imaginative twist to the style of resort wear.*

Wade Spees

**Jamaican Me Crazy** (843-785-9006; Coligny Plaza) Wacky resort wear, hip beach accessories.

**Kid's Express** (843-686-5790; Mall at Shelter Cove) Wide selection of fun and back-to-school clothes for youngsters.

**Knickers** (843-671-2291; Harbour Town) Classic outfits in linen, cotton, tweeds, and madras. An institution.

**Loose Lucy's** (843-785-8093; Coligny Plaza) A little bit of the 60s featuring tie-dye, old jeans, Indian prints, bandannas.

**Outside Hilton Head** (843-686-6996; Plaza at Shelter Cove) Top-of-the-line durable sports clothing (Patagonia, Woolrich, Teva), footwear, and accessories. Also at South Beach Marina.

**Porcupine** (843-785-2779; The Village at Wexford) Designer sportswear for women, lingerie, excellent shoe selection, swimwear. The classiest fashion stop on the island.

**Sweet Peas** (843-681-3811; 1 Mathews Court) Designer clothes for kids — the best and latest fashions.

## CRAFTS

**The Flying Cow** (843-785-3557); **The Wooden Menagerie** (843-842-8543) both in The Village Exchange, Palmetto Bay Rd. Large as life animal sculptures (in wild colors), folk art and paintings on boards, silly signs for your beach house or bathroom.

**The Gingham Doll** (843-689-9982; Port Royal Plaza) Craft supplies especially for needlework, sewing, and crochet. Doll clothes can be special ordered.

**Harbour Town Crafts** (843-671-3643; Harbour Town) Quality American handcrafts, large and small, whimsical and functional.

**Inspirations, Ltd.** (843-842-6606; The Village at Wexford) Home accessories and handpainted furniture; painted glassware; original "portrait" dolls.

**Smith Galleries of Fine Crafts** (843-842-2280; Village at Wexford) Over 300 American artisans are represented in media such as glass, wood, metal, clay, and textiles.

**Stamp Heaven Crafts** (843-686-3932; Village Exchange, Palmetto Bay Rd.) Zillions of rubber stamps and ink pads, cards, stencils, stationery, and paper products on which to create your stamped fantasy.

## GIFTS

**Creative Kitchens** (843-785-8516; The Village at Wexford) An excellent kitchen and fine houseware supply store. Cooks love it; anyone who needs a bridal gift should, too. Another location at Main St. Village (843-689-9460).

**Gullah Market** (843-681-7373; 103 William Hilton Pkwy.) Crafts by African-American artisans, fresh vegetables, flea-market bargains, and more.

**Hammock Company** (843-686-3636; Coligny Plaza) Limited edition wildlife and duck stamp prints; Pawley's Island hammocks, porch rockers, garden benches, swings; bird feeders and wind chimes.

**Legends Sports Cards** (843-681-4444; Main St. Village) Old and new trading cards, autographed memorabilia, and Ted Williams signature items.

**Magic Puppet** (843-785-3280; Coligny Plaza) Toys, puppets, magic tricks, Playmobil sets, books.

*Sweetgrass baskets woven by native islanders and for sale at the Gullah Market are trademarks of old Sea Island culture.*

Wade Spees

**Mole Hole** (843-785-8090; Coligny Plaza) Figurines and china collectibles; cards and oil lamps. Also at the Mall at Shelter Cove.

**Ship's Store** (843-842-7002; Shelter Cove Harbour) Everything for the sailor including charts, boat shoes, and nautical accessories.

**South Beach General Store** (843-671-6784; South Beach Marina) An old fashioned emporium.

**Stardust** (843-842-7346; 10 Park Plaza) Cards, tee-shirts with witty sayings, calendars, gifts for people who love cats.

**Uniquely Hilton Head** (843-785-3250; at Hall's Nursery, 852 William Hilton Pkwy) Small and large gifts for the garden including statues, furniture, and plants.

**YiaYia's** (843-671-4433; South Beach Marina) Fortunately, you are allowed to touch the merchandise, or most of it. A wild selection of souvenirs, joke gifts, accessories, Hilton Head logo stuff, and clothes. Good for all ages.

## GOURMET FOOD

**Chocolate Canopy** (843-842-4567; Crossroads Center, Palmetto Bay Rd.) Homemade chocolates galore.

**Cinnamon Bear Country Store** (843-661-5558; Main St. Village) Gourmet coffee, candies, and gifts.

**Healthy Days Natural Food Store** (843-785-7297; Coligny Plaza) Flours, herbal teas, sugar-free items.

**Heavenly Ham** (843-681-2022; 4 Mathews Ct.) Smoked meats, honey-glazed hams, ribs.

**Signe's Heaven Bound Bakery** (843-785-9118; 2 Bow Circle) Fresh baked breads, pastries, cakes, cookies, soups.

## SPORTSWEAR AND SPORTS EQUIPMENT

**Adventure Kayak and Canoe Co.** (843-816-5686 / 8 Archer Rd.) Ocean kayaks, canoes, Folbots, and accessories.

**Nevada Bob's Golf Shop** (843-686-4653; 1016 William Hilton Pkwy) All you need for the links at discounted prices. Club rentals.

**Outside Hilton Head** (843-686-6996; Plaza at Shelter Cove) Equipment for windsurfing, canoeing, kayaking, and camping. The most experienced staff around.

**Player's World** (843-842-5100; Market Place at Sea Pines Circle) Island's largest sporting goods store.

**Sportline** (843-686-8855; Heritage Plaza) Tennis racquets and same-day stringing; runner's accessories, in-line skates, and Oakley shades.

# CHAPTER SEVEN
## *Practical Matters &*
## *Seasonal Events*
## INFORMATION

*There's always room for a pick-up game in the old city.*

Wade Spees

What follows is information to make your visit to the Lowcountry run more smoothly. It's a modest compendium of essentials — what's here and how it works — intended to make planning your trip easier and enjoying your stay simpler. The chapter covers the following topics:

## AMBULANCE, FIRE & POLICE

The general emergency number in the Lowcountry is **911**, whether you're in Charleston, Beaufort, Hilton Head, or Savannah. Outside the cities, most of the counties have basic 911 service. Naturally, in an emergency, you can always dial "0" for the Operator's assistance in reaching the right agency.

A selected roster of other numbers, for emergencies or other business, follows:

**First Call For Help** (Information and referral service):
| | |
|---|---|
| Beaufort/Hilton Head | 843-524-4357 |
| Savannah | 912-651-7730 |

**Poison Control:**
| | |
|---|---|
| South Carolina | 800-922-1117 (from within S.C.) |
| Georgia | 800-282-5846 (from within Ga.) |

**Rape Crisis Hotline:**
| | |
|---|---|
| Charleston | 843-722-7273 |
| Beaufort/Hilton Head | 800-637-7273 / 843-525-6699 |
| Savannah | 912-233-7273 |

**Disaster/Hurricane Emergency Preparedness:**
| | |
|---|---|
| Charleston County | 843-554-5951 |
| Beaufort County | 843-525-7353 |
| Colleton County | 843-549-5632 |
| Hampton County | 843-943-7518 |
| Jasper County | 843-726-7740 |
| Chatham County | 912-651-3100 |

**State Police:**
S.C. Highway Patrol:
| | |
|---|---|
| Charleston Area | 843-740-1660 |
| Beaufort/Hilton Head | 843-524-0163 |
| Ridgeland | 843-726-8076 |

Ga. Highway Patrol:
| | |
|---|---|
| Savannah Area | 912-651-3000 |

**Police (non-emergency):**
| | |
|---|---|
| City of Charleston | 843-720-3892 |
| Town of Edisto Beach | 843-869-2440 |

| | |
|---|---|
| City of Beaufort | 843-525-7580 |
| Town of Port Royal | 843-986-2220 |
| Town of Hilton Head (sheriff) | 843-524-2777 |
| Town of Bluffton | 843-757-2263 |
| Town of Hardeeville | 843-784-3229 |
| City of Savannah | 912-232-4141 |

# AREA CODES, TOWN GOVERNMENT & ZIP CODES

## AREA CODES

The area code for the South Carolina Lowcountry is **843**. The area code for Savannah, Georgia and its metropolitan region is **912**.

## TOWN HALLS

*If you spend most of your time on the water, why not lash your mailbox to the dock?*

Wade Spees

The cities of Charleston, Beaufort, Hilton Head, and Savannah are governed by a mayor and city/town council. This form of government has been in place for some time, except at Hilton Head, where a desire on the part of residents to have some autonomy from Beaufort County — specifically to control the island's tremendous growth — spurred action more than a decade ago to form a "limited service" town government. Even today, as the area adjacent to Hilton Head (but technically "off-island") is booming with residential and commercial development, there is talk of southern Beaufort County, or Hilton Head itself, breaking off to form another county. We may well see secession in the Lowcountry in the 21st century.

In the meantime, and perhaps to avert such dividing of Lowcountry counties between the wealthy and less-wealthy areas, the trend in government is toward consolidation of services, whereby the cities or towns and the counties they are part of share in the cost and delivery of these services.

*Charleston, Beaufort, Walterboro, Ridgeland, Hampton* and *Savannah* are the region's county seats. For general information call:

| | |
|---|---|
| Charleston County | 843-723-6762 |
| Beaufort County | 843-525-7100 |
| Colleton County | 843-549-5791 |
| Jasper County | 843-726-7706 |
| Hampton County | 843-943-7500 |
| Chatham County | 912-652-7869 |

There are also smaller, scattered municipalities governed by smaller councils. For general information, contact the following town/city hall offices:

| Town | Address | Telephone |
|---|---|---|
| Beaufort | 302 Carteret St., 29902 | 843-525-7000 |
| Bluffton | Hwy. 46, P.O. Box 386, 29910 | 843-757-2642 |
| Charleston | 80 Broad St., P.O. Box 304, 29402 | 843-724-3737 |
| Edisto Island | 2414 Murray St., 29438 | 843-869-2505 |
| Folly Beach | 21 Center St., 29439 | 843-588-2447 |
| Hampton | 608 First St. West, 29924 | 843-943-2951 |
| Hilton Head | 1 Town Center Court, 29928 | 843-842-8900 |
| Isle of Palms | 1303 Palm Blvd., 29451 | 843-886-6428 |
| Port Royal | 1406 Paris Ave., 29935 | 843-986-2200 |
| Ridgeland | 108 E. Wilson; P.O. Drawer B, 29936 | 843-726-3351 |
| Savannah | Bay St., P.O. Box 1027, 31402 | 912-651-6790 |
| Thunderbolt | 2702 Mechanics Ave., 31404 | 912-354-5537 |
| Tybee Island | 401 Butler Ave., 31328 | 912-786-4573 |
| Walterboro | 242 Hampton St., P.O. Box 709, 29488 | 843-549-2545 |

# BANKS

South Carolina and Georgia banks are linked electronically to banking systems and debit card accounts throughout the United States. Money can be wired from your home bank or funds can be withdrawn from automatic teller machines provided your ATM/credit card corresponds with the regional networks. The following list provides information on several banks throughout the Lowcountry.

| Bank | Phone | Networks |
|------|-------|----------|
| *Charleston* | | |
| **Charleston Area Federal Credit Union** | 843-723-2761 | NCUA, Honor, Cirrus, Visa |
| **First Federal of Charleston** | 843-529-5800 | Honor, Mastercard/Visa, Cirrus |
| **First Union Bank** | 843-727-1110 | Plus, Honor, AFFN, Cirrus |
| **Nationsbank** | 843-723-6812 | Honor, Plus, Visa |
| *Beaufort* | | |
| **Nationsbank** | 843-521-6004 | Honor, Plus, Visa |
| **Palmetto Federal** | 843-525-8410 | Honor, Cirrus |
| *Hilton Head* | | |
| **The Anchor Bank** | 843-785-4848 | Honor, Avail |
| **First Union** | 843- 842-4200 | Honor, Cirrus, Plus, Visa,Mastercard |
| **Wachovia** | 843-686-9343 | Avail, Cirrus, Honor, Mastercard, Plus, Visa |
| *Savannah* | | |
| **First Union** | 912-944-2000 | Honor, Plus, Cirrus |
| **First Liberty** | 912-351-2201 | Honor, Plus |
| **The Savannah Bank** | 912-651-8200 | Avail, Honor, Plus, Cirrus |

# BIBLIOGRAPHY

Lowcountry life, past and present, is well documented, and its bookstores have ever-growing "local history" sections to prove it. Many volumes that had been out of print have been reprinted recently in response to new demand. Originals may be still found in second-hand bookstores, although at premium prices. Here is a suggested reading list of some classics, the books you're likely to find in residents' libraries.

These days, there are more "homegrown" histories available, courtesy of laptop publishing. Don't overlook them and the gems of local lore they contain. And, since the best part of a trip is often reliving it at home, check your local bookstore upon returning for further reading. The boxed quotes scattered throughout the text are taken from books included in the list below.

The list is by no means complete: think of it as a mere guide to the shelves.

## ART & ARCHITECTURE

Cole, Cynthia, ed. *Historic Resources of the Lowcountry.* Yemassee, SC: Lowcountry Council of Governments, 1979, second ed. 1990. 202 pp., illus., photos, index, $29.95. The definitive four-county survey of historic houses and sites with fine historical and architectural explanation.

Dugan, Ellen, ed. *Picturing the South: 1860 to the Present.* Atlanta, GA: Chronicle Books, the High Museum of Art, 1996. 213 pp., index ,$29.95. Based on a 1996 exhibit at the Photographic Galleries of the High Museum in Atlanta, Ga., the selection of pictures (from the Library of Congress Collections, private donors, historical societies, and museums) is honed to perfection and the accompanying essays (by several southern writers of the first rank) is excellent. The book manages to be moving without being melodramatic or sentimental.

Lane, Mills. *Architecture of the Old South: South Carolina.* Savannah, GA: Beehive Press, 1984. 258 pp., photos, $75. Exquisite, large format, black and white photos.

————*Architecture of the Old South: Georgia.* Savannah, GA: Beehive Press, 1986, 252 pp., photos, $75.

Ravenel, Beatrice St. Julian. *Architects of Charleston.* Columbia, SC: University of South Carolina Press, 1992. 338 pp., photos, index, bibliog., $19.95. First published in 1945, a detailed examination of the lives and works of the city's builders, engineers, and architects.

Rosengarten, Dale. *Row Upon Row: Sea Grass Baskets of the South Carolina Lowcountry.* Columbia, SC: McKissick Museum, 1986. 64 pp., photos, $10. A thorough and lovingly documented catalogue of a vibrant Sea Island art. It is the authoritative text on the shapes, weaving style, and uses of island baskets.

Severens, Kenneth. *Charleston Antebellum Architecture & Civic Destiny.* Knoxville, TN: University of Tennessee Press, 1988. 330 pp., photos, index, $49.95. A specialized topic explained in clear prose for the interested amateur or professional architect.

Severens, Martha R. *Charles Fraser of Charleston.* Charles L. Wyrick, Jr., ed. Charleston, SC: Carolina Art Assoc., 1983. 176 pp., illus., $14.95. The subject was a miniaturist of the 19th century whose portraits of local gentry, in the collection of the Gibbes Art Gallery, are exquisite and incisive.

Vlach, John Michael. *Back of the Big House: The Architecture of Plantation Slavery.* Chapel Hill, NC: University of North Carolina Press, 1993. 236 pp., illus., photos, index, $18.95. A serious, well-written, and fundamental study of the relationship of plantation "spaces" — the outbuildings, the quarters, the "Big House", the allées or avenues, fields, docks, and waterways — to the black and white people who lived there and to each other. Numerous plantation plans are cited.

## AUTOBIOGRAPHY, BIOGRAPHY, DIARIES & LETTERS

Bartram, William. *Travels through North & South Carolina, Georgia, East & West Florida.* New York: Viking Penguin, 1988. 452 pp., $7.95. The account of an 18th-century trip through the Lowcountry by the famous botanist.

Chesnut, Mary Boykin. *A Diary From Dixie.* Cambridge, MA: Harvard University Press, 1980. 608 pp., $12.95. A classic account, good on Charleston society.

Daise, Ronald. *Reminiscences of a Sea Island Heritage.* Columbia SC: Sandlapper, 1986. 103 pp., photos, $18.95. Archival black-and-white photos accompanied by text and stories of Sea Island Gullah culture. Daise and his wife, Natalie, are the creators and stars of the hit television series for children, *Gullah Gullah Island.*

Elliott, William & Theodore Rosengarten. *Carolina Sports by Land and Water, Including Incidents of Devil-Fishing, Wild-Cat, Deer, and Bear-Hunting, Etc.* Columbia, SC: University of South Carolina Press, 1994. Illus., $14.95. A reprint of Elliott's 1850s original, it is still funny, easy to read, and as full of suspense as ever.

Forten, Charlotte L. *The Journal of a Free Negro in the Slave Era.* New York: Norton, 1981. 286 pp., index, $8.95. The vivid impressions of a northern teacher who came to the Sea Islands to educate the newly freed slaves.

Georgia Writers' Project, ed. *Drums and Shadows.* Athens, GA: University of Georgia Press, 1986. $11.95. The collection of oral histories first published under the WPA program in 1940. It allows you to hear the voices of the coast.

Higginson, Thomas Wentworth. *Army Life in a Black Regiment.* New York: Norton, 1984. 279 pp., appendix, index, $6.95. Higginson, a Boston Brahmin, was the white commander of the First South Carolina Volunteers, headquartered in Beaufort, S.C. during the Civil War. Its honest, self-effacing narrative of camp life, countrysides, and skirmishes is invaluable.

Kemble, Frances Anne. *Journal of Residence on a Georgia Plantation in 1838–1839.* Athens, GA: University of Georgia Press, 1984. 488 pp., $11.95. Although the setting is the coastal Georgia plantation of the author's husband, Pierce

Butler, her insights into plantation life and the culture of black female slaves make this perhaps the best account of that time.

McTeer, J.E. *High Sheriff of the Lowcountry*. Beaufort, SC: JEM Co., 1995. 101 pp., $19.70. Newly reprinted, it contains the colorful recollections of the author's days as a Lowcountry lawman and his encounters with voodoo, rum runners, and local scoundrels.

Olmsted, F.L. *A Journey in the Seaboard Slave States*. Westport, CT: Negro Universities Press of Greenwood Pub., 1969. Illus., index, $35.00. A reprint of the 1856 edition in which the author acutely observes the coastal region and standards of living there.

Pearson, Elizabeth Ware, ed. *Letters From Port Royal 1862–1868*. New York: Arno Press, 1969. $14.00. In 1862, dozens of Northern abolitionists flocked to the Federally occupied area around Beaufort, S.C. to educate the newly freed slaves and manage the abandoned cotton plantations. This collection of letters by the Boston contingent is as pungent and moving a commentary on race relations and liberal expectations as exists.

Pennington, Patience. *A Woman Rice Planter*. Cambridge, MA: Belknap Press of Harvard University Press, 1961. The author was a Lowcountry native who managed her father's rice plantations after the Civil War and wrote about the experience for New York newspapers. The illustrations are by Alice Ravenel Huger Smith, a lyrical interpreter of the rural Lowcountry.

Pinkney, Roger. *The Beaufort Chronicles*. Beaufort, SC: Pluff Mud. 110 pp., $9.95. A new collection of remembrances and essays on small-town life and its simple pleasures.

Towne, Laura. *Letters and Diary Written from the Sea Islands of South Carolina, 1862–1884*. New York: American Bio. Series, 1991. 310 pp., $79. Another wonderful journal of a teacher; she established Penn School, the first school for freed slaves in the United States.

Verner, Elizabeth O. *Mellowed By Time*. Charleston, SC: Tradd St. Press, 1978. $15.00. Sketches and memories of old Charleston by a distinguished artist who favored etchings, pastel, and pencil drawing.


## CULTURAL STUDIES

Bluffton Historical Preservation Society. No. II  *A Longer Short History of Bluffton, South Carolina and its Environs*. Bluffton, SC: Bluffton Historical Preservation Society, 1988. 49 pp., photos, $9.95. An excellent local history with photographs of classic Lowcountry cottages.

Carawan, Guy & Candy, eds. *Ain't You Got a Right to the Tree of Life? The People of John's Island, South Carolina — Their Faces, Their Words & Their Songs.* Athens, GA: University of Georgia Press, 1989. 256 pp., photos, $29.95.

Johnson, Guion G. *A Social History of the Sea Islands.* Westport, CT: Greenwood Press, 1969. 185 pp., index, bibliog., $38.50. A reprint of the 1930 edition of a series in which scholars from the University of North Carolina examined the lives, speech, culture, and folkways of Sea Island natives. Others include *Folk Culture on St. Helena Island* by Guy B. Johnson and *Black Yeomanry* by T.J. Woofter, which, if you can find it, has stirring documentary photographs.

Jones-Jackson, Patricia. *When Roots Die: Endangered Traditions on the Sea Islands.* Athens, GA: University of Georgia Press, 1987. 189 pp., photos, bibliog., $19.95.

Parrish, Lydia. *Slave Songs of the Georgia Sea Islands.* Athens, GA: University of Georgia Press, 1992. 252 pp., photos, musical notation, $19.95. A reprint of the 1942 original by the wife of artist Maxfield Parrish, documenting the islanders' songs from the praise house to the play yard.

Taylor, John Martin. *Hoppin' John's Lowcountry Cooking.* New York: Bantam, 1990. 345 pp., illus., $24.00.

————*The New Southern Cook: 200 Recipes.* New York: Bantam, 1995. 287 pp., illus., $27.95. A superb follow-up to Taylor's first book, this one ranges a bit further but maintains the author's discriminating judgments and lack of pretension.

Terry, Elizabeth, with Alexis Terry. *Savannah Seasons: Food and Stories from Elizabeth on 37th.* New York: Doubleday, 1996. 340 pp., $30. Recipes and memories, written by mother and daughter, of the family's nationally acclaimed Savannah restaurant, which opened in 1980. There's a useful "source list" for ingredients available from speciality vendors by mail, too.

Vernon, Amelia Wallace. *African-Americans at Mars Bluff, South Carolina.* Columbia, SC: University of South Carolina Press, 1995. 200 pp., illus., photos, index, bibliog., $16.95. A wonderful documentary account of an African-American community north of Charleston, S.C.

Welty, Eudora. *The Eye of the Story: Selected Essays and Reviews.* New York: Vintage International, 1990. 355 pp., $14.00.

Westmacott, Richard. *African-American Gardens and Yards in the Rural South.* Knoxville, TN: University of Tennessee Press, 1992. 175 pp., illus., photos, index, bibliog., $24.95. One of the most thoughtful and inspired books ever written on African-American rural life (some in the Lowcountry), it focuses on several families and the way they create color, style, whimsey, and usefulness in their immediate landscape. It is part scholarly, part oral history, and the tone is just right.

## FICTION

Berendt, John. *Midnight in the Garden of Good and Evil.* New York: Random House, 1994. 388 pp., $22.00. A wild romp in Savannah — and it's all true.

Conroy, Pat. *The Water is Wide.* New York: Bantam, 1972. 320 pp., $4.95. This was the book based on Conroy's experiences as a Beaufort County school-teacher on isolated Daufuskie Island. His other books, including *The Great Santini* and *The Prince of Tides* have Beaufort as their setting (even in the movie version). His latest work (1995) is *Beach Music.*

Griswold, Francis. *Sea Island Lady.* Beaufort, SC: Beaufort Book Co., reprint of the 1939 original. 964 pp., $19.95. A big, fat Southern novel set in Beaufort.

Hewyard, Du Bose. *Porgy.* Charleston, SC: Tradd St. Press, 1985. 130 pp., illus., $20. A reprinting of the great tale, set in and around Charleston.

Humphreys, Josephine. *Rich in Love.* New York: Viking Penguin, 1987. 262 pp., $8.95. Set in Mount Pleasant, near Charleston, this novel (basis of the 1993 movie) captures the world view of a precocious 17-year-old girl. The author's other novels, *Dreams of Sleep* (1984) and *The Fireman's Fair* (1991), also have the Charleston area as their setting.

Naylor, Gloria R. *Mama Day.* New York: Random House, 1989. 312 pp., $9.95. A magical story set in a mythical place that nearly mirrors the Georgia/South Carolina Sea Islands.

Peterkin, Julia. *Scarlet Sister Mary.* Marietta, GA: Cherokee Press, 1991. 352 pp., $18.95. A reprint of the 1928 edition.

Powell, Padgett. *Edisto.* New York: Farrar, Strauss & Giroux, 1984. 192 pp., $11.95. A boy's coming-of-age on a Sea Island.

————*Edisto Revisited*: New York: Henry Holt, 1996. 145 pp., $20.

Sayers, Valerie. *Due East.* New York: Doubleday, 1987. 264 pp., $15.95. The first novel in a group that chronicles life in a town like Beaufort, S.C., where the author grew up. Others include *How I Got Him Back* (1989) and *Who Do You Love* (1991).

Worthington, Curtis, ed. *Literary Charleston: A Lowcountry Reader.* Charleston, SC: Wyrick & Co., 1996. 360 pp., $24.95.


## HISTORY

Bridenbaugh, Carl. *Myths and Realities: Societies of the Colonial South.* New York: Atheneum, 1963. 208 pp. Index, bibliog., $1.25.

Dollard, John. *Caste and Class in a Southern Town.* Madison, WI: University of Wisconsin Press, 1989. 466 pp., index, $14.50. A reissue of the 1937 work which, while not specifically about the Lowcountry, has everything to say about race relations in small towns throughout the region.

Jacoway, Elizabeth. *Yankee Missionaries in the South: The Penn School Experiment.* Baton Rouge, LA: LSU Press, 1980. 301 pp., index, bibliog.

Jones, Katharine M. *Port Royal Under Six Flags.* Indianapolis, IN: Bobbs-Merrill, 1960. 368 pp., illus., bibliog. A good general introduction to the area, with long passages quoting original documents.

Rogers, George. *Charleston in the Age of the Pinckneys.* Columbia, SC: University of South Carolina Press, 1984. 198 pp., index, $9.95. If there is one book you should read about Charleston's heyday, this is it.

Rose, Willie Lee. *Rehearsal For Reconstruction: The Port Royal Experiment.* New York: Oxford University Press, 1976. 450 pp., index, bibliog., $13.95. A beautifully written and meticulously researched account of the Northern abolitionists who went to the Sea Islands of Beaufort at the time of the Civil War. If you have a serious interest in the subject, the bibliography of this book is where you should start.

Rosen, Robert. *A Short History of Charleston.* San Francisco, CA: Lexikos, 1982. 160 pp., illus., photos, bibliog., $8.95. A good introduction to explaining Charleston by a native son.

Rosengarten, Theodore. *Tombee: Portrait of A Cotton Planter.* New York: McGraw, 1988. 752 pp., index, $15.00. This prize-winning book reproduces the diaries of an antebellum St. Helena Islander, Thomas B. Chaplin, and creates a context of explanation for them. This is the story — not the myth — of life on a cotton plantation, handled in vivid prose by the region's best historian.

Stampp, Kenneth. *The Peculiar Institution: Slavery in the Ante-Bellum South.* New York: Vintage, 1989. Index, $10. A classic study, first published in 1956.

Wise, Stephen R. *Lifeline of the Confederacy: Blockade Running During the Civil War.* Columbia, SC: University of South Carolina Press, 1988. 403 pp., illus., index, $16.95.

———*Gate Of Hell: Campaign for Charleston Harbor, 1863.* Columbia, SC: University of South Carolina Press, 1994. 218 pp., illus., index, $29.95.

Wood, Peter. *Black Majority: Negroes in Colonial South Carolina from 1670 through the Stono Rebellion.* New York: Norton, 1975. 384 pp., index, $9.95.

## PHOTOGRAPHIC STUDIES

Blagden, Tom. *The Lowcountry.* Greensboro, NC: Legacy Publications, 1988. 104 pp., photos, $49.95. Views of the coastal world by an immensely talented photographer. His words of introduction, of praise for the region's natural beauty, resonate with visitors and locals alike.

————*South Carolina's Wetland Wilderness: The ACE Basin.* Englewood, CO: Westcliffe Publishers, Inc. 1992. 110 pp., $29.95. A sumptuous study of the land and estuarine ecosystem in and around the Ashepoo, Combahee, and Edisto Rivers, much of which is being protected by federal, state, local, and private organizations.

Dabbs, Edith, ed. *Face of An Island.* An album of the early 20th century photographs taken on St. Helena Island by Leigh Richmond Miner and reproduced from the glass plates. A treasure.

Ellis, Ray. *South by Southeast.* Birmingham, AL: Oxmoor House, 1983. 122 pp., $50. Watercolors of the coastal region by noted painter and Hilton Head resident.

Isley, Jane, Agnes Baldwin, and William P. Baldwin, *Plantations of the Lowcountry.* Greensboro, NC: Legacy Pub., 1987. 151 pp., $19.95. Color photographs and meticulously researched histories of historic homes.

McLaren, Lynn, and Gerhard Spieler. *Ebb Tide, Flood Tide.* Columbia, SC: University of South Carolina Press, 1991. 105 pp., $40. Color photographs of favorite Beaufort sites...natural and man-made.

Schultz, Constance, ed. *A South Carolina Album. 1936-1948.* Columbia, SC: University of South Carolina Press, 1992. 143 pp. A collection of the photographs taken under the auspices of the Farm Security Administration, and later under the direction of its chief, Roy Stryker.

*Lowcountry pleasures can be as simple as finding a sand dollar.*

## RECREATION/TRAVEL

Baldwin, William P. III. *Lowcountry Daytrips: Plantations, Gardens, and a Natural History of the Charleston Region.* Greensboro NC: Legacy Publications, 1993. 283 pp., illus., photos, index, bibliog., $18.95. The best new guide of the area, written by a Lowcountry native. It is a model of organization (with maps and mileage clearly spelled out), good design, practicality, and a writing style that lends itself to reading aloud. The book you'll lend to anyone who takes your advice and visits the Lowcountry.

Ballantine, Todd. *Tideland Treasures.* Columbia, SC: University of South Carolina Press, 1991. 218 pp., $15.95.

Crowley, Rebecca Kaufmann. *Hilton Head Guidebook.* Beaufort, SC: Coastal Villages Press, 1995. 135 pp., $9.95.

Federal Writers' Project Staff. *The WPA Guide to the Palmetto State.* Walter B. Edgar, ed. Columbia, SC: University of South Carolina Press, 1988. 514 pp., photos, index, $16.95. A reprint of the superb guide.

Georgia Conservancy. *A Guide to the Georgia Coast.* Savannah, GA: The Georgia Conservancy, 1989. 199 pp., illus., index.

Moeller, Jan and Bill Moeller. *The Intracoastal Waterway*: Camden, ME: Seven Seas Press, 1979 (updated 1991). 149 pp., $16.95.

Trask, Fred. *A Guide to Historic Beaufort.* Beaufort, SC: Historic Beaufort Foundation, 1970. 125 pp., maps, illus., photos. The definitive guide, especially good in describing walking and driving tours.

Trask, George. *Beautiful Beaufort By the Sea.* Beaufort, SC: Coastal Villages Press, 1992. 48 pp., maps, illus., $7.95. A breezy, informal round-up of local points of interest and things to do.

Wright, Cantey Holmes. *The Edisto Book.* Columbia, SC: Mac Kohn Printing, 1988. 109 pp., map, illus. Good local history.

Wyrick & Co. *The Charleston Guide.* Charleston, SC: Wyrick & Co., 1987. 30 pp., $3.50.

## CLIMATE, WEATHER & WHAT TO WEAR

**B**efore there were house tours in Charleston and St. Patrick's Day in Savannah, there was the spring season for tourists who came to see the blossoms. And they weren't disappointed — azaleas bursting into bloom all over downtown, jasmine flowering on fence posts, dogwood and magnolia peeping out from under the shadows of live oaks in the woods.

In fact, there is something in bloom year-round in the Lowcountry, from late-summer mums to camellias to paper-white narcissus which scent the air at Christmas. This long season comes as a result of the semitropical to subtropical climate and the ever-present breezes that characterize the coastal region. Rarely do days pass in succession without sunshine. The annual rainfall for the region is about 51 inches.

---

### Endless Summer

From this early spring-time onward, there seemed no great difference in atmospheric sensations, and only a succession of bloom. After two months one's notions of the season grew bewildered, just as very early rising bewilders the day. In the army one is perhaps aroused after a bivouac, marches before daybreak, halts, fights, somebody is killed, a long day's life has been lived, and after all it is not seven o'clock, and breakfast is not ready. So when we had lived in summer so long as hardly to remember winter, it suddenly occurred to us that it was not yet June. One escapes at the South that mixture of hunger and avarice which is felt in the Northern summer, counting each hour's joy with the sad consciousness that an hour is gone.

—From *Army Life in a Black Regiment*, 1869
by Thomas Wentworth Higginson

---

The winters are generally mild — maybe 10 days of frost, and a half-dozen hard freezes. Spring comes early. Farmers generally break ground on February 1. In the old days, the cotton crop was finished by "lay-by time" in late August, when slaves, temporarily released from heavy field work, would tend to their cemeteries and families.

*Water and warm air, an unbeatable Lowcountry combination.*

Wade Spees

By May 1, it's hot, and that heat will penetrate every living thing through the end of September. They say the mean (and it sure is) summer temperature in the Lowcountry runs between 70 degrees and 88 degrees. Now that we've given a name — the Heat Index — to what it feels like when the 90 percent humidity is factored in, it's really probably near 95 degrees, or so it feels, for several months each year.

If you arrive in summer, be prepared to move slowly, wear hats, slather on the sunscreen, and drink plenty of liquids. Even on a hazy day the sun will burn you. Take extra precautions, too, if you're planning athletic pursuits: the tennis court is no place to be at midday.

The wild cloudbursts that drench the region in summer, and the often-spectacular thunder and lightening shows that accompany them, may cool things off a bit. More likely, they'll just bring mosquitos.

Then there are the gnats. Just when you're enjoying a creamy autumn day in the 70s, they find you. Avon's Skin So Soft has proved an effective repellent, as does staying out of the shade or standing in a breeze.

The seasons each bring their color, their migratory birds, their harvest of fish or shellfish, duck or deer. And twice a year it seems as if a whole new shipment of air is carted in, too — in late October, when the marsh has turned golden and the clouds pull themselves into exquisitely-defined cumuli; and again in late February, when the prevailing northeast winds of winter start to shift south and southwest.

But perhaps the best quality of Lowcountry weather is its subtlety and contradiction: the warm day in January that you were not expecting, the roaring fire in October that banishes the dampness and chill in the morning, but by late afternoon seems an inferno.

For clothing, always take more cotton shirts than you think you'll need: flowers should wilt, not people. Take comfortable shoes for touring (high-heeled shoes are often not allowed to cross the threshold of House Museums) and a light sweater or windbreaker. An overcoat or parka may be too much in winter; sweaters and shells work better.

**Weather Information**

| | |
|---|---|
| Charleston | 843-744-3207 |
| Beaufort | 843-524-2999 |
| Savannah | 912-964-1700 |

## HANDICAPPED SERVICES

Most of the region's accommodations, museums, restaurants, and touring services provide access and facilities for those with special physical needs — but call ahead to confirm details: some problems remain in retrofitting the older historic buildings for complete handicapped access. Your guides, hosts, or the Visitor Center's staff in each city will gladly assist you — several offer handicap-accessibility guides. See the section "Tourist Information" at the end of this chapter for addresses of city or county offices of tourism and travel.

## HOSPITALS

### Charleston

**Bon Secours St. Francis Xavier Hospital** Maywood Rd.; 843-402-1000.
**Medical University of South Carolina** 171 Ashley Ave.; 843-792-2300.
**Roper Hospital** 316 Calhoun St.; 843-724-2000.
**Trident Regional Medical Center** 9330 Medical Plaza Dr.; 843-797-7000.
**Veteran's Administration Medical Center** 109 Bee St.; 843-577-5011.

### Beaufort

**Beaufort Memorial Hospital** 121 S. Ribaut Rd.; 843-522-5200.
**Beaufort Naval Hospital** Ribaut Rd; 843-525-5600.
### Hilton Head

**Hilton Head Hospital** Hospital Center Blvd.; 843-681-6122.

### Savannah

**Candler General** 5353 Reynolds Ave.; 912-692-6000.
**Immediate Med** 2014 E. Victory Dr.; 912-927-6832.
**Memorial Medical Center** 4700 Waters Ave.; 912-350-8000.
**St. Joseph's Hospital** 11705 Mercy Blvd.; 912-925-4100.

## LATE NIGHT FOOD AND FUEL

The metropolitan areas of Charleston and Savannah, and the resort centers of Hilton Head, stay lit and active well after midnight — especially during the spring and summer — so finding gas or even grits should not be a problem. However, if you're traveling at night, remember that the Lowcountry is largely rural, traversed by long stretches of quiet highway. Unless you plan to gig for flounder and fry them up by the side of the road, it's best to travel with snacks.

## Charleston

**Circle-K Convenience Store** (grocery and fuel) 2284 Savannah Highway. Open 24 hours.

**International House of Pancakes** (food) 1521 Savannah Highway. Open 24 hours Sunday through Thursday, to midnight Friday and Saturday.

## Beaufort

**Huddle House** (food) Ribaut Road at Allison. Open 24 hours.
**Huddle House** (food) Sea Island Parkway. Open 24 hours.
**Island Plaza** (grocery and fuel) Highway 21, Frogmore. Open 24 hours.
**The Pantry** (grocery and fuel) 2231 S. Ribaut Rd. Open 24 hours.
**Winn Dixie** (food) Island Square, Lady's Island. Open 24 hours.

## Hilton Head

**Huddle House** (food) Northridge Drive. Open 24 hours.
**The Pantry** (grocery and fuel) Hwy. 278 and Arrow Road. Open 24 hours.
**Winn Dixie** (food) Northridge Plaza. Open 24 hours.

## Savannah

**BP Gas** 7203 Abercorn (grocery and fuel) Open 24 hours.
**International House of Pancakes** (food) 110 Mall Blvd. Open 24 hours on weekends.
**Kettle Restaurant** (food) 6801 Abercorn. Open 24 hours. Wheelchair accessible.

# MEDIA

## Charleston

### NEWSPAPERS AND MAGAZINES

*Charleston Magazine* (843-971-9811; P.O. Box 21770, Charleston 29413-1770) A glossy bi-monthly featuring stories about the city of Charleston, local politics, development, and some art features. Reviews and columns, too.

*The Post and Courier* (843-577-7111; 134 Columbus St., Charleston 29403) The daily paper of Charleston.

*Skirt!* (843-883-3281; P.O. Box 806, Sullivan's Island 29482) Irreverent, fresh, funny, and good-looking, with a feminist angle. Monthly.

*Upwith* (843-577-5304; 54 John St., Charleston 29401) A weekly with columns, reviews, and very solid features. Distributed free.

## RADIO

**WAVF-FM** 96.0; Alternative rock.
**WSCI-FM** 89.3; S.C. Educational Radio.
**WTMA-AM** 1250; Talk radio.
**WWBZ-FM** 98.9; Beach, boogie, and blues.
**WXLY-FM** 102.5; Oldies.
**WYBB-FM** 98.0; Classic rock.

## TELEVISION

**WCBD-TV** Channel 2, NBC.
**WCIV-TV** Channel 4, ABC.
**WCSC-TV** Channel 5, CBS.
**WITV-TV** Channel 7, PBS.
**WTAT-TV** Channel 24, FOX.

## *Beaufort and Hilton Head*

## NEWSPAPERS AND MAGAZINES

*The Beaufort Gazette* (843-524-3183; P.O. Box 399, 1556 Salem Rd. 29902) Daily. Local coverage, wire-service features and columns.

*Beaufort Magazine* (843-986-0511; 102 Sea Island Pkwy., Beaufort 29902) A glossy quarterly with profiles, features, facts, recipes, and local history.

*Hilton Head Monthly* (843-842-6988; 27 Bow Circle, Hilton Head 29928).

*The Hilton Head News* (843-785-5255; 5 Office Park, Pope Ave, Hilton Head 29928) Weekly.

*The Island Packet* (843-785-4293; P.O. Box 5727, Hilton Head Island, 29938) A solid, hard-hitting paper that has grown as the island has. Excellent local political coverage, a wide variety of local columnists, and wire stories. Monday through Friday; Sunday.

## RADIO

**WCHY-FM** 94.1; Country.
**WFXH-FM** 106.1; Rock.

**WHHR-AM** 1130; News/Sports.

**WIJY-FM** 108; Easy-listening music from the 60s-90s.

**WJWJ-FM** 89.9; S.C. Educational Radio.

**WYKZ-FM** 98.7; Rock, contemporary hits.

## TELEVISION

**WJWJ-TV** Channel 16, S.C. Educational Television.

**WTGS-TV** Channel 28, Fox.

### Savannah

## NEWSPAPERS AND MAGAZINES

*The Georgia Guardian* (912-238-2434; 528 Indian St., Savannah 31401) Weekly newspaper, published by the Savannah College of Art and Design.

*The Herald* (912-232-4505; 1803 Barnard St. 31401) Weekly, featuring news of the African-American community.

*Savannah Morning News* (912-236-9511; 111 W. Bay St. 31401) Daily and Sunday.

*Savannah Tribune* (912-233-6128; 916 W. Montgomery St. 31401) Weekly, featuring news of the African-American community.

## RADIO

**WGCO-FM** 98.3; Oldies.

**WJCL-FM** 96.5; Country.

**WLOW-FM** 107.9; Big Band, American Music Classics.

**WSOK-AM** 1230; Talk Radio, News, Sports.

**WSVH-FM** 91.9; Public Radio

## TELEVISION

**WJCL-TV** Channel 22, ABC.

**WSAV-TV** Channel 3, NBC.

**WTGS-TV** Channel 28, Fox Network.

**WTOC-TV** Channel 11, CBS.

**WUBI-TV** Channel 34, WB Network.

**WVAN-TV** Channel 9, PBS.

## REAL ESTATE

If you came to the Lowcountry and couldn't bear to leave it behind without owning a piece, take your place in line. Practically every new resident who has settled here recently was once in your position. Even the ones who thought the Lowcountry would be their "retirement home" have quit fighting the urge and moved in early. In Beaufort County alone, the rate of building exceeds 500 units each year.

There are hundreds of real estate agents, many independent, some affiliated with large national brokerage firms. One of them might be the proprietor of your bed and breakfast, and if not, he or she will probably have a suggestion. For starters, you should pick up the free, widely available, real estate magazines that are published weekly throughout the Lowcountry. These will give you a general idea of what's out there and how much it costs. Self-enclosed communities often have exclusive sales teams, offering every style of house — or building lot — from the grand to the modest. Once you're ready to look, select an agent in the place you like best. Walk-ins are welcome, and if you can't find what you're looking for, ask for referrals in other towns, too.

## ROAD SERVICE

Here is a list of some emergency road services in the Lowcountry.

### Charleston

**AAA Carolina Motor Club** (800-477-4222; 843-766 2394).
**Bouchillion Automotive Center** (843-744-6539) 24-hour towing.

### Beaufort

**Barnard Tire Co.** (843-524-4728).
**Ellis Welding** (843-524-5719).

### Hilton Head

**Coastal Towing** (843-689-3869) 24-hour towing.
**Mid Island Garage** (843-681-4636) 24-hour towing.

## Savannah

**Auto Intensive Care** (912-355-5388) 24-hour towing; especially useful if you're stuck on I-95 or I-16.

**Jackson Bros. Car Care Center** (912-236-0631) 24-hour towing.

## SEASONAL EVENTS IN THE LOWCOUNTRY

The following list is intended to draw your attention to annual special events in the Lowcountry that might coincide with the time of your visit. Some of them, like outdoor concerts in a park, offer informal pleasures that you can enjoy on a whim with your family. Others, like house tours, Spoleto performances, or tennis and golf tournaments, require a bit of planning: purchasing your tickets in advance is a good idea, as is securing lodgings, especially in the busy spring tourist season. For specific information regarding dates, schedules, performance times, admission or ticket prices (if applicable), call or write in advance, or check local newspaper listings. For lodging and dining suggestions, see specific venue chapters.

### JANUARY

Wade Spees

*Thousands turn out for annual oyster roasts at Boone Hall Plantation.*

## *Charleston*

**Lowcountry Oyster Festival** (843-577-4030; Charleston Area Convention and Visitors Bureau, P.O. Box 975, Charleston, SC 29402) A huge oyster feast, held on the grounds of Boone Hall Plantation. Games, entertainment, and contests for the whole family.

## *Hilton Head*

**1st Sunday Jazz** (843-842-4457; Hilton Head Island Jazz Society) An informal jam session held monthly at various island locations.

## FEBRUARY

## *Beaufort*

**Daffodil Daze Festival** (843-524-3163; Beaufort Chamber of Commerce, P.O. Box 910, Beaufort, SC 29901) A celebration of the annual daffodil harvest on a local farm. Bring your camera — the colors recall Monet.

## *Charleston*

**Lowcountry Blues Bash** (843-762-9125; P.O. Box 13525, Charleston, SC 29422; e-mail: emusic@mindspring.com; Internet: www2.discovernet.com/blues/index.html) Eleven days of performances by top blues players.

**Southeastern Wildlife Exposition** (843-723-1748 / 800-221-5273; 211 Meeting St., Charleston, SC 29401; e-mail: sewe@aol.com; Internet: www.southeasternwildlife.com) A comprehensive, multi-site exhibition of wildlife art in various media, and presentations promoting habitat conservation and wildlife appreciation. A huge, three-day national event that draws collectors, artists, hunters, and bird-watchers.

## *Hilton Head*

**Native Islander Gullah Celebration** (888-856-4982) A month-long look at island culture and its African roots.

## *Savannah*

**Georgia Heritage Celebration** (912-233-7787; Historic Savannah Foundation) A 12-day celebration of the founding of Georgia and the Savannah colony which features tours, re-enactments of Colonial life, lectures, art exhibits, music, dance, and crafts. At various city locations.

## MARCH

### *Beaufort*

**St. Helena's Episcopal Church Spring Tours** (843-524-0363; P.O. Box 1043, Beaufort, SC 29901) Tours of historic homes, gardens, and churches in Beaufort and on the Sea Islands.

### *Charleston*

**Drayton Hall Candlelight Concert** (843-766-0188; 3380 Ashley River Rd., Charleston, SC 29414) When this house is lit only by candles, it seems at its height of serene beauty.

**Festival of Houses** (843-723-1623; 40 E. Bay St., Charleston, SC 29401) The Historic Charleston Foundation's tours of private homes, plantations, gardens, and churches usually start toward the end of the month and last four weeks. A superbly-organized event — a tradition for more than 50 years — it will enrich your understanding of the Lowcountry.

### *Hilton Head*

**Family Circle Magazine Cup Tennis Tournament** (843-363-3500 / 800-677-2293; 140 A Lighthouse Rd., Hilton Head Island, SC 29928) For nine days, usually starting at the end of the month, the world's top women players compete at Sea Pines Plantation Racquet Club. Excellent tennis in a relaxed atmosphere.

**SpringFest** (Hilton Head Hospitality Assoc.; 843-686-4944 / 800-424-3387) Activities include musical performances; college tennis championships and exhibition play; festivals of food, wine, and chocolate.

### *Savannah*

**First Saturday Festival March – November** (Savannah Waterfront Association; 912-234-0295) Once a month in the good weather, spend the day on the waterfront where live bands, pushcarts, open-air theatre performances, and craftspeople bring excitement to River Street.

**Savannah Tour of Homes and Gardens** (912-234-8054; 18 Abercorn St., Savannah, GA 31401) For four days, Savannah's historic homes, churches, and gardens are open to visitors.

**St. Patrick's Day Parade** (912-233-4804; Parade Committee, P.O. Box 9224, Savannah, GA 31412) Savannah claims a substantial Irish heritage and celebrates it with abandon on this holiday. Mobs of people turn out to watch the downtown parade, which starts at 10 a.m. and dominates all other city activity for the day and night.

## APRIL

### *Charleston*

**Garden Club of Charleston House and Garden Tours** (843-571-3455 / 843-556-5476)

**Plantation Oyster Roast at Drayton Hall** (Historic Charleston Foundation, 843-723-1623).

### *Hilton Head*

**MCI Heritage Classic** (843-671-2448 / 800-234-1107; 71 Lighthouse Rd., Suite 414, Hilton Head, SC 29928) Falling about a week after the Masters at Augusta, this premiere golf tournament brings thousands of people and the top PGA players to Hilton Head.

### *Walterboro*

**Colleton County Rice Festival** (843-549-9595; P.O. Box 426, Walterboro, SC 29488) Arts and crafts, cooking demonstrations, and rice-husking celebrate the Lowcountry's rice-growing heritage.

## MAY

### *Beaufort*

**Gullah Festival** (843-524-3163; Beaufort Chamber of Commerce, Box 910, Beaufort, SC 29901) Held in late May, the festival features performances, plays, concerts of spiritual and gospel music, films, and lectures related to the West African heritage of the Sea Islands.

### *Bluffton*

**Bluffton Village Festival** (843-757-3855; Bluffton Town Hall, Bluffton, SC 29910) A very small, old-fashioned street festival featuring artisans, food, and entertainment, usually held the second Saturday of May.

### Charleston

**Confederate Memorial Day Observance** (843-722-8638; Magnolia Cemetery Trust, P.O. Box 6214, Charleston, SC 29405) Join the United Daughters of the Confederacy and other groups in a program honoring the Confederate War dead. (A similar celebration takes place in Savannah, too.)

**Piccolo Spoleto** (843-724-7305; Office of Cultural Affairs, 133 Church St., Charleston, SC 29401). The more informal aspect of Spoleto celebrates art, music, dance, and outdoor events which highlight regional artists.

**Spoleto Festival U.S.A.** (843-722-2764; P.O. Box 157, Charleston, SC 29402) Beginning in late May and lasting for about 18 days, Spoleto brings the best of international theater, music, art, and dance to Charleston. It's a magical time in the city.

### Hilton Head

**St. Luke's Tour of Homes and Gardens** (843-785-4099; St. Luke's Episcopal Church).

### Savannah

**Scottish Games and Highland Gathering** (912-964-4951; P.O. Box 13435, Savannah, GA 31401) Scottish dancing, pipe bands, and traditional games honoring Scotch heritage, usually held the first weekend in May.

## JUNE

### Colleton County

**Edisto Riverfest** (843-549-9595; Walterboro-Colleton Chamber of Commerce, P.O. Box 1763, Walterboro, SC 29488) Join a guided canoe and kayak flotilla as it winds down the Edisto River. Food, entertainment, and displays of equipment featured at two state parks along the way. Usually held the second weekend of the month.

### Hampton

**Hampton County Watermelon Festival** (843-943-3784; Chamber of Commerce, Box 122, Hampton, SC 29924) The oldest festival in the state celebrating the county's best crop. Held at the end of the month and lasting a week, featuring seed-spitting contests, beauty queens, and a big parade.

## *Hilton Head*

**King Mackerel / Cobia Fishing Tournament** (843-842-7001; Shelter Cove Marina).

## *Savannah*

**Concerts in Johnson Square** From June to August, enjoy two-hour lunchtime concerts every Wednesday and Friday, starting at 11:30 a.m., in one of the city's loveliest settings.

## JULY

**Fourth of July Fireworks** take place in several Lowcountry resorts as well as these locations: Brittlebank Park (Charleston), Parris Island (Beaufort), Hilton Head, Bluffton, Savannah's Riverfront, and Tybee Beach.

## *Beaufort*

**Beaufort County Water Festival** (843-524-0600; Chamber of Commerce, P.O. Box 910, Beaufort, SC 29901) A 10-day festival starting in mid-July that features special events each day and night: croquet, fishing, tennis, Ping-Pong, and golf tournaments, a juried art show, antiques show, kid's day, parade, and several outdoor dances. The air shows and acrobatic water-ski demonstrations are especially fun to watch.

## *Edisto Island*

**Edisto Summer Festival** (843-869-3867; P.O. Box 206, Edisto Island, SC 29438) A weekend of family-oriented fun on the beach, in the water, on the links. Street dances, local food specialities, and entertainment.

## *Hilton Head*

**Del Monte Banana Open Doubles** (843-785-6613; Hilton Head Beach & Tennis Resort).

## AUGUST

## *Hilton Head*

**King Mackerel Fishing Tournament** (843-785-7001; Shelter Cove).

## SEPTEMBER

### *Charleston*

**House and Garden Candlelight Tours** (843-722-4630 / 800-968-8175; The Preservation Society, P.O. Box 521, Charleston, SC 29402) More than one dozen different candlelight walking tours of private homes and gardens are offered over a period of about four weeks by the city's oldest preservation organization. Lectures and small concerts are also scheduled.

**MOJA Arts Festival** (843-724-7305; Office of Cultural Affairs, 133 Church St., Charleston, SC 29401) A celebration of the African-American and Caribbean heritage in the Charleston area. The influence on southern culture is traced through music, dance, art, food, stage performances, and more.

**Scottish Games and Highland Gathering** (843-884-4371; P.O. Box 21109, Charleston, SC 29413) Competitions in dancing and athletics held in a fair-like atmosphere at Boone Hall Plantation.

### *Hardeeville*

**Catfish Festival** (843-784-2231; Chamber of Commerce, P.O. Box 307, Hardeeville, SC 29927) Family entertainment, boat races on the Savannah River, and of course, catfish, are the focus of this festival, which takes place the third weekend in September.

### *Hilton Head*

**Hilton Head Celebrity Golf Tournament** (843-842-7711; Chamber of Commerce, P.O. Box 5647, Hilton Head Island, SC 29938) Held Labor Day weekend, at several island courses, the tournament draws lots of celebrities who play with a keen sense of fun.

### *Savannah*

**Savannah Jazz Festival** (912-356-2381; Coastal Jazz Assoc., P.O. Box 8004, Savannah, GA 31412) All styles of jazz played in spots throughout the city.

## OCTOBER

### *Beaufort*

**Historic Beaufort Foundation Fall Tour of Homes** (843-524-6334; P.O. Box 11, Beaufort, SC 29901) A weekend of candlelight and daytime tours of homes and gardens in and around Beaufort; the final day often features tours of outlying plantations, such as the rarely-seen *Auldbrass* designed by Frank Lloyd Wright and meticulously restored inside and out.

### Edisto Island

**Edisto Historic Preservation Society Tour of Homes** (843-869-1954; P.O. 206, Edisto Island, SC 29438) Day-long tour of homes.

### Hilton Head Island

**An Evening of the Arts** (843-785-3673; Chamber of Commerce, P.O. Box 5647, Hilton Head Island, SC 29938) A festive charity auction featuring work by local artists.

**Junior Davis Wightman Cup** (843-785-1152; Palmetto Dunes Resort).

**Head of the Broad Regatta**, Palmetto Rowing Club (843-681-4207; Broad Creek Marina).

### Ridgeland

**Gopher Hill Festival** (843-726-8126; P.O. Box 1267, Ridgeland, SC 29936) A one-day celebration with arts and crafts, music, and food. The Ridgeland area was long known as Gopher Hill, named for the gopher tortoise, a species which lives a protected life in the sand hills of Jasper County.

### Savannah

**Savannah Greek Festival** (912-236-8256; St. Paul's Greek Orthodox Church, 14 W. Anderson St., Savannah, GA 31401) A day-long celebration of Savannah's Greek heritage with food, music and dancing.

**Tom Turpin Ragtime Festival** (912-233-9989) A city-wide tribute to one of the innovators of ragtime music. Formal and informal concerts.

### NOVEMBER

### Charleston

**Holiday Festival of Lights** (843-762-2172; James Island County Park) See more than 100,000 holiday lights strung in the park, a dazzling display in a place that rarely knows a white Christmas. Family entertainment and special events scheduled through Christmas.

**Plantation Days** (843-556-6020; Middleton Place, Hwy. 61, Charleston SC 29414) The spirit of harvest days on a Lowcountry plantation is recreated through activities such as blacksmithing, wool dying and spinning, candle-making, and pottery. Traditional music and crafts, too, in the stable yards and green at Middleton Place.

### Hilton Head

**Hargray Hilton Head Island 5K and 10K Bridge Run** (843-689-3440).

### St. Helena Island

*Dancers from Sierra Leone — a country with linguistic and cultural similarities to St. Helena Island — perform at Penn Center's Heritage Days Festival.*

Wade Spees

**Heritage Days** (843-838-2432; Penn Center, P.O. Box 126, St. Helena Island, SC 29920) Held the second weekend in November on the historic Penn Center campus, Heritage Days celebrates Sea Island culture in its many forms. Thursday there is a special community sing; Friday there are lectures and presentations followed by an old-fashioned fish fry with musical entertainment; on Saturday, a parade and performances which include Gullah games and storytelling, dance, music, and demonstrations of traditional Sea Island crafts such as basket-making, net-weaving, and boat-building.

### Savannah

**Crafts and Cane Grinding** (912-897-3773; Oatland Island Education Center, 711 Sandtown Rd, Savannah, GA 31410) More than sixty artisans from the southeast come to sell their work and demonstrate how it's done; farmers grind cane to make syrup; folk musicians play outside.

## DECEMBER

### *Beaufort*

**Christmas at the Verdier House** (843-524-6334; 801 Bay St., Beaufort, SC 29902) The late-18th century planter's home is decorated during Christmas week as it might have been during holidays of long ago.

**Night on the Town** (843-525-6644; Main Street, Beaufort, USA) Join an informal, local street party as the downtown merchants welcome patrons to partake of holiday snacks and libations. There are decorations everywhere; jazz musicians, carolers, and even Santa make special appearances. An evening of small-town fun.

### *Bluffton*

**Christmas Parade** (843-757-3855).

### *Charleston*

*The decorations at Charleston's Manigault House recall the festivities of Christmas past.*

Wade Spees

**African-American Spirituals** (843-766-0188; Drayton Hall, 3380 Ashley River Rd., Charleston, SC 29414) "The Senior Lights" singing group of Johns Island present a moving concert of music of the Sea Islands at Drayton Hall.

**Christmas in Charleston** (800-868-8118; P.O. Box 975, Charleston, SC 29402) The season brings special tours and holiday events such as a parade of boats strung with lights and open-air marketplaces. Many restaurants and hotels offer holiday specials, too.

## *Hilton Head*

**Lowcountry's Twelve Days of Christmas** (843-681-4000; Westin Resort) A series of daily events (Dec. 15–26) including teas, fireside story telling, and illumination ceremonies. The holiday decorations are the island's best.

## *Savannah*

**Christmas in Savannah** (912-944-0456 / 800-444-2427; Convention & Visitors Bureau, P.O. Box 1628, Savannah, GA 31402-1628) All month long, Savannah comes alive with special holiday events: tours, performances, 19th-century style holiday presentations in old homes, crafts shows, and celebrations at the beach and on the river.

# TOURIST INFORMATION & ON-LINE ADDRESSES

Here is a listing of the organizations in the Lowcountry that cater to visitors' needs. You may benefit from them during your stay; or you may simply want to have their addresses in case you wish to follow-up on a yearly event or request further information. In many cases, booklets, videos, and pamphlets are available at a nominal charge; general information is free.

## FISHING AND HUNTING REGULATIONS

Licenses, permits, and wildlife stamps, whichever apply, must be in your possession while in the field or on the water. They may be purchased at tackle shops, sporting goods shops, and from the state.

**Georgia Department of Natural Resources, Game and Fish Division** Route 2, Box 219-R, Richmond Hill, GA 31324; 912-651-2221.

**S.C. Department of Natural Resources** P.O. Box 167, Columbia 29202; 843-734-3888.

## VISITOR INFORMATION

**Charleston Area Convention & Visitors Bureau** P.O. Box 975, Charleston, SC 29402; 843-853-8000 / 800-868-8118 / 843-853-0444 (fax); Website: http://www. charlestoncvb.com

**Edisto Island Chamber of Commerce** P.O. Box 206, Edisto Island, SC 29438; 843-869-3867.

**Georgia Website:** http://www.georgia.org.

**Greater Beaufort Chamber of Commerce** P.O. Box 910, Beaufort, SC 29901-0910; 843-524-3163 / 843-986-5405 (fax).

**Hilton Head Island Chamber of Commerce** P.O. Box 5647, Hilton Head Island, SC 29938; 843-785-3673 / 800-523-3373 / 843-785-7110 (fax); Website: http://www. info@hiltonheadisland.org.

**Lowcountry & Resort Islands Tourism Commission** P.O. Box 615, Point South, SC 29945; 800-528-6870; Website: http://www.come2sc@hargray. com.

**The Savannah Area Convention and Visitor's Bureau** P.O. Box 1628, Savannah GA 31402-1628; 800-444-2427 / 912-944-0456 / 912-944-0468 (fax); Website: www. http.savcvb,com.

**S.C. Division of State Parks** PRT, Edgar Brown Building, 1205 Pendleton St., Columbia, SC 29201; 843-734-0156.

**South Carolina Website:** http://www.travelsc.com

*The ideal pace for a Lowcountry visitor is to be slower than a scuttling crab.*

Wade Spees

# IF TIME IS SHORT

The Lowcountry divides easily into three parts: the major cities (Charleston and Savannah), the more rural areas (Beaufort, Edisto, Bluffton, and the Sea Islands), and the beach resorts (on Hilton Head Island, Kiawah, Isle of Palms, etc.). Concentrating on one of these locales is a sure-fire way to have a satisfying, if brief, visit.

Each place has its special qualities, refer to individual chapter openings for a sense of them. In general, the resorts are self-enclosed and limited in terms of history, culture, and sightseeing, yet their on-site recreational resources are exemplary and their use may determine your schedule. Beaufort or Edisto are lower-keyed destinations, where beachcombing and modest shopping might wrap around a day's worth of walking, biking, kayaking, or sightseeing. The cities, of course, are full of opportunity for touring and shopping. (A car is not necessary for a weekend trip to a city, although helpful if you want to explore the countryside or visit both Charleston and Savannah.)

Here are some recommendations:

## In *Charleston*

*Two Meeting Street Inn* (843-723-7322; 2 Meeting St.) is located in the Historic District, and waking up there makes you feel as if you're a native. *Maison DuPre* (843-723-8691; 800-844-4667; 317 E. Bay St.) is a lovely oasis, with a courtyard, a bit further uptown. These inns will be booked months in advance during the annual *Spoleto Festival* (843-722-2764), a series of music, dance, and theatre performances, and art exhibits, that occurs in late spring.

My favorite house museums and military sites are the *Heyward-Washington House* (843-722-0354; 87 Church St.) built in 1772 and representing the height of colonial living; the *Nathaniel Russell House* (843-724-8481; 51 Meeting St.) completed in1808; and the *Joseph Manigault House* (843-723-2926; 350 Meeting St.), designed in 1803 by a native son and a marvelous example of adapting European taste for the Lowcountry elite. Slightly father afield on Hwy. 61 are two nationally recognized historic sites: *Middleton Place* (843-556-6020) where the oldest landscaped gardens in America were laid out in 1741; and *Drayton Hall* (843-766-0188), an 18th-century Georgian home which is a magnificent, unfurnished example of the Palladian style. Military history buffs should visit *Fort Sumter National Monument* (843-722-1691; in Charleston Harbor) where the Civil War began; and *Patriot's Point* (843-884-2727; Mt. Pleasant) the berth of battleships and submarines.

Popular shops among locals are along *King St.* (antiques and clothing stores), *Queen St.* (boutiques and art galleries), *East Bay St.* (bookstores), and *Church St.* (classic men's, women's ,and children's clothing). *Fulton Five* (843-853-5555; 5 Fulton St.), *G&M* (843-577-9797; 96 Broad St.), and *Pinckney Street Cafe* (843-577-0961; 18 Pinckney St) are dining favorites.

## In *Savannah*

*The Gastonian* (912-232-2869 / 800-322-6603; 220 E. Gaston St.) and the *Magnolia Place Inn* (912-236-7674 / 800-238-7674; 503 Whitaker St.) are downtown luxury inns with a flair for style and comfort.

Historic sites of architectural and military interest include: the *Green-Meldrim House* (912-233-3845; Madison Square) where General Sherman lived during the occupation of the city; the *Owens-Thomas House* (912-233-9743; 124 Abercorn St.), a Regency-style urban villa designed by William Jay in 1816; and *Fort Pulaski* (912-786-5787; U.S. 80) a masonry fort that was, in 1847, state-of-the-art, and now is a great place for a picnic. Established in 1865, the *Beach Institute* (912-234-8000; 502 E. Harris St.) includes a permanent display of folk-art sculpture that celebrates the talent of Ulysses Davis and other African-American artists.

Antiques stores proliferate downtown on *Bull St.*, *Abercorn St.*, and *Whitaker St*; there are galleries and cafes in the *City Market*; *Factor's Walk* offers a variety of boutiques for clothing and crafts. Locals eat breakfast at *Clary's* (912-233-0402; 404 Abercorn St.) and dinner at the *Crab Shack* (912-786-9857; Chimney Creek, Tybee.) *Elizabeth's on 37th* (912-236-5547; 105 E. 37th) is one of the best restaurants in the southeast.

## In *Beaufort and the Sea Islands:*

*The Rhett House Inn* (843-524-9030; 1009 Craven St., Beaufort) and *Cassina Point Plantation Bed and Breakfast* (843-869-2535; Edisto Island) are the most gracious and relaxing inns outside the cities. The innkeepers may also arrange kayak and bicycle outings, prepare picnics, and suggest forays to *Edisto Beach State Park* (843-869-2156), *Hunting Island State Park* (843-838-2011) and other, more out-of-the-way places.

For a quick sandwich in downtown Beaufort, head for *Plums* (843-525-1946; 904 $^1$/2 Bay St.). On Edisto Island, *The Old Post Office* (843-869-2339; Hwy 174) is the best place for dinner.

For a sense of history, visit the *John Mark Verdier House* (843-524-6334; 801 Bay St.) the home of a wealthy 19th-century Beaufort merchant; *Penn*

*Center* (843-838-2432; St. Helena Island) the nation's first school for freed slaves; and the *Edisto Museum* (843-869-1954; Edisto Island), which reveals the history of the island, from the time of Native Americans to the present. *The Marine Corps Recruit Depot at Parris Island Museum* (843-525-2951) features the history of the Marines and the Corps' training.

Beaufort's *Bay St.*, and the narrow streets that lead off it, has a classic main street feeling: plate-glass display windows, awnings, and family-run stores. On St. Helena, *Red Piano Too* (843-838-2241; Hwy. 21 at The Corner) an art gallery and store, is the best place in the Lowcountry, perhaps in the southeast, to see native and outsider art on display and understand how that tradition fits in today's island culture.

# Index

# LODGING BY PRICE CODE

# DINING BY PRICE CODE

# DINING BY CUISINE

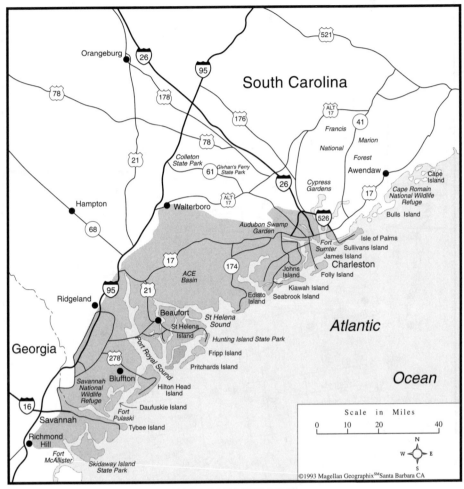

**THE LOWCOUNTRY**

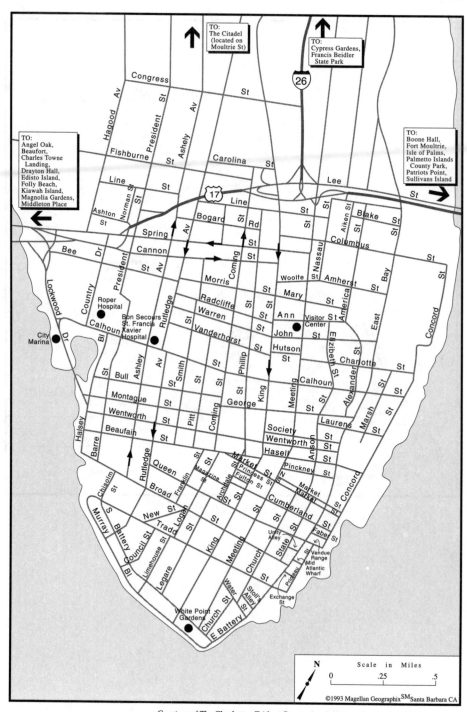

Courtesy of The Charleston Trident Convention & Visitors Bureau (used by permission)

# CHARLESTON

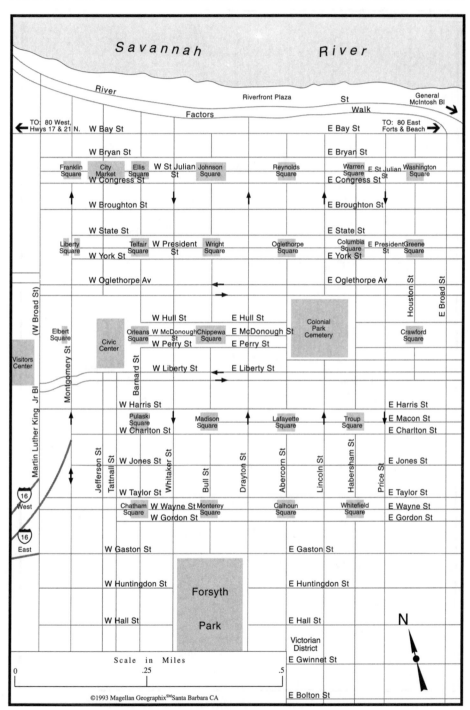

Courtesy of The Savannah Area Convention & Visitors Bureau (used by permission)

# SAVANNAH

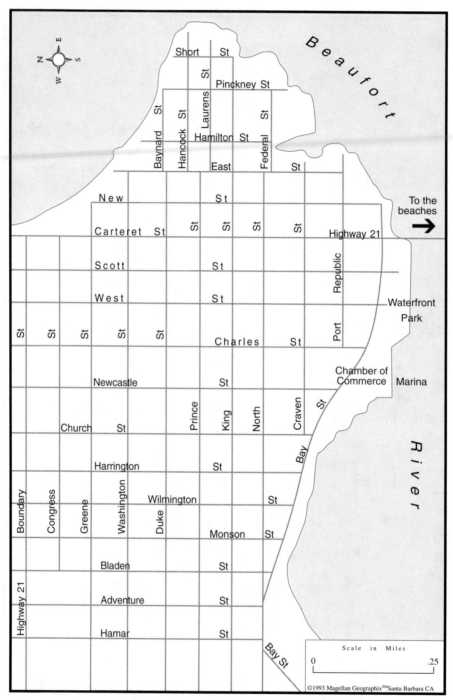

Courtesy of The Greater Beaufort Chamber of Commerce (used by permission)

**BEAUFORT**

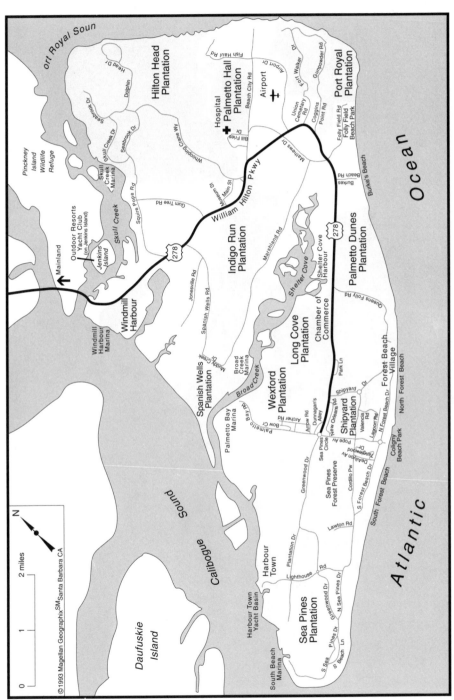

Courtesy of The Hilton Head Island Chamber of Commerce (used by permission)

# HILTON HEAD ISLAND

# About the Author

Cecily McMillan moved to the Lowcountry of South Carolina in 1980, having graduated from Harvard University and worked as a journalist for *The Real Paper* in Cambridge, Mass., and the *Baltimore News-American*. In addition to freelance writing on southern topics, she handled public relations for the South Carolina Education Television Network station in Beaufort, South Carolina. She came to know the Lowcountry further during her terms on the local planning commission, as a board member of a rural health center, as an officer of the Beaufort County Democratic Party, and as a young mother.

Her writing on the South has frequently appeared in the *New York Times* Travel Section and the Sunday Style Section, and in magazines such as *Southern Changes* and *Southern Exposure*.